LONELY REFUGEE

A Hungarian Australian American Memoir

Lonely Refugee:
A Hungarian Australian American Memoir

Book Design by Jeremy Berg
Photography by Elizabeth C. Fowler unless noted
Back Cover Photo by stephanieelizabethimages.com

Published by Starseed Books
6592 Peninsula Dr
Traverse City MI 49686

ISBN: 978-1-939790-18-7

Fowler, Elizabeth C.
Lonely Refugee:
A Hungarian Australian American Memoir/Elizabeth C. Fowler

Library of Congress Control Number: 2017931303

First Edition: March 2017

Printed in the United States of America

www.lorianpress.com

LONELY REFUGEE

A Hungarian Australian American Memoir

PHOTOGRAPH OF BEARER
PHOTOGRAPHIE DU TITULAIRE

Elizabeth C. Fowler

Acknowledgements

This has been labor of love that began with the spark of a desire to reclaim my family's history for my children. Once I accomplished that, I thought to mothball the project, but an inner call niggled and needled with remarkable persistence to get my story out to a larger audience. I am grateful to so many who have shepherded me along the way. To my writing buddies, Jack Hilovsky, and Anne Biklé: you stood by me week after week, month after month, year after year, holding my feet to the fire, and giving me sobering (to the ego) and invaluable critiques. To another writing buddy, Christy Anderson, who was only with us for a time but who first introduced me at a party as "a writer." I hardly believed it then, but you planted a seed of encouragement. To my friend and fellow life coach Karen Levine who's initial editing flurry rattled me—my writing is the better for your input. To my sister-in-law Mary Fowler, who gave me valuable editing feedback and reassurance. To Erin Brown, my editor, thank you for your attention to detail and your willingness to take a second look. To David Spangler, everyday mystic and inspirational teacher, who helped me formulate a spiritual foundation to live by. To Adrienne McDunn, Suzanne Fageol, Ruth Chaffee, and Freya Secrest, soul sisters and dear, dear friends who so often and so attentively listened and perceptively helped me transmute and metabolize my fears and frustrations. You remind me of the sacred contexts; you lift me up. To my mentor extraordinaire, Dave Ellis who I suspect had no clue what he was getting into when he committed over three years ago to read my weekly email check-ins. You have been a beacon through many a storm. Were it not for my commitment to you that goaded me to do even a smidgen of work on my manuscript every week, I would have abandoned this project months ago. To my brother Tom, who helped with historical information, gave me poignant, heartfelt feedback, and who did a superb job of editing the photos. To my sister Irene, who offered much needed love and support to get my story out there – you've had my back for so many years, Sis. To my publisher and dear friend, Jeremy Berg, who stood patiently in the wings. His comment *you may want to get it published just so as you can move on*, helped me get off my duff. To all that is sacred in and beyond the world, which is everything, my gratitude and awe. And finally, to my children Stephen and Stephanie who have supported and encouraged me every step of the way—you are my greatest, greatest pride and joy.

FOR STEPHEN AND STEPHANIE
With apologies for my unbridled habit of breaking into
song when prompted by words or phrases
YOU BOTH LIGHT UP MY LIFE

Contents

CHAPTER 1 – IN THE GHETTO

The four Palotas kids, Paul, Geza, Irene and me on the veranda of our
Surry Hills row house.

Heavy rains flooded our slum row house in Sydney, turning it into a living nightmare. I was two and a half years old, squirming in our renter's lap, terrified. Our tenant, Mac Mac closely resembled the witches in my nightmares. Wrinkled and sallow, garbed in grimy black, she smelled rancid, like my brother's really dirty socks mixed with tobacco and stale urine, like after I wet the bed.

My father, wearing galoshes stood in ankle high water. Bent over, he flung buckets of water furiously out of the kitchen. His piercing blue eyes were focused on the task at hand. A lock of his hair – prematurely grey since his twenties from the horrors of World War II – drooped over his moist forehead.

My mother, barely five foot tall, and shorter than my father by a few inches, still managed at this moment to tower over him. She alternately wrung her hands and raked her slim, shapely fingers through her thin, almost black hair. Her dark brown eyes flashed with anger as she yelled instructions. My father ignored her and kept ladling.

Mac Mac gripped me like a vice and tried to settle me down with her raspy cooing, "There, there, love."

I wanted none of it and screamed in Hungarian "Anyu, Anyu." I couldn't understand why Mum didn't answer me. Why was she arguing with Apu? And why was my father ignoring me too? Why didn't my parents save me from this witch? I was stuck. I couldn't escape. Even worse, I could not even be heard. My parents were totally caught up in their own dramas, their own traumas. To them I was invisible. I gave up the struggle, quieted down, and waited for release from Mac Mac's grip.

§

We inherited Mac Mac. She was living in the upstairs bedroom when my parents bought their first house in 1951 soon after immigrating to Australia from Hungary. The tenant laws in New South Wales provided continuous rent-controlled housing even amidst home sales and title transfers. My parents could not evict Mac Mac without finding her other, similar accommodations at the same ridiculously low rent she was paying. It took them months to find her another place and, in the end, they received aid from the local authorities because the filth in her room had become a health hazard. My parents never saw her throw out anything. After she left, they cleaned out piles stretching to the ceiling of newspapers and rotting rubbish and even disgustingly soiled feminine napkins.

My two-to-three times a week nightmares don't end with Mac Mac's departure. She wasn't their only source. My older siblings were too. My brother Paul – named for my father – was eight years my senior. Normally I loved his sparkling brown eyes and gorgeous smile. It lit up his whole face when he was happy. But one night, soon after the flood in our house and still feeling traumatized by that whole experience, I crept down the shadowy hallway towards our bedroom. Paul's head popped out of the doorway in front of me, and his grin signaled mischief.

"Watch out for the boogeyman," he whispered, nodding and averting his gaze behind me. I gasped, and froze in place, shaking.

A voice behind me yelled "Boo!" and I jumped, squealing in terror. I turned and saw my sister – named Irene, after my mother – who had conspired with Paul to scare me. Two years younger than he, she thought it fun to pull such pranks on her already "scaredy-cat" sister. Her dark hair and eyes – which all of us had inherited from Anyu – made her seem spookier in the shadows of the corridor.

My brother Geza peeked out from behind Irene. Age six and always eager to be one of the big guys, Geza joined in with a wobbly "Wooo," waved his hands about and poked me in my side. I wailed and cringed, stranded in the corridor, petrified, but I didn't run to Anyu or Apu. They were not much of a haven for me – more apt to tease me when I was afraid. So I slunk away from my sibs as they giggled and jeered – there was clearly no support from them either. I held my fear inside.

That night another nightmare surfaced – a variation of the usual witch theme. This time it was a gruesome boogeyman with darkened hollow eyes, a cruel grin that reached out for me with clawed hands, ready to choke me. I awoke with a start – chest pounding, throat clenched – and lay stiff and still on my bed. I saw the boogeyman sitting in the chair by the window. I stared, horrified, holding my breath.

The seconds stretched and I began to see more definition to the dark silhouette. Then a faint breeze blew through the open window and the silhouette flapped. The monster had morphed into a pile of my untidy sister's clothes. I shuddered and listened to Irene breathing quietly in the bed next to mine. Her slow in-and-out rhythm relaxed me, and I managed eventually to drift back to sleep.

As if Mac Mac and my siblings weren't enough, there was another monster in the Surry Hills house that scared me every day: this one in the bathroom wedged between the toilet and the tub. They called it a chip water heater. A primitive, tank-less hot water system popular in Australia from the 1880s until the 1960s, it consisted of a cylindrical unit with a firebox through which a pipe to heat water ran. My parents fed the firebox with newspapers and wood chips when we wanted hot water. I was sure there was a fire-breathing beast in that box. I flinched at every crackle and scrunched up my body tight as I could,

3

trying to avoid the boiling heat and the open, smoky flames that belched out just inches from where I sat on the toilet or in the tub. I feared it would one day set my hair on fire.

§

My parents worked hard and had little time to spend with me. With all our relatives still in Hungary, I had no cousins to play with; there were no aunts, uncles or grandparents to soften the edges of the nuclear core of Apu, Anyu, Paul, Irene, Geza and me. Moreover, we were foreigners – "bloody new Australians" as the Aussies disparagingly referred to us – and our neighbors shunned us. They averted their eyes when we ventured outside, but their avoidance didn't bother us for the ghettoes of Surry Hills housed mainly sots and seedy sorts.

My sibs were mostly gone at school and I envied their "grown up" ways and how they stuck together. They spoke English, I only Hungarian, for that is all we spoke at home. I longed to read and write and have homework like they did. Paul, Irene and Geza started out at the local parochial school but didn't stay there for long.

"You've got to do something!" Anyu yelled at my father the minute he walked in the front door after a long day at work. "Look, look at this," she said, continuing to poke Irene's scalp in Apu's face and separating the strands of her hair. "She has lice! They all have lice!" I wasn't sure what lice were, but the way Anyu spat the words out made me cringe. Maybe they were flesh-eating critters! I slinked as far away from them as I could so as not to be bitten, crouching in the corner behind a chair.

Anyu was still on her rant. "We avoided head lice in the cellars under Budapest during the bombings, and in the refugee camps in Austria, and Greta, only to come down with lice in this awful low-class neighborhood school! You must find a different school for these children."

"All right, all right," Apu replied, moving past her with a heavy sigh. "I'll look into it."

"You better, and quickly."

Apu checked out the surrounding neighborhoods and finagled a transfer to Bellevue Hill, an adjacent and well-to-do public school district.

My sibs rode the city bus to and from their new school and had all sorts of adventures together, which I envied and which they later recounted to me, bragging with pride. Each day they received just enough pennies for the bus fare. As the bus rumbled by an enticing lolly shop, they dreamed and drooled about the delicious treats: Minties, Pascall Jubes and licorice.

One day, Paul, always the one to come up with a brilliant idea, exclaimed,

"Let's go buy lollies with our bus money. We can walk home. It's not far at all."

Irene and Geza agreed without hesitation, their mouths watering, their stomachs growling in anticipation. Delighted with their gooey purchases, they munched as they walked, licking their sticky fingers, but soon, six-year-old Geza began to whine. "I'm tired. My legs hurt."

"It's not far now, just a few blocks," reassured Paul, though by now he'd begun to realize that the distance from school to home, over three miles, was quite a schlep.

"How much further?" moaned Irene.

"Quit being sissies. Come on, move," Paul urged. "Anyu's going to kill us if we don't hurry." The foolishness of their prank dawned as dusk descended, and their feet were dragging by the time they finally reached home. The front door flew open.

"Good god, where have you been? I've been frantic," my mother screamed. I had watched, startled, as she fretted about the house waiting for their return, checking the front window every few seconds and muttering to herself. Her worry now turned to rage when she noticed the candy-stained faces staring at her, wide eyed. "You spent your bus money on lollies? The wooden spoon for all of you! Bend over." Anyu's eyes glowed like coals, and her mouth stretched and tightened as she gave each of them a good whacking. Irene and Geza wailed with abandon. Paul just gritted his teeth. I watched in fascinated horror. I was crushed at missing out on the lollies. I wasn't part of the exclusive gang of three. Nevertheless, as I rubbed my butt in sympathy, I felt relieved that mine hadn't received a spanking.

I differed from my older siblings in one other important way. All three of them were born in Hungary under more auspicious circumstances, their births ushered in by respectful military physicians. I entered the world in March 1950, soon after my parents arrived in Australia. My shabby beginning occurred in a refugee camp in Greta, a reclaimed World War II army barracks about 100 miles North of Sydney, and 20 miles inland from the Pacific Ocean. My mother labored and delivered in the dingy camp, with only minimal ministration by the local GP. She didn't speak English.

"They left me alone, treated me like a peasant, did nothing for me. They couldn't care less about my suffering," Anyu said, her voice dramatic and sing-song. To the GP, she was low class and unwanted, even though she was one of tens of thousands of immigrants invited by the Australian government after World War II to provide much needed labor for the rich, yet sparsely populated continent.

I was born at a time when my mother had fallen to the lowest rung of the social ladder, far from her prestigious status as a high school principal and the wife of a lieutenant colonel in the Hungarian army. The privileges of her hard-earned education and that of her husband had evaporated and were worthless in this arid alien land. I was another sign of her fall from grace, and I felt it from the very beginning. Maybe that was why she remained so distant and unavailable. I reminded her of awful times every time she looked at me, but then so must have all her children. Paul and Irene were both born during the horrors of World War II, in 1942 and 1944 respectively. She delivered Geza in 1947 during the post-war Communist occupation and oppression, shortly before the arrest warrant for Apu forced my family to flee.

The stories Anyu told of her life in Hungary trickled down through my childhood years. I felt her disdain for me from my earliest memories. "You are a little Aussie," Anyu often teased with a grating edge to her voice. When Apu called me a little Aussie, I felt his endearment and his comment didn't smart like Anyu's did. Apu shared very little about his life in Hungary as I was growing up. He didn't open up until years later when I was in my forties. Yet, even as a child, without them saying anything, I felt the pain of Anyu and Apu's uprooting and their struggles in our adopted country. They remained distant, absent, and unavailable. I felt a burden, a pain, and so I instinctively remained as unobtrusive as possible. I didn't want to bother them. I wanted to lighten their load any way I could. I often pictured myself wrapped in pillows and blankets, crouching in a corner, hidden in a protective cocoon. Only in later years did a part of me emerge that clamored more and more for their – or anyone's – attention, for their affection, and for their love.

§

In the Greta refugee camp my father worked any and all odd jobs he could find including radio repair, office payroll, and accounting. He even served as a camp policeman. My mother cooked and helped supervise the camp kitchen. I have a picture of her dressed in a white smock and headscarf, where she, along with other refugee women, toiled over large cauldrons in the stifling hot bungalows. The inland arid bush country temperatures often topped a blistering 100 degrees Fahrenheit.

My parents remained in the Greta camp for a year. Then, having obtained a loan from more established Hungarian immigrants in Sydney, they used the money for a down payment on their first home, our row house in the slums of Surry Hills. Apu again worked any and many jobs to support us: on a wireless assembly line, in an Eveready battery factory, in a weaving factory, as an airplane instrument repairman at Kingsford Smith Aviation Service, even as a taxi driver at night. He attempted to start businesses in radio repair and painting contracting. Both failed. He ventured into eucalyptus oil production. He was gone for weeks during which he and his partners endured grueling work in the arid bush, cutting down trees and extracting the pungent oil only to find oil prices plummeting with the discovery of synthetic menthol.

Even though Anyu stayed at home, I couldn't get her attention. She stayed busy with housework or cooking dinners in an "in-home" restaurant for several Hungarian single men. By my father's account, she earned more working three to four hours a day than he did working two jobs and running after extra income in his spare time. I mostly kept to myself.

When Apu brought home the first knitting machine, it was a novelty for him, a way to earn a few extra shillings. I sat mesmerized as he and Anyu took turns sitting with the small manual model on their laps, sluicing it back and forth. With each arm-shifting pass, I delighted in how the collars and cuffs for sweaters were slowly churned out below, row by row, like a pasta maker. I also liked the machine because it enabled my parents to sit in one place, rather than run around in and out of the house toiling at their various jobs. It was a rare opportunity when I could sit with them, watch them, and just be with them in the same room.

Apu had finally discovered a viable income source. In contrast to his multiple odd jobs, these knitted pieces were sold at relatively handsome prices to a Hungarian acquaintance who owned an established knitwear factory. Little did my parents know when they bought that first manual machine that knitwear would become their source of livelihood, providing not only a means for their financial recovery, but also a measure of affluence over the next fourteen years.

CHAPTER 2 – MOVING ON UP

My father, Paul, and Daddy's girl.

My mother, Irene, my sister, Irene, and me. Formal photos taken in our Union Street house.

To make room for the new knitting machines, my parents purchased a larger house in the North Sydney neighborhood. Our two-story row house at 97 Union Street, like the ones adjacent to it, had a postage stamp-sized front yard, bordered by an intricate wrought iron fence identical in design to the tiny second-story balcony railing. We moved soon after the birth of my youngest sibling Thomas Leslie and lived there from the time I was three until I was nine.

"I thought I was too old to get pregnant. I didn't know I was until I felt the baby move," Anyu related some time after Tom's "accidental" birth. She smiled at my toddler brother as I held him on my lap, playing *csip-csip-ckóka* by gently pinching the back of his plump little hand and bouncing it up and down in time to the well-known Hungarian children's ditty. I quieted down, clasping my hands around Tom and hugging him. I wanted to hear more from my mother, but knowing Anyu's ways, I also began to feel a little apprehensive. Anyu looked down at the slub-knit polo shirt in her lap and jabbed her needle through the hole in the button with her thimbled finger.

"But this time, unlike the horrid refugee camp where you were born," she said, shooting a disdainful glance at me, "I had an established and competent Hungarian physician attend me. He treated me like a lady of status. When my labor began, he admitted me to the fancy hospital. Since it was evening, he ordered a sedative and I slept all night. At the civil hour of eight the next morning, he marched into my room and announced: 'Now we will proceed with the birthing.'" Anyu puffed her chest out for emphasis and looked at us with pride.

I held Tom even tighter as a shiver ran up my spine. I turned away from my mother's cold smile in order to hide my flushed face. My brother stilled in my arms, somehow sensing my upset. I gazed blankly at the quieted overlock machines in our factory living room. Not even the fuzz and the lint balls around the machines stirred in the quiet that now filled the room. Anyu's tale of Tom's birth only served to make me feel worse about my own inauspicious refugee camp beginnings. I belonged to Anyu's tragic past, times she wanted to forget. I hung my head.

My younger brother went by "Laci," a Hungarian diminutive of Leslie, but Thomas was on his birth certificate after the maternity nurses informed my mother that Leslie was a girl's name. Tom was the fifth and last child and arrived when I was three. My parents honored him by calling the new business Tomknit and they proudly hung a shingle by the front door of our new home. I thought this to be another nod to Tom's more genteel birth and a slight to mine. After all, they didn't call the business "Elizabethknit."

§

The corner pub down the hill from our house had a regular clientele of sots who bellowed and upchucked on the footpath at all hours. Motorcycles vroomed three doors down from us in the other direction where a group of bodgies and widgies, members of the Aussie grease subculture, hung out. The guys had tattoos and duckbill-slicked hairdos. Chest hairs sprouted from under their grey singlets, and their bellies fell out of their grimy jeans. The girlfriends dyed their hair canary yellow and orange, layered on thick black eyeliner, wore tight tops and even tighter pedal-pushers.

One time I passed them by on my way to get some butter and paprika for Anyu at the milk bar two blocks away and they were sitting in the tiny front yard guzzling big bottles of Tooheys beer. One of the bodgies called out, "Hey, lovey, wanna sip o' my beer? Aw, come on." The others snickered and hooped. What on earth did they want from a scrappy four-year-old in worn and unmatched shorts and top? Did they smell my fear? I sped past them blushing and trembling. After that, I didn't dare go by their house when they were outside. Despite the colorful goings on, our North Sydney neighborhood was a definite step up from the seedier one in Surry Hills.

§

We inherited another tenant with the new house. This lady, unlike Mac Mac, was nice enough. She wore pretty pastel colors, trim cardigans, and her light hair was always groomed as if she had just stepped out after a shampoo-and-set at the beauty parlor. But we needed her room, and my parents wanted her out. My older siblings were only too happy to help oust her and took matters into their own hands.

This proved another opportunity for adventure. I was four by then and since Tom's birth, no longer the youngest. Paul, Irene and Geza allowed me to tag along, but since my assigned role was a purely supportive one, I was expected to hang back from the main action. My older sibs plotted in a huddle in the boys' bedroom.

"Oh, I know," Paul exclaimed leaning back against the pillow of his sloppily made bed, his hands clasped behind his head, "Let's plonk Tommy in front of the renter's door sitting on his potty."

Irene giggled. "Great idea! She'll be disgusted with the smell and leave for sure."

Geza, sitting on his bed next to Irene added an enthusiastic, "Oh yeah." I huddled on the floor, my knees up to my chest questioning this dubious tactic. I could see us getting into big trouble – Anyu and Apu wouldn't like it – but I said nothing.

Tom was posted outside the renter's door sitting on his chamber pot. The tenant was hardly ruffled and merely smiled at him as she passed by. A more creative plan was called for and we again gathered in the boys' room. This time Tom was with us, and I was keeping him occupied on the floor playing peek-a-boo while the others resumed their plotting.

"Well, that was a flop," Irene said.

Paul was undaunted. "No worries, I have an even better plan that's sure to work. Let's collect Tom's poop and wrap it up as a Christmas present for her." We all cracked up. I held my hand over my mouth to keep from spluttering. Even baby Tom joined in with a giggle.

"You've got to be kidding," Irene gasped in between guffaws. "We'll get the wooden spoon for sure if we do that."

"Yeah, we'll really get into trouble," Geza added, sobering some. I again stayed out of the conversation, not wanting to challenge – or to commit. Little Tom sensed the sober turn in the room and quieted down, laying his head against my chest. Paul finally spoke up.

"Yeah, we probably will get spanked, but it'll be worth it, won't it?" Silence. Irene looked at her hands, twisting them this way and that. Geza fiddled with the corner of his pillowcase.

"Well, who's in?" Paul asked, first giving Geza, then Irene, a hard stare.

Irene hesitated but then replied, "Oh, okay. It'll be worth the paddle on my butt just to see the renter's reaction." She grinned.

"That's the spirit." Paul chuckled.

"Oh, me too, I'll do it," Geza said with a half-smile.

They didn't ask for my assent. I didn't want to give it anyway.

My mother didn't suspect a thing, even when my sibs started to help out emptying Tom's pot.

"Oh, this is the one. It's a huge piece," Irene exclaimed.

"Pooh, it smells awful," Geza said, scrunching his nose.

Paul laughed as, using wooden popsicle sticks, he gingerly transferred Tom's poop from the pot to a cardboard gift box, "That's the point, idiot. The stink's what'll get her out of here. Okay, Irene," he continued, "Now it's your turn. Wrap it up nice and sweet." Irene grabbed the pretty red and green Christmas paper with a flourish and covered the box beautifully.

"Needs a bow too," Geza added.

"I know, I know. Give me a chance," Irene said, snipping the ribbon then tying a lovely bow.

"Perfect." Paul nodded, grabbed the box, and held it up high. "Everybody ready?" He chortled.

"Yep, let's do it," Irene and Geza replied, almost in unison. They marched to the tenant's room and gently rapped on the door. I lagged behind, watching with trepidation.

My siblings had angelic expressions on their faces when the renter answered the door.

"Hello ma'am," Paul began. "We wanted to present you with a Christmas gift."

"Oh, what delightful children you are!" she exclaimed. "You are so thoughtful! Thank you for the lovely gift. Look, I will place it right here under my Christmas tree." We could barely suppress our giggles as we said our goodbyes and scuttled back to our rooms.

It took no time in the sweltering December heat for the poop to reek and seep through the box and glittery wrapping paper. We heard the tenant's screams through the door and muffled our giggles.

"You goddamn bloody kids!"

Our tenant moved out soon after. That was one time my parents didn't paddle us for our escapades.

§

On the main floor of the Union Street house, the family kitchen bisected the two areas that housed the knitting factory. It had a concrete floor and served as a sort of breezeway between the detached addition on the back that housed the giant knitting machines and the main house. Apu oversaw the mechanical monsters that rhythmically chugged away night and day, the runners sluicing back and forth across hundreds of needles, knitting one row with each pass. The noise was deafening, and my father blamed the machine cacophony for the hearing loss he developed in later years. He spent many hours under and behind those brutes, fixing and refitting them, smeared in oil, often swearing.

The front room was Anyu's domain and smelled of steamed cotton and wool. It housed the steam presser, the cutting and design tables, the blade fabric cutters, the overlock and finishing machines.

Apu, in addition to programming and servicing the knitting machines, handled the hiring and firing of employees as well as the buying, selling, and the marketing of the knitwear. Anyu, in addition to designing and cutting out the sweater parts, handled the accounting and billing.

All of our employees were immigrants, either Hungarian, Greek, or Italian. Anyu wasn't fluent in English, but the little "pig English" she spoke worked well enough as the common language. It became the communication standard in the factory. Apu, perhaps with a premonition of the escape and relocation that was to come, had learned English while still in Hungary spending hours listening to the BBC on the radio. He was fluent in other languages and loved chatting with employees and business associates in English, German, and Italian. He once mused that he would have preferred to join the diplomatic corps rather than entering the Ludovika military academy in Budapest. The family tradition of a military career passed on to him as an obligation when his older brother, Zoltán, contracted tuberculosis and was therefore ineligible for military service.

My favorite times were after the employees left for the day. The noise quieted and we had the house to ourselves once again. My parents often continued their work, but at least they had fewer distractions. I especially liked Thursday evenings when my mother, sister, and I listened to the hit parade on the radio. We sat in a circle surrounding cardboard boxes filled with partially finished garments, and sang along (my mother and sister out of tune) to songs like Doris Day's "Que Sera, Sera;" Perry Como's "Hot Diggity;" Pat Boone's "Love Letters in the Sand;" and one of my mother's favorites: Marti Robbins' "A White Sport Coat."

Some nights we put finishing touches on the sweaters by snipping and pulling the overlocked edges back through the seams of the sleeves and garment sides. Other times we took the long sheets that had cascaded out of the knitting machines – the collars and bodies of the soon to be made garments – and separated each piece by pulling out the connecting threads. As I tugged and twirled the cotton strings around my fingers, they became red and sore but I didn't mind. I cherished spending those rare, pleasant opportunities with my mother. I stole glances and studied her petite frame bent over her work. Her shapely legs were crossed neatly at her ankles as she worked steadily on the garment in her lap. I remembered how proud Anyu was of her good-looking legs and how Apu must have loved them too, for he often bought her elegant Schiaparelli stockings. I warmed to see Anyu's brown eyes sparkle as she sang along. This was a rare time when her eyes glowed with joy rather than disapproval or disdain. This was a rare time when I was included in her joy.

I also cherished time with my father for I adored him. I always thought Apu a handsome man, with his soft blue eyes and thick shock of grey hair, ever ramrod military straight stretching his five-foot-seven frame for every bit of height he could garner. He prided himself on his self-discipline, his ability to maintain his high school weight throughout his life. I was happy to study the violin when I learned it was the instrument he played when he was young. It turns out I had a good ear and could sing in tune. Maybe these qualities endeared me to him, for he so loved music. I soon came to be known in the family as his favorite and I wore this special status like a badge. I relished the attention – so rarely showered.

One hot summer day we kids were standing about in the kitchen.

"Anyu, we're sweltering. Can't we go to the beach?" Paul asked, leaning over the sink and splashing some water on his face.

"I'm fine to do that," she replied, "But you'll have to persuade your father."

Apu was the only driver in the family. We peeked into the back room where my father lay under a broken knitting machine, his face and hands splattered with grease, fuming and cussing because his latest fix had failed.

"Well, that doesn't look promising." Irene groaned, sitting back down at the table with a flop. Anyu turned to me.

"Why doesn't 'Daddy's girl' sweet-talk your father." she smirked.

My siblings immediately surrounded me. "Oh yeah, great idea," they said, nudging me into the machine room. I hesitated at the threshold but they motioned me wildly to continue, big grins on their faces. I took a deep breath, braving Apu's foul mood, and crawled under the machine. I lay down next to him. My bare legs, flip-flop straps hanging between my toes, stuck out parallel to his legs, which were covered in stained ragged khakis, and scuffed brown shoes.

"Please Apu, please can't you take us to the beach? Please? It's so hot!" Apu stopped twisting his wrench, paused for a long moment, and then carefully laid the tool back with the others on his tray. He crawled out, and grinning, helped pull me out from under the machine. He wiped his hands on a rag and dabbed a grease spot from my nose.

"All right, kiddo, let's go," he said.

At times like this, I didn't mind being singled out, for I was getting what I craved – attention and approval.

When I had nightmares that were so overwhelming that I could no longer lie frozen in my bed, it was to Apu that I ran. Even though he chided me for being afraid, he was still more supportive than my mother and easier to hug. It never entered my mind to reach out to Anyu. There was some inexplicable aura about her that emanated *don't come close, don't bother me.* Though I adored and preferred my father, I never confided in him. I didn't confide in either of my parents – or my sibs. I didn't want to show any weakness for that was sure to bring on either swift criticism or ridicule. I wanted to put forward my strengths to garner their attention. I longed for their approval. And on this day, when I persuaded my father to take us to the beach, I had gained both his and my mother's approval. I had even been a hero, of sorts, to my siblings.

§

Though I was his favorite, Apu was also terribly strict and some of my worst childhood memories were when he took me to dental visits. Without warning, he would lead me up the steps to the dental surgery. I would panic as the realization of what was to come hit me. I would try to bail, then balk, then freeze. I became a cornered animal with no way out. "Don't cry, be strong," my father admonished with his typical military stolidness as he dragged me up the steps.

The "dentist" my father took me to was a fellow Hungarian, and not truly trained as a dentist. He practiced as an otolaryngologist – ear, nose and throat physician and surgeon – in Hungary. Thanks to the quirks in the Australian professional laws, he was unable to obtain a license as a physician, but succeeded in getting a license to practice dentistry.

Apu dumped me at the office. I was left with the dentist and his wife who served as assistant, receptionist, and Girl Friday. Neither of them was friendly, and both lacked empathy. I tensed with fear as I was led silently to the chair, crying and apprehensive about what I knew was to come.

I always had cavities. I faltered, a faint attempt to keep from reaching the chair but the dentist had me cornered and pushed me on, painfully squeezing my arm. Feeling powerless and small, I lacked the ferociousness to put up any real resistance.

So I obeyed and sat down in the chair. The dentist probed until he found cavities and he fixed them, right then and there.

"Sit still and don't move your head," he warned me.

His wife added, "If you do, it'll jar the drill and do great damage."

Both had sour looks on their faces. I was petrified and with good reason. Those were the days before high-speed and water-cooled drills, when it was unheard of to use local anesthesia. The shrill whine pierced my ears, the reek of burnt bone filled my nostrils, the pain seared hot and lingered for a long time. I cried silently, tears streaming down my face. I squeezed my eyes shut like caged baby chicks having their beaks burned off.

I never understood why my father always dropped me, inescapably and without any heads-up or preparation, into such a traumatic situation. I have to think that he believed that this would be the best for me, but his thinking was totally misguided. How could he, with his military training, which certainly taught him the importance of going into battle prepared, think that it was better for me to get hauled off to the dentist without warning?

Afterwards, when Apu would return to collect me, he would inevitably deliver the *coup de gras*, patting me on the back as he proudly said, "What a good soldier you were!" I'd fume with embarrassment and rub my aching jaw, but I didn't say anything. I didn't want to make waves – besides, Apu had just complimented me and his approval was what I craved.

My father often ignored and minimized pain. He'd laugh at any injuries we suffered as kids. Decades later when my toddler son had a hard fall in our driveway and badly scraped his knee, my father joked about it.

"It's nothing," he told my little boy. "It didn't hurt. You don't have to be a baby and cry."

Firmly, I turned to my father saying, "No Apu, his knee does hurt," as I gathered Stephen in my arms, holding him, comforting him and allowing him to cry. He soon settled.

My father was taken aback by my vehemence and forthrightness. He still didn't agree with me and maintained his military bravado, but from then on, he refrained from challenging my childrearing. He still quipped about my permissiveness but never again did he intervene directly with my kids.

In fact, my father had little contact with my children. Doting grandparent did not describe him – or my mother for that matter. This didn't surprise me. Why would I expect them to be any more hands-on as grandparents? I wondered if it wasn't better, overall, for my children to have my parents less involved. I didn't want their Spartan child rearing ways to affect my children negatively.

§

The bedrooms in the Union Street house were upstairs, accessed by a narrow flight of steps, its walls festooned with fungal flora that looked like a petri dish in full bloom. Many Sydney houses like ours were damp and moldy and impossible to dry out because most residences lacked central heating. The dank cold and humid summers took their toll on walls and carpets. Sydney's climate was subtropical, but I have never been so cold living anywhere as in the winters. At night, I slept with a hot water bottle, but by morning, the heat had dissipated, and my feet felt frozen. Occasionally, my father allowed my sister and me to have the kerosene space heater in our room. The family had just one heater. Mostly it was for my mother's comfort, but sometimes we were allowed to have the heater in our bedroom if we had a cough or as a reward for good behavior.

Unbearable at the other end of the climate spectrum were the Sydney heat waves. On the long languid days of summer, temperatures topped 100 degrees Fahrenheit with near hundred-percent humidity. Citywide alerts cautioned us to avoid the sun, and all the beaches were closed. The torrid conditions kept me sweating and awake on sultry nights, my body sticking to the deep well of my lumpy mattress. We suffered through those extremes of Sydney weather, because our house, like most in those days, had no air conditioning.

Even cars were without climate control systems. On hot muggy Sundays, all seven of us crammed into our sweltering Ford Falcon to attend Hungarian Mass on the other side of town.

"Ooh, you just sat on my new dress," Irene said, pushing me away.

"Sorry," I mumbled, lifting my butt and squeezing closer to Tom on the other side.

"Ouch, the seat is blazing," Tom whined, his legs sticking out of his short pants and burning on the sun drenched red vinyl.

"Let's get going so we can at least have a breeze," Anyu grumbled to Apu who couldn't start driving fast enough to suit her. Irene leaned out the window to allow the breeze from the moving car to cool her down. Geza, on Tom's other side, also got to sit next to the window, as he was older. My parents and Paul were crammed across the bench seat in the front of the car. Each traffic light – and there were dozens of them – added to our misery for then, even the hot breezes weren't there to give us any relief. We inevitably arrived at Mass crumpled, sweaty, irritable and far from saintly.

For most of the year, though, the Sydney climate felt deliciously temperate and comfortable, and we had no need for climate control systems. As a child, I didn't fully appreciate the wonder of spending countless hours and days running around in shorts and flip-flops, totally in tune with the ambient temperature with nary a goose bump or bead of perspiration on my bare skin. What a gift to revel in the freedom and comfort of it all and to flow with my surroundings.

§

It was a huge deal when my father brought home a brand new television set, making space for it in the front room of our house, amidst the overlock and steam press machines. We all hooped and hollered as he and Paul lugged in the clunky, wood-framed console. My mother sat silently in the corner, her arms folded. "Hold on, hold on," Apu said with a laugh as we kids crowded around the TV. "I have to turn it on first." We backed off a little, waiting in excited anticipation as he plugged the set in and pulled out the on/off knob.

"There's no picture, is it broken?" I asked.

"It takes a while to warm up, stupid," Paul said. The screen brightened.

"Oh look, it's a flea dance," Tom squealed as he waddled up to touch the screen.

"You're in the way," Geza said. "Get out of there!"

Apu set the antenna on top of the console and attached its wires to the screws in the back. "This should help get us a better picture," he said moving the rabbit ears up and down and twisting it this way and that.

"That's it, Apu, right there," Paul interjected. "No, you went past it, come back a little."

"But the picture's flipping, and it's making me dizzy" Irene protested.

"Well, don't look at it then, bird brain," said Paul.

"Will you kids stop it?" Apu turned to look at us. "I'm trying to figure this out."

Paul quieted down and – always one to love fiddling with mechanical things – studied the console. "Here's a button that says vertical hold."

"Okay, try that," Apu said, sounding more frustrated.

"Look, I got it," Paul cried clapping his hands. "See, the picture's still now."

I hollered, "Oh, you can hear them talking; turn the volume up." We heard a man's voice and saw a gravelly picture of him sitting at a desk.

"He's talking about the news," Irene exclaimed, delighted.

"There are still shadows beside the figures," Apu noted, but try as he could – and as we all tried later – we never did get those grainy "ghosts" to disappear. It didn't matter. We loved watching anyway. We were even fascinated by the silent test patterns, which aired most of the time because broadcasts were initially limited to just a few evening hours.

Televisions were first introduced in Australia in time to telecast the 1956 Olympic Games from Melbourne. My father was one of the first of our friends to purchase a set. He bought it for my mother to make up for not taking her to see the Games. At the last minute, my parents decided to attend the Olympics after all and drove to Melbourne with friends. They relished reconnecting with my father's military academy friends who participated in the games as fencing and boxing trainers.

My father often boasted about the athletic abilities of the Hungarians. Indeed, the tiny country with a population of just ten million ranked in the top ten in most summer Olympic Games in the last fifty years of the twentieth century. In several Olympics, it placed in the top five.

I shared my father's pride in the athletes of his homeland. I wanted to believe that we as Hungarians were better, that we were superior, that we were among the best in the world. That's what Apu touted and tried to instill in me. Yes, I felt pride, but I also felt an underlying doubt, a sense of being less than. Though he didn't talk about his inferiority complex until decades later, I somehow sensed, even as a six-year-old that he, too, felt less than like me, and that he masked his unworthiness with Hungarian pride and bravado.

Hungary ranked fourth in medal standings in the 1956 Olympics, behind the Soviet Union, the U.S., and Australia, the host country. Those Melbourne games proved an emotional forum for Hungarians to vent their frustration and rage against the Communist occupation. Just a few weeks earlier, in a bloody battle, the Soviet army had crushed Hungarian attempts to revolt. The animosity climaxed when the Hungarians competed against the Soviets in the semi-final water polo event. The Hungarian and Russian competitors kicked and hit each other amidst cries of *"Hajrá Magyarok!"* (Go, Hungarians!). When one of the Hungarian players emerged from the pool with a bloody nose, many angry spectators jumped onto the concourse beside the water, shook their fists, shouted abuse, and spat at the Russians. To avoid a riot, police entered the arena with one minute to go, shepherded the crowd away, and ended the game. The subsequent newspaper headlines of "Blood in the Water Match" may have been an exaggeration but the vitriol and angst of the Hungarians and their sympathizers were not. The Hungarians beat the Soviets and went on to win their fourth gold medal in water polo, defeating Yugoslavia in the final game.

My father's national pride and compassion for the suffering of his compatriots prompted him to help provide opportunities for several 1956 Hungarian revolution refugees. He hired some at the knitwear factory and for the most part, they worked out well. He and Anyu had built enough of a financial base by then that they were able to purchase an inexpensive rental home for one of the displaced families. They wanted to provide better initial living quarters than my family had had in the grim Greta refugee camp. But this outreach gesture didn't turn out so well.

"My God, they've punched holes in the walls, stopped up the drains. Hell, I had to pull out clothes that they had stuffed down the toilet," my father bellowed one afternoon pacing about the kitchen and banging on the counter. He added, "This time those goddamn gypsies have gone too far!" Anyu gave him a withering look, and then resumed stirring the *császármorzsa* ("emperor's crumbs") she was preparing for dinner.

"Maybe it wasn't such a good idea for you to buy that rental house in the first place," she said. "How are you going to get out of this mess? They're not even paying rent. We're losing more and more money, month after month."

"I know, I know," Apu replied, dragging his hand through his thick hair. I stood by the kitchen table, my eyes locked on my shoes and the concrete floor.

Császármorzsa, made of toasted pancake dough and served with either milk coffee or cocoa, was my brother Paul's favorite. Anyu often made it as a last minute eat-no-meat Friday dinner dish. I loathed it. My parents were arguing yet again, and that soured the upcoming meal even more. I hated their heated discussions. They worried me and I feared they might split our family apart. I quietly set the table, placing the spoons next to the chipped bowls, remaining as inconspicuous as possible.

With the help of city officials, my father finally managed to evict the tenants. Sick at heart, he sold the rental house at a significant loss. Even though I hated that the rental episode was a frequent source of my parents heated quarrels, I was proud of their reaching out to support their compatriots.

§

With my parents so busy with the knitting business, I wound up spending a lot of time taking care of my younger brother, Tom. I was six and he barely three, but we'd walk more than two miles from our Union Street house to the North Sydney Olympic Pool. There we swam and frolicked for hours in the salt water complex picturesquely set between the Sydney Harbour Bridge on one side and Lavender Bay on the other. We even ventured into the sixteen-foot deep end with only lifeguards supervising us.

One time as we were walking home from the pool I ran ahead of Tom. With his chubby short legs, he couldn't keep up and began to wail, "Lizzie, Lizzie, please stop. Please, please wait for me." I got a perverse pleasure out of his distress and stayed just beyond his reach. He soon became completely unglued and panicked, screaming in terror. "Don't go, don't go, don't leave me!"

My mean streak softened. I ran toward him and gathered him up in my arms. He hiccupped and sobbed and firmly grasped his arms about my neck. I felt a guilty pang and hugged him tighter. Nevertheless, I persisted in pushing the boundaries with Tom, taunting and teasing him. The most frequent sin I reported to the priest at nearly every confession was "being bad to my little brother." I passed on to poor Tom what my older siblings did to me – and more.

When Tom was four, he and I walked up to the North Sydney retail area to buy another matchbox car to add to his growing collection. A poster of a Holden sedan in a shop window caught our attention. Excited, we strolled into the store to purchase it. The chubby shopkeeper with painted blonde hair and a smock over her muumuu took our shillings and handed us a Sydney Opera House lottery ticket, popping the stub in a large box. I balked and asked, "Where is the matchbox Holden?" With her hands on her hips, she replied, "It's a raffle, love, and you have a great chance of winning a real car."

My brother and I stumbled out of the shop and burst out crying. Tom wailed, "I want my matchbox car." I was terrified that we'd win the car and that my parents would be furious with us. The huge car would be a major inconvenience for them, a big burden. What would they do with it? Where would they park it? I felt certain I would be severely punished.

Facing my parents and the perceived burden of owning and caring for a real car loomed as a far greater catastrophe than the embarrassment of returning to the shop to beg for the ticket stub to be destroyed. We crept back into the store, holding hands, with tear-stained faces and hiccupping pleas. "Please, could you take the lottery ticket out of the box?" The bemused shopkeeper assured us with a grin. "Sure, love, I'll make sure you won't win the car." I handed her the lottery ticket and she gave us the matchbox car we had originally wanted to buy. Relief flooded me. I had averted what I felt sure would have been an unmitigated disaster. We walked home, tear-stained but relieved. Our parents, caught up as usual in their factory work, didn't notice a thing. This time I felt relieved to escape their attention.

§

The knitwear business accumulated a few good years of solid gains. My parents had weathered several lean years where anxious discussions of looming bankruptcy peppered their conversations, giving me the willies. Now with their flush profits in the bank, they were ready to relocate the knitwear factory to an industrial area warehouse and, after seven years, separate it from our family home.

CHAPTER 3 – LOOKS LIKE WE MADE IT

Our stately home on Milner Crescent in Wollstonecraft.

My younger brother Tom and I dancing the twist at brother Paul's 21st birthdaybash. I'm wearing my sister's hand-me-down dress and my first ever high heels.

My father burst into the front room. "I've found us a house," he declared with a huge grin. My mother, seated at an overlock machine, snipped the edge of a loose thread on a garment and looked up at him with a smile. I stood in the doorway, out of their line of sight. "I just went through it with Sándor and he agrees with me that it's a great deal at nine thousand pounds and he said to jump on it." Sándor was a Hungarian friend of ours, Tom's godfather in fact, who happened to also be a real estate agent. Apu leaned against the overlock machine and took Anyu's hand. "The house is on a corner lot and that's more desirable and it's in Wollstonecraft, an upscale neighborhood. We've made it, Irene. We'll finally be able to move out of the slums." My mother patted his hand, "All right then," she said. I smiled and hugged myself. Maybe this time, in a new house, my parents would be happy. My hopes rose and joy bubbled in my throat.

We moved in late 1959, and the stately home became our family mansion for the next six years, from the time I was nine until age fifteen. We had arrived. We had finally transcended our marginal existence as immigrants and refugees.

The house perched on a corner lot, the rear of which abutted the North Shore railroad line, and the tracks ran right behind the property. The deafening rumble and rattling of windows as trains passed every few minutes became part of our daily cacophony. We hardly noticed it after living in the house for a few weeks.

Ever the trickster, my brother Paul loved to pull a railroad line joke: he and his mates picked random numbers from the phone book for homes located in train station neighborhoods, and rang them up in the middle of the night. In an innocent voice he asked, "Hello sir, do you happen to live on the North Shore line?" When the groggy, barely awake resident slurred, "Umm, yeah . . . yes we do," my brother yelled, "Well get off the bloody tracks, the train is coming!"

§

The front of the house had a formal garden, my mother's pride and joy. Her most peaceful times were spent watering in the late summer afternoons, hose poised in her hand, fanning the water spray over the garden, a soft smile buttering her face. She planned the flowerbeds that edged the pathways with Lőrinc Bácsi, ("Uncle Lőrinc.") He was my godmother's husband and he spent most Saturdays planting, pruning and mowing, perspiration soaking his short, squat body. Using his first name followed by "uncle" was the Hungarian traditional sign of respect for our elders.

Behind the flowerbeds bloomed a row of rose trees and beyond them a lawn, which Lőrinc Bácsi kept manicured to perfection. A hedgerow of azaleas lay under the windows, delighting me each spring with their resplendent splashes of gold, salmon, pink and scarlet blossoms. In the middle of the front lawn stood a large poinsettia tree, big enough to climb.

On the lateral street side of the house a frangipani tree scented the walkway and in back, a vivid purple bougainvillea stuck up every which way over the garage like a bed-head hairdo. On the other side of the house, by the side door, a passion fruit vine bore delicious fruit, invariably snatched by one of us kids as soon as one turned from green to wrinkly plush plum. Many a time I waited eagerly for one of these luscious treats to ripen, only to find that one of my sibs had plucked it first.

The backyard had two clotheslines strung from wooden posts since we, as most families in Australia in the sixties, had no clothes dryer. Our "modern" washing machine came equipped with an attached set of electric rollers to wring out the washed clothes.

One time my mother accidentally fed her arm into the wringer. I was playing in the back yard and her screams and sobbing startled me. She ran out of the laundry hugging her left arm, already swollen like a sausage. Apu flew out of the house to see what had happened.

"This looks serious: I'm taking you to the casualty ward."

"No, oh no," Anyu whined hysterically. "I don't want to go to the hospital." She flapped her uninjured arm pushing my father's helping hand away.

"Come on, Irene. We have to go," he coaxed, braving her swats and putting his arm around her. He gently led her to the car. I felt relieved to see her return home a few hours later with her arm in a sling for comfort and with the good news that the X-ray showed no fracture.

In contrast to her usual strong-willed ways, Anyu had a morbid fear of doctors and of undergoing surgery. She was petrified that she would die. When she needed an operation for an abscessed cyst in her jaw, she screamed and resisted. Apu, somewhat embarrassed at her frantic outburst, especially when she acted out in front of the doctors, did his best to settle her down and talk sense into her. After much babying and coddling, he was able to persuade her to undergo anesthesia, and she fortunately came through the surgery without complications.

My mother stepped into the role of a child when confronted with health problems. My father became the tolerant and directive parent. The roles they customarily played in their relationship at such times reversed – she shifting from her usual controlling manner to one of submissiveness; my father replacing his acquiescence with a calm but firm control. I was puzzled by my mother's childish behavior and, like my father, embarrassed by it. This was another instance that I empathized with him and failed to appreciate my mother's terror.

I thought she used her dramas as a way of capturing Apu's attention. I failed to see that perhaps her underlying motive was a cry for help, a need to be taken care of, a primitive demand to be loved. Her acting out served to cover up her feelings of vulnerability.

After her jaw surgery, my mother vowed she would not have any further operations and it wasn't until she was in her eighties, when her vision became so compromised from cataracts, that we were able to persuade her to undergo surgery. She had the procedure performed on a single eye and declared that that was all she needed. She could see just fine and refused to have surgery on the other eye.

In her late eighties, Anyu fell and fractured her hip. I rushed to the ER as soon as I heard and found her already drugged for pain. By then, the seeds of Alzheimer's were planted in her brain: she was leaving notes for her Hispanic housecleaner in Hungarian; she kept repeating herself and didn't remember events.

"Anyu, you have broken your hip and you need surgery to fix it," I told her. She smiled at me through a drug-induced daze and patted my hand. She offered no resistance, a marked shift from her previous attitude towards medical procedures. Though relieved that she was willing to proceed with surgery without a fight, I felt sad to see that the combination of the sedatives and dementia had robbed her of her spunk and tenacity. A part of me mourned the vibrant drama queen mother who was no more.

§

Built in the 1930s, our Wollstonecraft house stood as a venerable dark brick edifice festooned with a wood columned porch and leaded glass windows. The entry expanded to a sunny nook off to the right where my mother kept long trays held up by wrought iron stands that she filled with her beloved potted plants: cyclamens, rubber plants and palms. This nook was also where our dangly, lopsided Christmas tree stood every December. The pine tree options in the hot Aussie summers were spindly at best, but I loved them anyway.

The large living area was elegantly paneled in strips of dark oak topped at six feet with a narrow wooden ledge. One year my parents hosted a fancy formal party and my mother placed candles all along the ledges. Proud of what she considered to be an original and elegant decorative motif, she puffed out her chest and smiled with pleasure as she lapped up guests' compliments.

Two of the "bedrooms" opened onto the verandah and had no outside windows. These interior rooms could not be advertised as bedrooms because they did not meet the code standards. My parents scoffed at these requirements and much to their delight, the fewer bedroom listing lowered the price of the home. I for one never worried that my health was hampered breathing "stale" air in my bedroom. My sister and I shared one sub-code bedroom, my middle and younger brother the other.

The enclosed L-shaped verandah with its leaded glass windows was the family hangout. The daily sun tracked along its curved span from the northeast to the southwest. I had a favorite spot at one end where I wiled away many lonely hours playing a ballgame that I had learned at school. I threw a tennis ball for seven straight catches off the wall, then seven bounce and catches, seven reverse bounce and catches, seven turns and catches. I repeated the whole sequence with each hand, then with ever-increasing numbers of claps in between. The rhythm and successful repetitions fed my need for a sense of accomplishment. When I dropped the ball, I would fume and beat up on myself. Each failure fueled my lack of self-confidence. I would flush, remembering how quickly I had been eliminated in that same ball game at school and I'd throw the ball hard against the wall in utter frustration.

In this same section of the verandah, my younger brother, Tom, spent his solitary hours painstakingly laying out scores of soldiers, cowboys, and Indians, and reenacting strategic battles he'd read about in his history books. On late, dark nights, the rest of us stumbled over the sharp soldiers, cursing poor Tom.

In the middle of the L-shaped verandah lay a beige shag area rug topped by comfortable, well-worn rattan furniture. The brightest light graced this corner and here is where I loved to read novels – including my Enid Blyton *Famous Five* mysteries – and where, in the era prior to permanent press, my sister and I ironed everything from shirts and handkerchiefs to bed linens.

My parents set up a ping-pong table at the other end of the verandah. The scant clearance between the table and the walls hampered cross table shots, but despite these restrictions, we kids delighted in sparring with each other. Once in a while my forehand slammed perfectly, and this fueled my competitive streak.

"Oh ho, gotcha with that slam," I cried with glee. "Tied at seven all."

"It won't last, I'll get you yet" Tom said, picking up the ball and preparing to serve.

"See! Gotcha back," he said, face aglow as an ace serve flew by me.

"Well, you haven't won yet." I growled as I reached down to pick up the ball. My next two serves landed in the net.

"Damn," I muttered to myself.

"You're losing it, sis." Tom was gloating. I could have slugged him. I felt prickly all over and my nose began to itch with tears. When my next two slams also landed in the net, my shoulders slumped and my throat filled. I didn't say a word. My game had fallen apart. Tom was relentless, though. He had found his rhythm and was making shots impossible for me to return. I lunged and landed against the wall with a thud. Then I gave up trying to reach the cross table shots.

"Ha, ha, you can't hit a thing," he said as he lobbed another shot out of reach. "Try and get that one," he teased. I flushed bright red, with rage as much as from the exertion.

"You don't have to rub it in," I whined, completely undone.

"But it feels so good to see you squirm. Twenty to ten. Game point. Come on, give it to me," he taunted. I didn't even try to return his serve. I let the ball whiz right by me.

"I'm on a roll, let's play another game," he said with a chuckle.

"I'm done and you're mean," I yelled, slamming the paddle on the table. I turned and stomped away, hiccupping and heaving with my tears.

§

We removed the ping-pong table to make room for dancing at my oldest brother's black-tie twenty-first birthday party. Middle brother Geza served as disc jockey, playing record cuts on the hi-fi stereo relocated to the room adjacent to the dance area. I had turned thirteen that year and Anyu let me wear my first grown-up party dress to Paul's coming of age celebration. The dress was a pink dotted-swiss, full-skirted frock that was a hand-me-down from my sister. Grinning and blushing, my hair salon-coiffed, and wearing sling-back shoes – my first ever heels – I was thrilled to be allowed to join the grownup festivities, and to participate in my brother and sister's much coveted social life. I was at the same event with their friends, older boys that I had frightful crushes on.

"May I sit next to you?" Frank asked, pointing to the empty seat next to me with a flourish, his face framed with curly dark hair, his eyes dancing behind dark rimmed glasses.

"Of course," I answered, flushing with delight, for one of my sister's boyfriends had just spoken to me!

"Great party," he continued, "And I must say, you look very pretty tonight." I blushed and couldn't think of a thing to say. I was brain dead.

"Smile for the camera," Klári Néni ordered, looking down at her lens and snapping a shot of Frank and me. She, a good friend of my parents, was a professional photographer and was shooting my brother's bash. I smiled brightly for the pictures and then looked down at my clasped hands, bashful again.

"I saw you dancing with Tommy a while ago." Frank smiled. "You looked like you two were having fun. Would you do me the honor of dancing with me too?" I grinned like an idiot.

"I'd love to!" I replied gingerly placing my hand in his outstretched one as he helped me up and led me to the dance floor. I was over the moon! One of the grown up boys had shown me some attention, and I'd been asked to dance by someone other than my baby brother! Now, if I could just keep from stepping on Frank's toes. But Frank was a good dancer and easily led me in rock 'n roll moves to Elvis' "Return to Sender." "Thank you," I said at the song's end, breathless as much from the gracious attention Frank had given me as from the exertion. My teenage hormones raged. Frank bowed and moved on.

"Well done, sis." Tom grinned. "You looked good out there on the dance floor." I thanked him. I gazed about and espied tall and taciturn med student, Mick. He was the boy I most idolized. He didn't ask me to dance and hardly noticed me, but at least I was in the same room, attending the same party.

Later that evening Paul asked me to dance. In fact, he cut in when he saw me being held tightly, widely swaying to and fro in a slow dance.

"That guy was completely smashed," he muttered as he steered me away. "Stay away from him." Too naïve to know any better, I hadn't realized how drunk the fellow had been. I felt grateful to Paul for watching out for his kid sister.

§

My birthday party that year was a very different story. I had turned thirteen and was feeling rather grown up and excited, having finally been allowed to invite some of my schoolmates to my own party.

"Oh, what lovely panties! Thank you so much Lisa," I exclaimed, patting the matched set of lacy bikini briefs in pastel pink, green and blue. She smiled, her freckled face framed with flaming curls. "I'll love wearing them. They're so feminine."

"Open mine next," Shari said. A somewhat chunky girl with close-cropped dark hair, she pushed her gift into my lap. I untied the lovely purple satin ribbon and tore into the shiny wrapping paper.

"So beautiful." I smiled.

"It's a teacup and saucer and dessert dish. You can start your trousseau with it," Shari said with pride. I gingerly picked up the teacup.

"Such delicate china. I love the floral pattern. Thank you so much." I opened two more tea sets, all fine china with dainty flower designs. I felt so grown up and I felt so happy to be closer to some of my Aussie schoolmates.

Then, my parents came into the room with a large box. "For you, from us," Apu announced with a proud grin. The box wasn't wrapped and the cellophane window showed a doll: an oversized, gaudy, bridal-clad confection. I was stunned!

"Thank you," I muttered, but inside I was seething. My parents had gifted me with my first doll at age thirteen! I was a teenager, for God's sake! What on earth were my parents thinking? I avoided eye contact with my friends. They smiled and didn't say a thing. I shivered to think what they had made of this dumb gift. Good grief, they must see me as an overgrown baby.

The dratted doll had come several years too late. It seemed to me as if my parents were trying to make up for their omissions in my toddler years by buying the biggest and most ornate doll they could find. I never played with that doll. It sat on my bed for a day or two but then I stuffed it in the back of my closet so I could obliterate the embarrassment I'd endured in front of my friends.

§

I looked up to my older sister, Irene. She was pretty and I have to admit I was a bit jealous of her perfectly straight teeth. In contrast, my front teeth were overlapped and my incisors inched halfway up to my nose. Irene was popular and had boyfriends that I coveted. She attended parties and balls and wore gorgeous evening gowns designed by my mother.

I sometimes accompanied Anyu and Irene when they drove to the other side of Sydney to confer about fabric choices, and for measurements and fittings with a Hungarian dressmaker. I thought the chubby widow very elegant in her black, short snug skirt, paired with an angora grey sweater, the look finished nicely with dark shaded hose. She loved her sewing work and smiled and laughed as she pinned and adjusted my sister's gowns. "Ah, she's beautiful, no?" the dressmaker would coo as Irene stood for a fitting.

My sister was the center of attention. I stayed on the sideline, witnessing the hoopla and excitement as the invitations to attend dances and balls poured in, hoping my turn would come soon. I got to wear Irene's gowns as hand-me-downs years later. The pink dotted-swiss cocktail dress that she wore to a cadet dance I wore to Paul's twenty-first birthday party. The apricot silk ball gown with the lace top that she wore to a Hungarian White Rose Ball, I wore to my fifth-year high school dance. To a cadet dance I was invited to, I wore a makeshift long black skirt and beaded knit top my mother threw together at the last minute. The dressmaker created no gowns for me, but then I received far fewer invitations than Irene had, and attended far fewer dances than my sister. I was less of a poster child for my mother's fashion sense. I wistfully sang Streisand's "Second-hand Rose" from *Funny Girl* to myself. It fit how I felt: the slighted, second-best daughter.

My sister glowed in her most elegant ball gown of all, an aqua one-shoulder chiffon creation with a wide, white, satin beaded belt. My mother copied the dress from one Elizabeth Taylor wore in the movie *Elephant Walk*. When Irene's date arrived to escort her to the Hungarian White Rose Ball, my sister breezed into the room like an apparition, her gown flowing around her, her hair styled in a soft chignon. She looked like a goddess. The young man's jaw dropped. He clicked his heels in military fashion style and abashedly kissed her hand. Unlike her other hand me down gowns, I didn't get to wear that most coveted of all her dresses until twenty years later.

Anyu had a great eye for design and my sense of fashion came from her. Over and above being responsible for creating new season samples and the fact that the family's livelihood depended on our knitwear being fashionable, my mother loved to flip through *Women's Day*, *Vogue*, and *Seventeen* magazines simply to check out the latest styles and see what the movie and TV stars were wearing. She loved the chic and the glamor.

My mother dressed well and nearly always wore a stylish hat and soft leather gloves when she was out and about, except perhaps on the hottest days of summer. She wore trendy low-heeled leather pumps even to work where she stood at the cutting tables for grueling hours on end. She never gave in to wearing more comfortable sneakers or orthotic shoes, despite her aching corns.

Anyu designed the new sweater styles each year for the knitwear factory, creating and cutting brown paper patterns for these original *"ötlet"* ideas. Some of the most vehement arguments between my parents raged over my mother's tardiness in completing designs. While working on homework in my room one evening, I heard them arguing in the living room.

"Please, would you get them done? You know we have to get the samples out to the stores by the beginning of the month," my father begged.

My mother shot back. "You keep hounding me, and I'm fed up with doing all the work around here. I'm the one that works the hardest."

My father finally lost his cool and shouted back at my mother, *"A rosseb egyen meg!"* Ah, a pox on it! He then stormed out of the house and headed back to the factory to work and to stew.

My mother went about the house as if nothing had happened. Her lip curled in a small smile, which looked to me like she was basking in a victory, like a cat that had swallowed the canary. She had achieved the upper hand, gotten a rise out of my usually even-tempered father, and she had deflected her responsibility for getting the samples done. I took my father's side. I felt his pain and frustration at my mother's putdown. I knew he worked just as hard as my mother, and was just as smart, and I resented that she didn't support him. I hated even more that she belittled him.

§

Sometimes I wished I had a sister with whom I could be close, but Irene remained distant for the most part, caught up in her own teenage struggles. My parents gave her a transistor radio and it remained glued to her ear, a constant companion in bed, in the car, at the beach, everywhere. Transistors were the newest fad and my sister used hers as a way to tune out the family. The radio was the size of a shoebox, with a stylish blue leather exterior, whose luster quickly wore out from constant banging and carting around. It was heavy as lead from all the tubes and the battery inside, but my sister didn't seem to mind lugging it around.

Irene often disappeared for hours without letting anyone know where she was. My mother wrung her hands and fretted over her disappearances. My father fumed. When my sister would finally show up, she'd refuse to tell any of us why she'd left and where she had been. A stony silence filled the house for days after one of her absences.

One evening my father picked her up after an outing with friends. He became incensed when he saw her smoking on the street corner, her fingernails painted a bilious green. He yelled at her as he shoved her in the car. "You look like a prostitute," he fumed. Though he made her remove the nail polish, he could never get her to stop smoking – not even decades later.

Even though I admired my sister, I mostly avoided her. She was prickly and testy and I didn't want to provoke her, or raise her hackles, but I couldn't escape her wrath entirely.

She often recruited me to curl her hair. Her instructions were exacting. "No, no, not sideways. Roll the curler towards the back." She checked my work in a hand held mirror as I struggled to loop her stick straight hair around the rollers. "Tighter, tighter. The curl is too loose. You missed a piece of hair, right there. Quit being such a klutz." I believed her. Her criticism deepened my insecurities, and made me fumble even more. When I inadvertently pulled her hair, she screamed, "Ow! You idiot. Stop yanking my hair!" I kept at it, finished the job amidst the yelps and the put-downs. I saved the tears for afterwards. I didn't want to hear her disparaging "What a baby!"

Years later, my sister acknowledged that she had acted like a spoiled brat and apologized for her diva behavior. But when we were kids, I thought I deserved her criticism. I was the less smart, less popular, and awkward younger sister. The way she treated me meshed completely with my poor self-concept.

Though I didn't have a great relationship with my sister, I will forever be grateful to her for helping me over one major hurdle: she enlightened me about periods. Anyu didn't teach either of us about menstruation. Without any discussion or instruction, she simply handed us a box of pads when we reached menarche. Irene spent most of her teen years believing that periods were a family disease until she learned about the menstrual cycle in a biology class she took her first year at university. As soon as I began to have periods, my sister took me aside. She brought out her biology textbook, showed me the anatomic illustrations of the female organs, and taught me what our mother had failed to teach her: the physiology of reproduction. Her caring attention saved me from the grief and guilt she had suffered alone for years. Her thoughtfulness more than made up for the times she ignored me, the times she yelled at me, and for the messes that collected on her side of our bedroom.

A few years later, in my fourth year of high school, the nuns, in a progressive and groundbreaking move, put on a sex education class. Mother John Bosco, who had left her medical practice to join the nunnery, taught the class. In order for us to participate, we were required to have our mothers accompany us. The nuns wanted full transparency and disclosure about the sensitive information they were about to teach. I cajoled my mother into coming. There was no way I wanted to face the shame of being the lone student unable to take the course. In the classroom, the Aussie mothers chitchatted amongst themselves. My mother and I remained silent. She didn't know any of the other mothers and she hardly spoke any English. I squirmed, feeling embarrassed, and relief flooded over me when the social niceties were over and the presentation finally began.

I'd already heard the material of the lecture from my sister, so there were no surprises for me, but I wondered what my mother's reaction was. How much of the English did she understand? How much of the subject matter – like ovarian cycles and optimum time for conception – was new to her? Was she embarrassed by the explicit information? Anyu sat through the presentation with a faint smile on her face – as mysterious as the Mona Lisa. Afterwards, all she said was that she liked the lecture. I was afraid to ask her about any particulars and it didn't enter my mind to confront her about her lack of instruction with me. Had I challenged her, I feared her comeback would have been that the school took care of it anyway so that took care of it.

§

In the Wollstonecraft house, my parents' bedroom also served as the dining room as well as the TV room. An imposing table blocked the view between the twin beds, which edged against the walls on either side of the room. The beds were camouflaged during the day as divans. My mother fashioned bright red and green abstract patterned slipcovers and bolsters for the beds to hide their nighttime function.

My parents placed the television set in the dining room, ensuring that they maintained control over what and how much we watched. On the rare occasions when I became ill, I spent most of the day alone, my mother at work in the knitwear factory, my sibs at school. I'd lie on Anyu's bed watching old movies on TV like *The Court Jester* with Danny Kaye and *Madame Curie* with Greer Garson. This proved a double-edged privilege, as I loved watching TV, but felt miserable and alone, sick in bed.

I found the unusual setup of dining room, bedroom, sitting room, TV room rather strange, even as a youngster. The separation and obstruction of the beds by the dining table, and their daytime camouflage reflected how I viewed my parents' relationship. I hardly remember them hugging or kissing. Apart from their arguing, they covered up their feelings amid the hard work of running their knitwear business and raising the family. I didn't fully realize the gaps in their relationship, their lack of affection for each other. I couldn't make sense of their behavior. All I could pick up on was a generic malaise that existed between them.

A modern china sideboard butted up against one wall of the dining/master bedroom. It had a fold down door in which polished stones were embedded in fiberglass. My mother cherished this ultra-modern piece so much that she had it shipped when we emigrated to the United States five years later.

Anyu loved modern furniture. She wanted to dispense with everything old or antique, all of which she associated with her musty, impoverished childhood environment. It's as if she wished to leave all the pain of her Hungarian life behind, a life that had betrayed her and was now lost to her. It was her attempt to begin anew, to fit in in a new country, to blend in with the changing world currents. Now that she could finally afford new furniture, she only wanted the newest, most avant-garde styles. As with her fashion sense, she hungered for the latest designs, the newest fads: white extra shaggy rugs, a royal blue coarse weave couch with stark straight wooden legs and sharp angles.

I didn't care for the modern furniture. It felt cold and unyielding, and mirrored all too well the relationships within our family: relationships that were monochromatic like the white and blue primary colors of the décor, hard like the rocks in the dining room sideboard. The traditional Hungarian embroidered throw pillows my mother added to the couch did little to warm the furnishings, just as our Hungarian heritage did little to deepen our connections with each other. I didn't know how to relate sincerely with my sibs or my parents. I didn't know how to share my feelings, my worries. I had no confidantes. I felt isolated, my life stark, and this detachment and coldness was reflected in every new piece of modern furniture my mother proudly brought into our home.

§

"Dinner's ready," Anyu called. My brothers quickly appeared, dragging the oblong kitchen table out from the wall so that all seven of us could fit around it. Anyu stood at the ancient gas stove and ladled the Lipton's chicken noodle soup, fortified with a can of green peas and extra noodles. Irene and I took turns carrying the bowls the step or two to the table.

Anyu and Apu took their seats at either end. Tom, Irene and I scrunched together with our backs against the wall. Paul and Geza got to sit on the open side. Led by Apu, we all mumbled the quick blessing:

Edes Jézus légy vendégünk áld meg amit adtál nékünk. Amen.

Dear Lord Jesus, be our guest. Let this food by thee be blest. Amen.

The bottle of cod liver oil appeared in Anyu's hand. We kids let out a chorus of "eews!" It was the same drill every night.

"Cut it out and show me your spoons," she said. We each dutifully held them out to be filled with the foul smelling oily swill. We scrunched our faces at the ghastly taste and dove into our soup. It's a wonder the cod liver oil ritual didn't turn me off of soups for life but my love of potages didn't wane at all.

"You'll have to get some Johnny Walker for Jozsi's birthday party," Anyu said looking at Apu. He glanced at her. She held his gaze.

"I can stop by the bottle shop on the way home from the factory." He sipped another spoonful of soup.

Paul grinned. "You'll get to check out all the Aussie drunks getting pissed before the pub closes at six."

"Why do they close at six?" Tom asked.

"It's the only way to keep the sots from carousing all night. Kick 'em out early and make 'em go home to their wives," Paul said. He laughed and so did the rest of the family. I tittered nervously to fit in, but I felt uncomfortable. Paul loved pub-crawling with his mates and boasted about his drinking – why was he making fun of the Aussies who did the same thing?

"They had to pass a law to get the drunks to go home," Apu said. "Those Aussies hit the pubs as soon as they knock off work. They're lazy bastards. They put in their nine-to-five, make union wages." And he added as he always did. "They have no ambition." Apu looked pointedly around the table at each one of us in turn. "We Hungarians are smarter and we work harder. Don't any of you forget that." He cast his eyes down at his empty bowl and his mouth tightened. "The Aussies are jealous of our success. They hate us for that."

What had the Aussies done to Apu? I was too scared to ask. I looked at my sister as she slurped her broth directly from the bowl, leaving the delectable, drained noodles and peas for last. I relaxed a little, joined in, and did the same. We grinned at each other. After we finished licking our bowls, Anyu plonked the next course into them: a grilled pork chop and a lump of potatoes sautéed with onions.

"Close your mouth when you chew, *Csámcsogó*" (muncher)," — my father yelled at Paul. My brother grinned in embarrassment. The drama repeated itself almost nightly. I didn't understand the reasons for Paul's lack of a learning curve and cringed when my father shouted at him. I made sure to keep my mouth closed when I chewed.

§

During the workweek my mother quickly slapped dinner together after a full day in the factory. She fixed a soup every day of the year, sometimes the embellished Lipton's soup, but mostly browning a quick roux, adding paprika, some vegetables and noodles.

But on Sundays, my mother poured her heart into the lunch fare. She made beef broth from scratch, spread and salted the fatty marrow from inside the soup bones onto toast points, serving them as appetizers. She then added cream of wheat dumplings to the savory broth. Alternately, she'd fix a chicken soup, spiced with a paprika roux, filled with vegetables and tiny pasta that she individually twirled and shaped with her fingers, setting each nugget on a clean tea towel. For the main course, she'd fry Wiener schnitzel, or she'd chop onions till her eyes watered, adding them to her versions of the traditional Hungarian *gulyás* (beef stew) or chicken paprikas. When we had roast or fried chicken, the distribution was always the same. My sister and I nibbled on the wings, maybe a drumstick and my mother gnawed on the back. The boys and my father ate the bulk of the bird.

Baked delicacies became the most awaited *pièce de résistance* of our Sunday meals. Our mouths watered as Anyu prepared her raised dough delights. We didn't mind when she recruited us to help out with the arm-aching task of beating the dough until the requisite blisters appeared. I snuck globs of the sweet yeasty dough while resting my weary arms, but my mother invariably noticed me snitching, and rapped my knuckles, a smirk on her face. The smack was worth it.

With the yeast dough she baked either *darázsfészek* (walnut rolls) – like cinnamon rolls except with loads of butter, walnuts, and sugar substituted for the cinnamon filling – and *arany galuska* (golden dumplings), rounds of dough dipped in the same buttery walnut mixture, layered and baked in a casserole. My mother gained fame amongst our Sydney Hungarian friends for her *fánk*, donuts so delicate that a central ribbon formed in the rising when fried on each side in peanut oil.

My mother limited my duties in the kitchen to setting the table and washing and drying the dishes. She never encouraged me to assist her with cooking. The few times I volunteered to help her chop or stir, she pushed my hand out of the way and took over the task herself. I believed I was a klutz. I was naturally left-handed, as was my brother, Paul. My parents called him *suta balkezes* – "lame left-handed" – and forced him to use his right hand. To avoid similar ridicule, I taught myself to write right-handed, but for most tasks that I didn't think of, like using a knife or scissors, I reverted to my natural left-handedness. I wasn't surprised that my mother had no patience with me. She could do it all better and faster. The last thing I wanted to do was to irritate her and so I avoided helping her in the kitchen.

§

In 1964, when I was thirteen, Anyu and Irene journeyed to Europe and to Communist Hungary for four months. By then, the knitwear factory had grown into a flourishing enterprise whose profits provided the financing for the trip. The passage of a few years had dissipated the intensity and backlash of the 1956 Hungarian Revolution, and the communist restrictions had loosened toward returning natives. Anyu took this opportunity to visit her ill mother in Szentes, the small town where she grew up, southeast of Budapest in the plains country of the Tisza River. Her heart forever remained in those farming flatlands. Years later, when we took her on trips to the Cascade Mountains outside of Seattle, she would complain about the heights.

"These steep roads make me dizzy," she'd say, squeezing her eyes shut. "These mountains are horrible!"

"But look how gorgeous the glaciers and crags are, Anyu," I'd exclaim.

"Bah," she'd scoff, "There's nothing more beautiful than the great plains where I grew up." I could never get her to appreciate alpine country.

Anyu was the oldest of three sisters born to an assistant merchant father and a seamstress mother. My grandmother provided the financial support for the family once her husband became disabled with chronic heart problems resulting from rheumatic fever as a child.

My grandmother worked at home dressmaking and making alterations for customers, but she loathed her seamstress work. Anyu complained that she too had succumbed to a similar hateful fate in Australia, working in a knitwear factory to help support the family. Surprisingly, in contrast to her early dislike of making a living doing handwork, Anyu, in her later years took up knitting, needlepoint, crocheting, and other crafts with considerable relish. It was her way of staying connected, remembering her mother, and occupying her many hours alone.

Anyu worked her way out of humble beginnings by applying herself, excelling in high school, garnering a scholarship to attend the University of Szeged. She was the only family member to study beyond high school and she earned a degree in mathematics and physics. As a rare female at the university, professors doted on her and she soaked up the attention. My mother's "minority" status in academia foreshadowed my own entry into the male bastion of medicine in the 1970s.

Growing up, I listened to Anyu's repeating lament. Delivered with a faint smile that unsettled me, she would sigh, "Ah, my university years were the best in my life; it's all been downhill since then." When she, yet again, breezily dropped the statement, dramatically gazing out of the verandah window of our Wollstonecraft home, I could no longer let it go. I tried to make light of her comment, desperately wanting to hear that she liked her life right now, her life with me, with all of the family.

"But we are part of the best years of your life too, aren't we?" I exclaimed.

She replied without hesitation and with a grin and an icy stare. "I never wanted you." I roiled inside, kept a smile plastered on my face and thought to myself that she must be teasing, but her gaze remained steady and unrelenting. Anyu then marched away with a sickening grin on her face, as if she relished the pain she had caused. I felt crushed and conflicted. Shaking, I turned and shuffled to my bedroom, collapsing on my bed. For years, my feelings of being unwanted battled with any sense of worthiness I was able to muster.

§

My mother lived a paradox. Despite her intelligence, her university education, and her years of teaching high school math, science, and gymnastics in Hungary, she believed in the superstitions of her small town upbringing. For example, she would never sit with thirteen at a table – that presaged bad luck, and she yelled and threatened to leave unless some of us were banned from the table. In later years, when our family grew with in-laws and children, the large gatherings were often marred by her embarrassing outbursts.

My mother refused to have pictures taken with all of the family together. That too was bad luck, and meant that one of us would die soon. With each new moon, she took out coins from her purse and pretended to spit on them saying, "Poo poo, your mother, father come here, poo poo, your mother, father come here." This assured that her money would multiply.

On New Year's Eve, a blond man had to be the first to wish her happy New Year or else she'd have bad luck all year. This role belonged to my father until, in later years when my parents' relationship soured, the obligation passed on to my blond brother-in-law. The rest of us knew to stay mum until the New Year wish had been delivered by the appropriate good luck charmer. Also, on

New Year's Day several protocols needed to be followed for luck to come that year: don't spend money for then you will spend all year; don't eat chicken or other fowl for then your luck will fly away; do eat lentils for beauty, rice for money, pork for luck. For my mother, these superstitions were more than quaint traditions; she was dead serious, and raged when crossed or teased about them. I keep my mother's New Year's Day superstitions, partly for tradition's sake, partly as a way to remember her.

§

Even though my relationship with Anyu was fraught with disdain and distance, I cried, inconsolable after she and my sister left for Europe. Apu and I had seen them off in Adelaide and travelled back to Sydney by train. At first he tried to make me laugh.

"You look funny with your red nose and your sniffing. Careful, people will think that I'm abusing you," he'd say with a grin. I cried harder. At the station I couldn't keep from blubbering. Apu's face flushed with embarrassment in the dining car as more and more people gave us strange looks. "Quit being a baby," he whispered. Try as I might, for I desperately wanted to please and obey him, the tears refused cooperate. The novel overnight ride in a fancy sleeper car didn't help either. The next morning I was still red nosed, wet faced and hiccupping. It took being dragged by my exasperated father to see a live musical, *The Black and White Minstrel Show*, to finally make my tears subside.

As the sole remaining female in my chauvinist family, I set about cooking for the boys. Excited to fill my mother's shoes, I stepped up to the challenge of preparing meals for my father and three brothers. I wanted to impress them and so I decided to make the donuts for which my mother was so renowned. I mixed the flour, heated the yeast in milk, and added the eggs and sugar. I didn't ask my brothers for any help. I beat and beat the dough until my arms ached, but the blisters I longed to see never appeared. I waited and waited for the dough to rise but it never did. My initial confidence turned to nerves as the culinary failure dawned on me. I ended up frying unleavened dough.

"Concrete blocks." My brothers guffawed. "Let's drop them and see if they fall through the floor." To my shame, they had figured out what I had done wrong. "You boiled the yeast didn't you? Hah, you killed the poor little yeasties." I was appalled: my brothers had immediately figured out what I hadn't the whole time I had been stewing, waiting for my dough to rise. I felt stupid and burst out crying.

My father silenced them with a slap or two and took pity on me. He immediately arranged for us to dine at a local restaurant for evening meals. I was more than happy to relinquish my cooking duties. My family teased me for years about my concrete donuts.

It wasn't until I married that I began to cook again. In those first weeks as a new bride, I sent a flurry of letters to my mother begging for her recipes. I keep her letters of treasured Hungarian dishes in my recipe box to this day. I remember Anyu with mixed emotions as I check the ingredient portions written in her bold, loopy European script and prepare yet another batch of walnut rolls or donuts. I recall how I received her love in the form of food that she prepared and which I relished – to excess at times. Less treasured, I also remember the pain of her putdowns, her shoving me away from the kitchen, her inaccessibility.

I've become quite proficient as a cook, and have even tackled those dratted donuts. To my delight and my brothers' grudging compliments, I cook delicious donuts that rise so beautifully when fried that wide circular ribbons festoon their middles. I felt redeemed to receive my mother's compliments, but mostly I adore that my children love my donuts.

§

My mother and Irene returned from their European tour with hundreds of color slides, some old pictures, and many stories. One picture and one tale touched me deeply.

Anyu returned with her wedding pictures. She looked gorgeous in a floor-length, all-white traditional Hungarian costume, replete with a bodice and veiled headpiece. The netting of her bridal bouquet trailed almost to the floor capturing strands of ferns and white carnations. Anyu gazes with a faint smile at the camera. Apu, decked in the full dress regalia of a lieutenant, holds a glove in one hand, lightly touches the tasseled sword at his side with the other. He looks admiringly at my mother.

The marriage was perhaps doomed from the start as my father's brother, Zoltán, openly disapproved of Anyu, thought her and her family too low class, and tried to talk my father out of marrying her. To demonstrate his displeasure, Zoltán failed to show for the wedding – and he the best man! My father, rather than openly facing the shame, married my mother privately in the church a few hours ahead of the scheduled ceremony. My parents showed up at their reception already hitched. The conflicts that marred my parents' wedding presaged those that occurred around my own wedding thirty-some years later.

The story about Anyu and Irene's trip that touched me the most was about what happened when they attended a performance of Erkel Ferenc's opera *Bánk Bán* in Budapest. The libretto describes the experience of the Hungarian people exploited and supressed by foreign royalty. Despite the very real fears of retribution and arrest at the opera performance – there were Russian soldiers in attendance – the aria of *Hazám, Hazám, Te Mindenem* (My country, my country, you are my everything) brought the Hungarian audience to its feet. Proud and united, with tears streaming down their faces, they stomped and cheered and clapped a resounding standing ovation. The Hungarian spirit could not be supressed by the Communist occupiers.

My sister brought back an album of the opera highlights. I remember my father's reaction when he played the homeland aria for visiting Hungarian guests. Oiled with a few *fröccs*, a combination of red wine and soda water, the swelling strains of the aria brought tears to his eyes. These he brusquely wiped away. I felt his homesickness as my own and my eyes also filled with tears. I, too, felt exiled even though I was just fourteen and had yet to step on Hungarian soil.

§

With the knitwear business thriving, my parents could afford household help and they hired Jutka Néni (Néni is Hungarian for aunt and, like Bácsi – "uncle" – for a man, Néni is the respectful address for one's elders). Jutka Néni cleaned our Wollstonecraft home once a week, wiping and sweeping, vacuuming, and washing and scrubbing from one end of the house to the other. She wasn't our first cleaning lady, but she was unquestionably the best. Before her, my parents had employed my godmother, Dori Néni, and while she wasn't a bad cleaner, she was no comparison to Jutka Néni. Dora Néni stirred the dust. Jutka Néni banished all traces of it.

Dora Néni was the kind of godmother I would have liked to replace with a sweeter version. My parents chose her for my christening from the slim Hungarian pickings in the Aussie refugee camp. Dora sprouted sparse thin strands of short-cropped, black-dyed hair, smelled of stale cigarettes, and wore loose dentures. Her raspy smoker's guffaw spooked me. I cringed when she teased me about my budding breasts or my academic accomplishments. I silently groaned at her predictable gifts: flannel pajamas from Woolworths – always the same – and boring. I yearned for chic, frilly, feminine baby-dolls and bemoaned the formless, fashion-less fuddy-duddies that, to my chagrin, stayed sturdy, never wearing out, only to be replenished year after year in larger sizes that matched my growing frame.

In contrast to Dora Néni, I loved Jutka Néni: her broad smiling face with the gold-capped eyetooth, her plump frame, and arms with extra buns adjacent to her elbows. Jutka Néni was of good Austrian peasant stock, so my father said. She grew up close to the Hungarian border and so, like many of the residents in the area, learned colloquial Hungarian. She immigrated to Australia as a mail order bride and married Feri Bácsi, a taciturn, wiry man with a partial pointer finger amputation who talked as if there were rocks in his mouth. Theirs was a marriage of convenience, an opportunity for Jutka Néni and her teenage son to have a better life. Jutka Néni was humble. On one of her cleaning days, she and I lunched together on a simple meal of bread and butter, topped with thinly sliced raw onion and a dash of salt.

"Onions are very healthy for you," she declared. I giggled. "No, really," she insisted. "Onions clean your blood." I wasn't so sure of that but I decided to believe her, for Jutka Néni, with her rosy cheeks, certainly looked to be the picture of health. She grew serious and studied her hands. "Look how ugly they are," she fretted, "Rough, red, cracked, calloused. You know I was invited to go to a wedding and almost didn't go. I felt too embarrassed by these worker's hands. Then I came up with the idea of wearing gloves. I couldn't eat any of the food at the reception but that was okay." she shrugged. "As long as I could hide my worn down hands, I felt all right." I could relate to her feelings of inferiority and I felt bad for her. I delighted in Jutka Néni's salt-of-the-earth company. When she was with me, she looked me in the eye, and spoke to me as an equal, totally present. I hardly ever shared this experience with my father – and never with my mother.

I mourned the loss of Jutka Néni when she moved to the outskirts of the city that summer, and I felt apprehensive about returning to school.

CHAPTER 4 – SCHOOL DAYS

Standing at the entrance to our Wollstonecraft home. I had to wear the hat and gloves at all times outside of the school. The clunky suitcases in the background were laden with heavy school books.

The bell rang for lunch my first day back. I was in my second year of high school. Most of my classmates rushed from their desks and clustered into cliques. They had socialized over the summer holidays and had easily reconnected when classes began. I listened to their laughter as they hurried out of the classroom. Their faced were animated; their heads butted together as they shared secret confidences and gossiped in hushed voices. I followed them out, alone, jealous, and frozen with fear. Who would want to have lunch with me?

Because I felt like a foreigner, a Hungarian, I didn't make any close friends at school, and it never entered my mind to invite them over to my house for other than a rare birthday party. I didn't often receive invitations to their homes either, and so, over the longs weeks of summer, I had had no contact with any of my classmates.

My father's reaction to my last report card hadn't helped my sense of feeling like an outsider. When I had handed him my results, beaming with pride, Apu immediately exploded.

"What do you mean you came in third in your class. You should be first. You are smarter than these Aussie kids."

My mood had instantly plummeted and I hung my head, crushed to hear the criticism. I hadn't dared to tell him that there were girls who wrote so beautifully and fluently in English, avid readers who knew so much more about literature. Some knew more about Australian and world history than I did. I didn't understand parts of problems sometimes and I often made silly computation mistakes on my math homework. My father's response had hurt and confused me, and alienated me further from my Australian peers. It pitted me against them because it was my duty to strive to beat them. I was told that I was better than these girls, but my experience was the opposite.

I coped by compartmentalizing at home. I didn't share school happenings except for the basics. "Yes, I have homework... Yes quite a bit of it," or "No, not so many assignments tonight." I mostly stayed numb, avoiding confrontations and conflicts. My parents didn't want to hear any of the particulars of my classes anyway. They didn't have the time. They never seemed interested. It was easier to stay mum. I strove to report only my accomplishments.

In some ways, I had looked forward to my Second Year. I loved turning the pristine pages of new textbooks, writing in fresh notebooks, and learning new material. But now, on my first day, all those hopes were dashed. I grabbed the two smelly salami sandwiches and the apple from my locker and headed to the quadrangle. I didn't see one welcoming face. My heart lurched. I still didn't fit in. Even after seven years at this school I was still the outsider, the "bloody new Australian."

I gazed around, checking to see where I might sit. The cliques weren't an option. They'd for sure give me a dirty look and then ignore me. I couldn't face that kind of public humiliation. A plump classmate sat alone. I couldn't sit with her either. No one liked her and I would be even more of an outcast if the girls associated me with her. With an awkward twist, I walked in a different direction. I frantically looked around, seized by panic, my face flushed. "Dear God, everyone can see that I have no place to go, no one to sit with."

Then I saw Sue chatting with another girl and there was room next to them on the bench. I thought they might be more open. At least they weren't losers, and at least they had spoken to me last year. With apprehension, I slowly approached them. Sue looked up and smiled. Relief rushed in and I smiled back, but then I was flooded by another wave of self-consciousness. What on earth would I say after "Hi?"

Variations in this scene were often replayed, day after day, in my school years.

§

The die was perhaps cast on my first day of kindergarten at Saint Mary's, the North Sydney neighborhood parish school. An Italian girl who lived down the street from us, a year older than I, cornered me in the quadrangle with her friends, lifted my skirt, and squealed, "Let's see if the bloody new Australians wear underpants like we do!"

I flushed, my head floated, and my vision blurred. The girls shrieked with glee. I pulled my dress down and cringed into the recesses of the playground. I'd vaguely learned about the disparaging taunt from my family before this, but with this incident, the "bloody new Australian" status was indelibly tattooed on my psyche and for years fueled my sense of being an outsider.

Fifty years later, in 2001, as my brother Paul lay dying of bile duct cancer, he shared a story that occurred around the time that I began kindergarten, when he was attending a select public technical high school in Sydney. Even though Paul's gaunt, jaundiced, cancer-ridden body sank into the living room couch, his eyes burned with intensity. His wife, Jennifer, and I along with the rest of my siblings – Irene, Geza, and Tom – encircled Paul protectively, leaning forward in our chairs to catch his every softly uttered word.

"On a field trip, as we boys climbed on the bus, I was about to take a seat towards the front when the teacher snarled at me, 'Get in the back of the bus, you bloody new Australian! You greasy buggers are the dregs of this country and don't even deserve to be here.'"

A hush descended in the room. None of the five of us sibs uttered a word. I grieved that Paul had lived with this pain for years before he could even share it. A strong bond of compassion and acceptance enveloped us, all the more poignant as this occurred so rarely in our family. A loving presence charged the room and poured into my heart. Thanks to Paul's gut-wrenching honesty, my sense of living as an outsider for so many years was not only validated, but its pain abated.

Discrimination in Australia! Hard to imagine with the general image of Aussies: the "good on you mate" types; the down under swaggering friendly sorts; the easy going champion athletes like Rod Laver, Dawn Fraser, and Ian Thorpe; the amiable world travelers encountered in foreign countries. Hard to imagine that in the fifties and sixties when I grew up, Australia was firmly and decidedly prejudiced against certain white populations.

The fact that the British treated the native Australians abominably has been acknowledged to varying degrees. The attempted annihilation of the aboriginal population included not only massacres and mass poisonings, but the decimation of thousands of natives who succumbed to British imported diseases such as smallpox and measles. Furthermore, an estimated 100,000 children of the so-called "stolen generations," graphically depicted in the movie *Rabbit-Proof Fence* and in the memoir *My Place* by Sally Morgan, were ripped from their mothers between 1869 and 1969 to be "civilized" and "acculturated" – first in "Christian" orphanages (whose treatment of these children was severely less than Christian in character) and later with white families.

The Australian government officially promoted flagrant racism not only toward native aborigines but also toward other races. I learned about the *White Australia Policy* in fifth grade. "This policy is traced to the 1850s and was formally enacted in 1901," the nun droned on. "It excludes all non-Caucasians including Asian, Mid-Eastern and African populations from settling in Australia. The policy's political intent is to keep the overcrowded nearby Asian hordes from overrunning the country. That is a real threat to our relatively under-populated country that has vast natural resources." I squirmed in my seat. I glanced around at my classmates. They were busy taking notes, or doodling or they were completely distracted gazing out the window. The nun had presented the facts with an almost *belle indifference*. There was no commentary and no questioning. The overwhelming impact of discrimination weighed heavy on me and seemed insurmountable. What about the prejudice my family and I felt in the face of such obvious intolerance towards people of color? I kept my eyes lowered and began to doodle, digging my pen hard into my workbook page.

For my family endured discrimination far subtler than that directed towards the aborigines or other non-white ethnic groups. We, the Hungarians, along with the Greeks, Italian, and Polish immigrants were the "bloody new

Australians" who poured into the country as part of the great European diaspora following World War II. As part of the *Populate or Perish* government initiative, we provided a boon for the Australian continent that hungered for labor to fuel its expansion.

Yet, from the moment we landed, the "native" Aussies of British stock blackballed us. In part, they resented the immigrants who often times proved more industrious and therefore were more successful than they were. Racial slurs abounded: abo and boomer (for the native aborigines), wog, dago, wop, and kike were just a few of the often-bandied terms. "Bloody New Australian" served as a generic smirch for all central and southern European immigrants that the English and Irish Aussie descendants spat out with vehemence.

My parents with their accented English were forever branded every time they opened their mouths. We children who learned to speak Aussie English without an accent, fared somewhat better, but with foreign names like Palotás and Brezezicki and Pellegrino and Papallo we were similarly pigeonholed and taunted. Neighbors smashed our front windows in North Sydney when I was five. "They resent us for being too industrious," my father said with a scowl. In a defensive effort to fit in and to normalize, the immigrants themselves began to taunt one another, as my underwear-examining Italian classmate demonstrated so clearly on my first day of kindergarten.

The Australian government finally repealed the White Australian Policy in the 1970s, but by then my family had already emigrated to the United States.

§

After my shaky school beginnings in kindergarten, I transferred to Loreto Convent Kirribilli where I spent the next eleven years: six years of elementary and five of high school.

Mary Ward, an Irishwoman who desired more educational opportunities for women, founded the Institute of the Blessed Virgin Mary (IBVM) in the seventeenth century. Known as the Loreto nuns, the teaching order expanded over the next two hundred years and schools spread around the world. Loreto schools were established in every Australian state with two in the Sydney area: our rival school Normanhurst to the north and my own school in Kirribilli, just north of the Sydney Harbour Bridge and the city. Loreto Convent was a posh young ladies school. I credit my parents for wanting the best instruction for their kids. They prioritized education and were willing to pay for it.

Paul, Irene, and Geza started out in Sydney's public schools but once my parents achieved some financial stability, they transferred them to private Catholic schools. Tom and I, the two youngest, attended only private schools. According to my older sibs, we were more spoiled. I have to admit that when it came to schooling, Tom and I were indeed privileged. In other ways, though, I thought we received much less attention from our parents. By the time Tom and I came along, the novelty of having children had faded, and our parents delegated much of our care to our older siblings. I didn't think Tom and I won out in the end and I recoiled when the others accused me of being spoiled.

My first day at Loreto Convent Kirribilli, I felt proud to wear my brand new school uniform: a royal blue blazer with the school crest emblazed in gold on the breast pocket, a beige blouse, royal blue tunic, brown socks and clunky tan shoes, all topped off with a panama hat and gloves. The pride turned to terror when I arrived at the school. Just as I had my first day of kindergarten, I sobbed and clung to Apu's leg. The nun was dauntingly garbed in a thick black habit, and veil, belted with rosary beads, with an over-starched white collar and a white wimple that framed her eyes, nose and mouth. I liked her smile as she gently grabbed my arm and pulled me away from Apu.

"Here, Elizabeth, this is your hook. I'm going to have you place your hat and blazer right here and let's put on your brand new pinafore."

My father pulled the smock out of a brown paper bag. "Here it is, Mother."

I sobbed as I removed my gloves and unbuttoned my blazer. Apu helped me put on the royal blue pinafore and I grabbed onto his leg again.

"Now it's time for your father to leave Elizabeth." I gave a wail but then looked about the classroom. The other girls were already seated at their desks, looking at me with interest and – were they mocking me? I shut up immediately. I didn't want to make a scene. Apu patted me on the head and left. Mother led me to an empty desk towards the back of the room. I huddled and hunkered down, brusquely wiping away my tears.

I soon settled into the routine of shaping my letters and numbers in pencil as perfectly as possible. I loved schoolwork and after a day or two, got over my separation anxiety. I quickly picked up English. One day, as I was warming to my new environment, I decided to befriend my desk-mate and I gaily began to chat with her. The next thing I knew, the nun had appeared beside me, and was rapping my knuckles with a wooden ruler. She had sped to my desk without my even noticing and had shocked me into silence. From then on, I quickly learned to behave – to be a good girl – just like I had learned to be at home.

§

Loreto was a two-and-a-half mile walk from our house on Union Street. It seemed like an inordinately long trek as a kid, but my toughest journey ever occurred on a day in 1957, when the nuns sent me home from second grade ill with the Asian flu. I was one of thousands to succumb to a severe pandemic that year. I trudged home alone, disoriented, feverish, and aching. When at last I stumbled into the house, my parents were alarmed to see me arrive home early and so sick. The nuns had not called to notify them of my coming.

I lay in bed, deathly ill for over two weeks. Though feverish and aching all over, I discovered a hidden benefit in my suffering: for the first time ever, I had my mother's complete attention. She checked on me frequently, took my temperature, felt my forehead – rare moments of physical contact. She fed me comfort foods that I loved: fresh squeezed orange juice and grated apple. She also gave me "sick-bed" egg drop soup that I cared for much less, but which I dutifully downed to please her. The bedclothes developed a sweet gamey odor from my raging fevers and sweats. I inhaled deeply over and over savoring its smell, associating it with my mother's ministrations. I lay in bed for hours, drifting in and out of consciousness. I had nothing to do, nowhere to be. Without any effort on my part, I was able to draw my mother's attention, something I found so difficult to do when I was healthy, when I tripped over myself trying to impress her with perfect grades and good behavior.

§

I did well at Loreto, getting high grades and gold stars for deportment and attitude – until third grade.

"Who was the vandal that scribbled in Cathy's workbook? I demand the culprit fess up right now!" roared the nun as she waved the despoiled book high up in the air. I wasn't worried, for I hadn't done the damage, but then my desk-mate, Cara, raised her hand and spoke up.

"Mother, Elizabeth scribbled in my book too." My face flushed red, and I glared at her, and then stared at the nun in utter disbelief. Cara and I had playfully drawn faces on each other's workbooks, but this was totally different from the mischievous scribbles someone had anonymously drawn in another classmate's book. My desk-mate had ratted me out in her own defense, to avoid being accused. The nun believed she had found the criminal and she pounced. With a self-satisfied glare she bore down on me, her spittle flying in my face as she hissed, "You are to stay behind after school." I bowed my head to avoid the stares of the other girls. I felt cornered and completely defenseless. I shook, dreading what was to come.

After class, the nun grilled me to confess, rapping my head with her silver nun's ring. With tears streaming down my face, I professed again and again, "I didn't do it, Mother." She didn't believe me.

"You impudent, insolent girl, of course you did it!" I didn't give in, and she finally sent me home in disgrace to contemplate my abominable behavior. After a fitful night, I returned to school the next morning desperately hoping that she would drop the issue, but she kept me behind at recess, and continued the interrogation. My classmates averted their eyes and slinked by as Mother again thumped on my head with her ringed finger. "Confess that you did it, you cheeky girl."

Finally, in desperation, I cried out, "Mother, if I had done the scribbling, I would have owned up to it long before now."

She finally paused, realized my innocence, and dismissed me. "Oh, go to the playground. Off with you."

She never apologized, either for accusing me, or for her anger. The culprit of the scribbling went off scot-free. My classmates avoided me for days. I was the tainted one, the accused. I chalked up my classmates' avoidance as more evidence that, as a "bloody new Australian" I was— yet again – the outsider and therefore less than. I had no close friends in my class to turn to, no one I could commiserate with, or in whom I could confide.

I didn't relate this episode to my parents or my siblings. It never even entered my mind to do so. Our family didn't come to each other with problems or worries. We only showed our strengths and our achievements. I had no confidantes.

It hurt being ostracized that way – and the notebook incident was just one of many times my classmates shunned me. Another instance that occurred while I was in grade school I unwittingly brought on myself. I had always wanted curly hair like my Hungarian friend Suzy. My mother gave in to my incessant whining, perhaps feeling some pity for me as she too suffered stick-straight hair. She took me to a hairdresser for a permanent, where I willingly submitted to the torture of beautification. I wanted to scream as the hairdresser hooked, and then yanked each tuft of hair through a tiny hole in a rubber square, but I bore the agony in silence for it was of my own doing: I wanted curls. When the stylist proudly turned the chair to show me the finished perm in the mirror, I cringed inside but faked a smile. I had wanted soft curls, but had ended up with a mass of frizz. My siblings joked and jeered. "Hey frizzy." I couldn't hide my hairdo at school, and the "in-crowd" girls a year ahead of me quickly dubbed me "golliwogg." My alienation deepened. Not only did I have to bear the pain of being a "bloody new Australian," my classmates had taunted me with another denigration in using the Negro racial slur. I slinked around for weeks, avoiding everyone until that humiliating perm grew out.

I also sensed my difference from the other girls at lunchtime. I mostly brought my meals from home, embarrassed at my mother's chunky, smelly, bacon grease and green pepper, sardine or "bully beef" – how my brothers referred to Spam – sandwiches. I coveted my mates' lunches. They ate delicacies that their mothers had carefully wrapped in crisp wax paper. They nibbled on the slimmest millimeter slice of devon (baloney) on white bread cut into perfect triangles. The crusts had been removed with engineering precision. Occasionally, my mother allowed me to buy lunch delivered to the school by a deli down the street. I thought this a huge treat! On these special days, I, too, could be as refined as my classmates, and I savored delicious devon sandwiches, thin and elegant in freshly baked and buttered Tip Top brand white bread. On days I bought my lunch, I felt like I could fit in – a little more at least.

Later, the deli deliveries were replaced with a lunch kiosk inside the school. Volunteer mothers manned the lunch counter, heating delicious meat pies in large ovens. My mother, of course, didn't volunteer. I envied the girls whose mothers worked the kiosk and socialized with the nuns. My Aussie classmates called out "Hi Mummy" so naturally, and with such familiarity, that my heart sank. Oh, how I wanted that easy interface with my mother. At those lunch times, I hated that she barely spoke English, and I hated that I was Hungarian. The luscious pies served piping hot, and dripping with thick, juicy gravy provided a substitute oral gratification for the pain I held inside.

Two major brands of pies were produced in Sydney at the time: the Big Bens were square delicacies. The Scott's pies were round with perfectly stamped, carefully fluted edges. My brother Paul, with his usual irreverent humor, often remarked that you didn't ever want to buy a meat pie on a Monday as they gave you "the trots" from the bacteria that multiplied and flourished over the weekend in the stilled meat grinders. Fortunately, with all the meat pies I consumed over my growing years, I never came down with that particular food poisoning malady.

§

In fourth grade, I was thrilled to be introduced to something that had arrived all the way from America, the land of my dreams: multiple choice testing. Loreto had invested in a U.S. English comprehension series. The nuns introduced the new educational aid with great fanfare and I delighted in fingering the shiny laminated eight-and-a-half-by-eleven cards. Each card contained a literary excerpt followed by comprehension multiple-choice questions with the levels of difficulty coded in different eye-popping colors. Choosing an answer from four or five options forever changed how I learned and retained information. I was used to answering open-ended questions, and I therefore needed to recall the information to build an answer. Now all I had to do was to recognize answers, which required much less mental effort. I realized almost immediately that using multiple choice distinctly lowered the quality of my learning. Nevertheless, I delighted in being exposed to a piece of the United States, and smiled each time I came across words such as labor for labour, neighbor for neighbour. This, along with American TV shows like *The Mickey Mouse Club* fueled my fascination and my desire to go to America.

§

Mother Maria, my fourth grade teacher, wore coke bottle glasses and had a toothy, unsettling grin that at times came across as a leer. I thought her a tolerable teacher for the most part until the day she called a student to the front of the class to work a math problem on the chalkboard. Poor Patty had no idea how to even begin figuring it out and she had less and less of an idea as the nun taunted her more and more. Mother raged out of control, banged the girl on the head with her silver nun's ring. *What is it about nuns using their silver rings as weapons?* I squirmed in my chair. Mother kept at Patty. "You are a stupid, really stupid girl. Shame on you!" Patty wailed, totally broken up and broken down. By now, she was completely incapacitated, incapable of solving two plus two, let alone the more challenging problem on the board. I knew the answer and tightened my head muscles in an attempt to send the solution to her, but to no avail. "Oh, go on with you, go sit down, you dimwit." Mother dismissed her with a shove. Patty slunk back to her desk. I knew she wasn't the brightest in the class, but no one deserved that kind of treatment. No one. I felt so embarrassed for her, but failed to go up at the end of the class to console her. None of my classmates did. She walked out to recess all alone. I did to Patty what my classmates had done to me when the nun had accused me of scribbling. I felt uncomfortable about approaching her. I had no idea how to help her.

§

When I moved on to higher grades, I liked my teachers more, and I felt blessed to have some wonderful role models. My favorite nun was Mother John Bosco, a beautiful woman who left her medical practice to follow a call into the nunnery. One time a novice nun nervously fluttered into our classroom, grasping a tear-stained student by the shoulder, interrupting as Mother John Bosco wrote on the blackboard. In a low, grave voice the young sister asked, "Mother, would you please assess this student's serious injury?" The ex-physician glanced at the child's scraped knee. "She will be just fine with a rinse and a Band-Aid." She reassured the flushed and anxious nun. With a hint of a smile and a twinkle in her eye, she turned back to the board and resumed her teaching. I was in awe of how she handled the episode: her deference, competence, and her playfulness.

Mother John Bosco's unassuming air, warm sense of humor, and matter of fact teaching style encouraged me to study and excel. Her past life as a medical doctor intrigued and inspired me. I wanted to be like her, to emulate her – minus the nun part of course.

Another nun at Loreto impressed yet daunted me, and that was Mother Angela, the mistress of schools. This Irish beauty, who spoke with a brogue, was as gorgeous as any pinup model. Her billowing, dowdy habit couldn't hide her lush figure, and she turned even priests' heads. I wanted her sharp wit, brilliant mind, and self-assuredness. She spouted fluent Latin, wowing yet confusing us in every Latin class. She disciplined errant students in a swift, yet just fashion. Some older students posted a banner on her office door with the invocation from Dante's *Inferno*, "Abandon all hope ye who enter here." Bemused rather than offended, Mother Angela left that quote pinned on her door for several weeks.

§

My class paved the way for a new statewide educational system in New South Wales. Named the Wyndham Report after its founder, the new system meant we no longer had five years of high school leading to the leaving certificate statewide exam. Instead, a sixth year was added with exams at the end of the fourth and sixth Forms. Needless to say, there were glitches in the implementation of the new curriculum, as the expectations were not well known. We, the guinea pigs, embraced the new program with both pride and trepidation.

The new scheme proved a huge benefit for Loreto as it required the school to expand its science program. Before the Wyndham Report, Loreto did not consider these necessary subjects for "Loreto Ladies." The school focused on grooming young women for Christian wifely and motherly duties – and for vocations to the nunnery. Indeed, my parents had to hire outside tutors in physics and advanced math and calculus for my older sister, as none of these subjects were offered at Loreto at the time. I certainly benefited from the state's new curriculum, as the sciences were my strong subjects. So, along with elocution, Christian Doctrine, and the humanities, I now studied physics, calculus, and biology taught by some newly hired competent teachers in those fields.

My older brothers had such strong teachers. One of their favorites was Mr. Fortnum and they loved to mimic him. Paul would sing-song in a lilting parody:

"Aah, Riley, no homework again today? Twenty-five lines by 4 o'clock. I see your smirk, son, so you can now make that fifty lines!"

Their parodies of Mr. Fortnum were steeped in the utmost respect for they had true admiration for his strong teaching abilities and high standards. Both Paul and Geza achieved honors in the statewide matriculation exams in the classes that Mr. Fortnum taught.

Mr. Fortnum must have thought my brothers good enough sorts because when his daughter transferred to Loreto in the fifth grade, he urged her to seek out the Palotás boys' younger sister.

Patricia warmed to me as much as I gravitated to her. I was amazed that she wanted to spend time with me, even though I was a "bloody new Australian." For the first time, I had someone with whom to play. I didn't have to worry about whom to approach. Patricia found me at every recess and every lunch. We sat on the school's grassy hill, chewing on grass blades. We walked to the train station together, chatted on the platform. She'd head across the Harbour Bridge to Croydon. I rode in the other direction to Wollstonecraft, except on days that I took ballet lessons. Then, I happily boarded the train with her.

"I'm beginning pointe classes," I said, opening my ballet bag and pulling out my brand new pointe shoes. The train lurched to a start.

"That's great. We won't do that for a while at my school."

"Yeah, my school's the best. It's part of the Royal Ballet."

"I like my ballet school as well," Patricia answered. "They use a different technique is all."

"It's not as good." I puffed myself up. Patricia said nothing, just smiled. She didn't badmouth and she was soft spoken – always. I wonder how she put up with me, always brash, always opinionated.

The year Patricia befriended me, I got wires and a retainer plate to help straighten my crossed and bucked teeth. They weren't full braces, as my dentist wasn't trained as an orthodontist, and wasn't versed in banding techniques. I was the first in my class to have orthodonture, a rare occurrence in Sydney at that time, and I was mortified. My parents scoffed:

"Little Lizzie, the movie star! You want to be beautiful don't you? You want to be a Hollywood actress so you have to have straight teeth. We're giving you that. You have nothing to complain about."

No sympathy, no empathy, no concept of how to console. I had no idea of what it felt like to be consoled – until Mr. Fortnum.

The week after I got the braces on my teeth, Mr. Fortnum met Patricia at the school as we were leaving. He had the same angular facial features as his daughter. The family resemblance was striking. While his strong bone structure gave him an air of strength and masculinity, Patricia's high cheekbones and narrow, oval face, chiseled chin, and shock of thick, straight, light brown hair were hauntingly beautiful. As Mr. Fortnum greeted us, I could tell he *saw* my wires. More importantly, he *noticed* my discomfort. I saw the kindness in his eyes as he said, "It's hard to have the discomfort and the obviously visible wires and bands, isn't it? It's tough, even though you know it will help make your teeth look better."

For the first time in my life, I had the experience of really being seen. I was dumbfounded! My heart ached and went out to this man, this almost stranger, because he *got*, he totally and completely got who I was, and what I was feeling. He met me in my world, at my level. I was deeply touched by his understanding and compassion. His words comforted me and for the first time since the braces were put on my teeth, I felt the knots of self-consciousness and embarrassment ease inside me. Mr. Fortnum's caring comment was like a long draft of cool water on a parched tongue. I was just eleven at the time, but I've never forgotten that moment. It took only a few seconds for him to say what he said to me, but his ability to connect with what I was feeling has had an indelible, lifelong effect on me.

I've tried to follow his example throughout my life. I haven't always succeeded. I failed miserably for years, for my parents' poor communication skills were deeply ingrained in me. Children really do learn what they live by and I slowly, eventually came to realize that I had a lot of new learning to do. I had to shift from my parents' aloofness, harsh judgments, and dismissiveness, and to emulate in my behavior the degree of awareness and empathy I had received from Mr. Fortnum. I work at it every day with the people in my life – my children, friends, patients, and clients – and belatedly with my first husband.

Growing up, I thought my upbringing pretty normal. My parents provided me with a host of opportunities – private schools, music lessons, dance lessons. My family ate well, feasting on delicious Hungarian dishes that Anyu prepared. Nevertheless, a subconscious void remained – one which I didn't recognize until I was in my thirties. I didn't feel a strong bond with my parents or siblings. Hugs were a rarity, and I never confided my hurts or joys with either my parents or my brothers and sister.

Child development pundits today use the term attachment disorder for what I experienced as a child. As an adult, I discovered just how pernicious and insidious my attachment wounding was. I realized how I had to scrape the bottom of an empty emotional barrel as a child, to collect the few scraps of loving experiences. My parents simply didn't have the emotional resources to fill the barrel. Though they gave all the love and care they were able to provide, their childhood patterning and war traumas left them with little ability to effectively bond or demonstrate love. As a child, this inability to express love proved to be crazy-making for me.

As an adult, I felt that in some predetermined way, I was destined to carry the burden of an early life path devoid of significant intimacy, bonding, or touch. Navigating and overcoming these deprivations has been a lifelong pursuit for me, an ongoing challenge. As I absorb the lessons, though, I find myself blessed with connections and the kind of intimacy I have long been hungry for and now get to both give and receive, share and teach others.

I was in my early forties, when during a therapy session, I experienced a full-body awareness that fueled my premonitions and brought me some remarkable insights. I sensed that my mother did not wish to birth me, that she and I had made a pre-incarnational pact where she would provide only the basic survival needs to raise me. The Hungarian phrase that she used was *kutjaköteleség* or "dog's duty," meaning that she would provide only the bare minimum of succor, that of food and clothing, housing and education. I had agreed to this pre-birth pact and understood that my life's work lay in dealing with, and integrating the consequences of these parenting deficiencies.

It is ironic that a "dog's obligation," the instinctual behavior that mammals exhibit includes plenty of touching and nurturing of the young pups. My mother used the term with the opposite intention, to signify the absolute minimum of care rather than the true instinctual level of intimate affection.

I was oblivious that such intimacy even existed – until Mr. Fortnum.

§

"Attention, girls, I have the names of the junior school sports captains." The whole class hushed and sat up straight, excited to hear who the nuns had chosen. "The green captain is Patricia. . . , the vice-captain . . ." I checked out. My head felt like cotton wool, my brain buzzed. I flushed with jealous rage. Patricia was now a leader, and I was not. She would be more popular than I. Why couldn't the nuns have elected someone else? That way Patricia and I could have stayed on the same footing. I hated that the nuns singled her out instead of me, even though she clearly deserved the accolade – she was a swift runner and an excellent athlete. I knew that she was a far better choice as captain, for my running skills were mediocre at best, but that didn't quench my envy.

Patricia glanced at me and smiled. I looked away, my lips pursed, my eyes flashing. She came up to me at recess. "Elizabeth, are you all right? You looked upset in class . . ."

I turned away with my nose in the air. I snuck a peek at her a moment later. She looked stunned and hurt, but then smiled as other girls came up to congratulate her.

I never sought Patricia out again. I was a complete fool and I threw away her friendship. Patricia took the slight graciously and never badmouthed me. After a few weeks, I sorely regretted my flare of jealousy, but I was too afraid, too full of pride to approach her and apologize. My guilt over how badly I treated her haunted me for years.

§

In my fifth high school year at Loreto Convent, I was elected by the nuns to become a prefect, a school leader. This prestigious honor took me completely by surprise. Giddy and grinning, I stood in line at the school telephone with the seven other newly elected prefects, each of us taking turns to call our parents with the thrilling announcements. This proved a confirmation for my parents that the pain and terror of their war- and immigration-disrupted lives had, at last, come to some good.

My father's pride knew no bounds. After my phone call relaying the news, he immediately went out and bought a used Mercedes sedan. He picked me up at the school gate that very afternoon and, with a big grin and a puffed out chest, ceremoniously opened the car door, and with a flurry, motioned with his arm for me to be seated. I smiled, proud yet baffled and embarrassed by the grand gesture, and sheepishly slipped into the front seat, wanting to avoid the attention and scrutiny of my classmates. I had become the family mascot, the symbol of success and assimilation in a foreign society.

Also in my fifth year of high school, I lucked out having another wonderful mentor in Noelann Gandon, my drama teacher. A local theatre producer (termed director in the U.S.) she was an authentic bohemian eccentric, an irreverent Loreto ex-student with bright red lips and fingernails, a harsh smoker's guffaw, and a loose tongue from which the expletives "bloody" and "damn" flew with gay abandon. I felt comfortable confiding in Miss Gandon. I'd stroll over in the late afternoons to chat with her in the faculty break room. She listened and laughed with me. Unlike other grownups, she gave me information without infusing any personal vested interest, and she treated me as an equal. Miss Gandon volunteered information without strings. Her wisdom stemmed from personal experience in the world of drama. When I felt brave enough to confide in her that I wanted to be a movie star, she advised, "Start early. Hollywood looks for youth above all."

Miss Gandon chose for us to perform *A Man for All Seasons* by Robert Bolt in the school music festival. In the tryouts, I read for the lead part of St. Thomas More in an even, quiet tone, thinking that's what the role required. My classmate Michelle read with more inflection. Miss Gandon glanced over, somewhat puzzled at my monotone read and awarded the part to Michelle. I was shocked and sorely disappointed, but I learned quickly. The next role we read for was Thomas Cromwell and I effused with lots of modulation in my voice. I got the part.

I loved the camaraderie with my fellow actors, and for the first time had a sense that I fully fit in at school. At last, I belonged to a cohesive group. The structure of daily after-school rehearsals solidified our social and personal connection. I reveled in being part of the smart, accomplished, chosen, in-crowd group of girls. I dove into the art of acting. I lost track of time when on stage. Miss Gandon kept at me to deepen into the role, and when I finally exploded, the well of emotion that I drew on startled me – and delighted Miss Gandon. I felt in my element, and lost all sight of self-consciousness when I escaped into my role as the manipulative and diabolical Cromwell. I could somehow release the inner anger and mixed-up turmoil that I'd held onto for so long. In spitting out Cromwell's vitriol, I released the pressure of a multitude of unidentifiable, free floating, and deeply imprisoned emotions.

Not only did I have the joy of finally belonging to a much admired peer group, I also had the experience of immersing myself into a role and expressing deep emotions. As if that were not enough, I also had the pleasure of acting in professional costumes that Miss Gandon obtained on loan from the local Royal Theatre production of the play. We young thespians felt honored and thrilled to act in these gorgeous, richly brocaded, and fur-trimmed gowns. Our performance was hailed as a resounding success by the school, and we received favorable reviews in the *Sydney Morning Herald* newspaper. Even my father, rarely one to complement, commented on how professional the production was.

I felt on fire when I acted. I thought I had found my life's work and so I was overjoyed when Miss Gandon invited our drama group to her professional production's cast party. I, along with a couple of classmates attended the backstage affair where we met a group of actors and stagehands. Many were dressed in brightly garish clothes, one man in a chartreuse corduroy jacket and a crimson ascot, another in a black beret, turtleneck, skin-tight pants waving a cigarette in a holder in grand circles as he spoke in scratchy high-pitched tones. The women wore tight, slightly worn dresses of velvet and satin and huge hoop earrings. Voices intermingled and interrupted each other, rising and falling several octaves. I felt decidedly uncomfortable. I thought these people were weird. In a rare show of sharing my inner thoughts, I voiced my apprehension to my father who came to drive me home. "Are you sure that those are the kind of people you want to spend years with in an acting career?" he asked. My dad had said aloud what I feared most. I did indeed feel uncomfortable about being part of such an eccentric group. His calling out my hidden fear felt so raw that I withdrew in a haze of confusion. His stating the obvious left no forum for exploring my inner conflict. A pin had burst the bubble of my movie star fantasy and I nursed my deflated dream in silence.

My acting dream had begun with *The Mickey Mouse Club*, and grew with

American TV shows such as *77 Sunset Strip, Surfside 6,* and *Dr. Kildare.* I longed for all things American.

When I went to the beach, I often stood at the water's edge, gazing at the horizon, and imagined the shores of America at the other end of the ocean's expanse. I dreamed of being in Los Angeles, in Hollywood. I pictured myself a movie star, receiving accolades from adoring fans – and from my idols: Richard Chamberlain, Efrem Zimbalist Jr., and Troy Donohue. Little did I know that my family would be moving to the U.S. in just a few short years.

I waded in the shallows and the salt water, like soft embers of joy, percolated through my feet and coursed up my body and into my heart, lighting it up with a soft glow. The ocean was affirming my desires. I splashed and grinned as I choked up with tears, making the waves glisten even more. I felt the ocean as ally, and so began my lifelong love of, and connection with beaches.

CHAPTER 5 – GIRL ON THE BEACH

Younger brother Tom & I at the beach on our inflatable boogie board type floats.

On summer weekends thousands of swim-suited bodies dot Sydney's sandy coasts frolicking in and out and under the pounding surf. Aussies immerse themselves in their beach culture and this was one new tradition we immigrants adopted with pleasure.

Suzy, skinny, blue eyed with a mass of unruly blonde curls was my best friend outside of school. Indeed she, a fellow Hungarian, was my only early childhood friend, and we loved going to the beach. My earliest beach memories are times spent with her at sheltered Balmoral Bay near her house. We built sand castles and ran in and out of the water, splashing and chasing one another under the watchful eye of her dour mother. The water felt so deliciously cool and refreshing on hot summer days.

I was grateful to Suzy for her friendship. I would have felt very much alone without her. The Australian-born kids from our neighborhood avoided us. Because I went to a private school, my classmates came from all over the area. This distance, as well as my feeling like a foreigner kept me from seeking their company outside of school hours.

With Suzy, though, I had a delightful companionship. We were forever busy and never bored. When we weren't at the beach, we were playing with her kitten in her backyard or tossing knucklebones (jacks) – a favorite childhood game – for hours. In her bedroom, we built elaborate tents out of sheets and blankets.

We rode in the back of her contractor father's pickup truck. Suzy said something to me but the wind was swallowing her words.

"I can't hear you," I yelled.

"I can't see a thing." She yelled, louder this time. She laughed, pulling strands of golden hair out of her mouth, and turning this way and that in an attempt to keep the curls out of her face.

"I can feel the wind in my mouth – it's making it dry." She licked her lips and opened her mouth wide. I imitated her and felt the rush of air fill my mouth and throat. I coughed and laughed.

The pickup hit a huge bump. Suzy sailed halfway down the truck bed. I hit the side. We squealed in delight, scrambled back to the front. Suzy banged on the rear cab window. As her father looked around, she waved her arms and screamed, "Another bump, another bump." She bumped against me again and again to pantomime what she wanted. Her dad grinned and nodded.

From then on he revved the engine to accelerate with more inertia, turned corners more sharply and aimed for every pothole. When we stopped, he gave the brakes a hard stomp. Suzy and I screamed and chortled as we were jostled about. Her dad was laughing as he came round the back, opened the rear gate, and helped each of us down in turn.

"When can we do it again, Api?" Suzy asked, giving him a huge hug. "Can we go somewhere where it's really, really bumpy?" My friend was fearless.

Sadly, though, I never felt completely comfortable around Suzy's mother. Her disturbing wet lips gave me the creeps and she acted superior. For instance, she had Suzy wash her face every morning, and when she noticed that I hadn't washed mine, she looked disapprovingly at me and asked pointedly, "Doesn't your mother have you wash your face every morning?" I flinched and a flush of embarrassment lit up my cheeks. Why indeed didn't Anyu have me wash my face? All of a sudden, I felt dirty and I squirmed. What else did Anyu fail to tell me about basic cleanliness practices? I shuddered to think I might be showing up at school dirty and smelly. No wonder my classmates shunned me! As that realization dawned, my cheeks burned even redder. Suzy's mother's stare unnerved me and before I could defend myself – and my mother – I stuttered, "N-no, ma'am."

"Well," she huffed. "How else would you get the sleepy bugs out of your eyes?" Suzy hid her smile in her towel. I leaned over the sink and splashed the freezing water on my face. Never again would I let another morning go by without washing my face.

Suzy's mother had definite opinions about food products. Never shy about voicing them, she was certain that Ovaltine tasted much better than our family's Nestle Quick chocolate milk, that her Peters ice cream was far superior to our Streets brand. I felt leery in her presence, always a bit on edge and anxious as I wondered when the next implicit or explicit judgment would come.

But that woman served soft-boiled eggs the best way ever. I loved them! Every morning on sleepovers, she sliced toast into strips and we dipped them into soft-boiled eggs nestled in tiny cups. I looked forward to breakfast at Suzy's house, all the more so because they often followed a night filled with homesickness.

In fact, the only time I really withdrew at Suzy's was at dusk when I became uncontrollably and inexplicably homesick. No matter how great the days were, when darkness descended, I began to feel teary and longed to be home. I could make no sense in the downturn of my feelings but when they descended, even Suzy couldn't cheer me up. On one occasion, I became so upset that my father had to drive over to pick me up. I felt miserable and mortified. I eventually learned to tolerate the loneliness of most sleepovers, yet I still often cried myself into a fitful slumber. By the next morning, though, I would have brightened, eager to eat toast strips and soft-boiled eggs, and to embark on more adventures with my beloved Suzy.

§

While my early childhood summer outings were usually spent at the sheltered Balmoral Bay beach, Suzy occasionally joined our family on our jaunts to Queenscliff.

Queenscliff, the northern portion of the several mile long Manly Beach, quickly became our family favorite. Many a summer weekend, all of us piled into our green and white Holden station wagon, and my father drove through a maze of suburban streets. Freeways had yet to be constructed in Sydney. In child time, it took forever to get there. We hooped and hollered as the car crept over the hillcrest revealing the first birds-eye glimpse of the gleaming expanse of Manly Beach and the endless ocean horizon beyond. My skin prickled, and my innards roared and soared to see the gleaming ocean every time we came over that rise.

Our beach outings spanned whole days. We camped out on the grass patch above the sand in the shade of a row of Norfolk pines. My mother had fixed lunch the day before: fried chicken or wiener schnitzel sandwiches, potato salad with just vinaigrette and onions, whole watermelons. Later in the day if we got hungry again, we could head to the milk bar across the street for meat pies and ice cream.

We spent long hours in and out of the pounding waves – mostly in – emerging from the surf only for eats and drinks. I watched Suzy catch a five-foot wave. She rode it for a while, her grinning face sticking out from the edge of the curl, and then she disappeared into the wash. A few moments later, she emerged with a squeal and jumped up and down, flailing her arms, and then swimming back.

"Great ride! C'mon," she said. "Here's a good one." She turned to the shore and began to paddle furiously. The wave was too high, too scary. I began to paddle, but my strokes were half-hearted. "I missed it," I yelled, but Suzy was out of earshot. I bobbled about, giving myself silent pep talks: *Don't be a scaredy-cat. You can do this.* I resolved to try the next wave with her.

"I missed it," I repeated, when Suzy returned.

"Next one," she said. We both watched the rises and falls, ready to take off when the perfect swell came along. One soon did – thankfully, a smaller one.

"Now!" I squealed. Choking back my fear, I paddled and kicked with abandon. I could hardly believe it! I was sailing through the inside of the wave, water all around me. It felt as if I'd been hurled topsy-turvy into a magical place. I rode about fifteen feet, Suzy a little further. I stood up in the sand, ecstatic, and jumped up and down. Suzy grinned and pointed.

"Watch out!" The wave tumbled over me. I flailed about the churning wash and came up coughing and spluttering.

Suzy swam back to get me. "Hey, are ya okay?"

"I'm great," I said looking her straight in the eye with a grin. I did a mini dive and pummeled my way back out, ready to catch the next wave, basking in my newfound confidence.

I heard a shrill whistle. "Come out of the water immediately. Everyone out!" yelled a husky voice through a bullhorn. I shot a panicked look at Suzy – her face looked just as scared. Without a word we sped through the water as fast as our arms and legs could propel us. We ran through the shallows and up the sand bank, joining scores of others who were also fleeing. The brawny lifeguards, with their tiny Speedo trunks and chin-strapped plastic caps lined the water's edge, waving swimmers and surfers in, yelling and whistling.

"Look, Suzy! Shark fins," I shrieked, shivering and panting. Out in the distance a pair of black triangles cut through the water.

She followed my pointing finger, her eyes wide. "Geez, oh geez!"

"Strewth, I'm glad we've got life guards!" I sank down on the sand, hugging my legs to keep them from shaking. Suzy plopped next to me. We grinned at each other, relieved. We chatted and drew in the sand for a few minutes until the lifeguards yelled that the coast was clear. We raced back into the water without a second thought.

At the end of the day, we took bracing cold showers in the beach bathrooms.

Piles of sand, enough to build a sand castle with, washed away from our swimsuits and onto the concrete floor of the shower stall. It felt delicious to be salt and sand free. Dressed in dry shorts and tops, we walked the beach, rehashing our day. We headed back to the family hangout feeling spent, yet achingly good.

When I didn't have my friend Suzy to play with, I hung out for hours in the surf with my younger brother Tom. When we were eleven and eight, our parents gave us matching inflatable rubber floats for Christmas. These were like boogie boards, and they helped to give us a longer, more exhilarating ride. The extra floatation gave me more confidence and I ventured with Tom to catch bigger waves. That meant we also caught our share of dumpers that churned us round and round and under the sand. These rogue waves submerged us long enough that our breath ran out and we sucked in sand and water. We had to dig our heads out of the sand, spluttering and coughing. Afterwards we sat at the water's edge stunned and gasping for a time, waiting to catch our breath. Later, we bragged about our dumper wave sagas, sharing our war-with-the-wave stories again and again.

I spent the most cherished times in the water with my father. We swam out beyond the surf and bobbed atop the gentle waves. Apu taught me how to float, steadying me by placing his hand under my back. When I panicked and struggled, he said, "Relax; the salt in the water makes it heavier. It'll hold you up, see?" I soon settled, delighted and proud that I had been able to follow my father's instructions. We lay on our backs next to each other, our ears popping in and out of the water, rhythmically muffling the sounds of the surf and the cries of the swimmers beyond. "Look how blue the sky is," my father marveled. "We are out here, away from everything with no worries." I realized how rare these carefree moments were for my father, away from the demands of the factory and my mother's harping. My heart went out to him. I wanted to help. I wanted to protect him. I wanted to keep him safe and happy. I wished I could keep him out in the water forever.

"We're getting to look like prunes," Apu said, his voice pulling me out of my reverie. "It's time to get out of the water." My spirits dove when he moved to swim back to shore. Our special time was over.

In contrast, my mother was deathly afraid of drowning. The only water she dared venture into, beyond ankle depth, was the sheltered saltwater pool carved into the rocky edge of Queenscliff. She stepped in the pool up to her waist at my father's urging, scared yet enjoying the refreshing cool. The mixed emotions reflected in her hesitant smile. She rejected my father's suggestions to learn to swim and her inability proved a source of embarrassment for him and for me. I couldn't understand her reticence, since all of us, including our father, had learned to swim with ease as children. Growing up in the Hungarian plains, kids like my mom didn't have places to swim and so, without the early exposure, she developed and harbored a lifelong fear of water.

Despite her own fear, neither Anyu – nor Apu for that matter – ever felt the need to supervise our swimming at the beach. Extensive lifeguard systems made the Sydney beaches extremely safe. The lifeguards constantly patrolled, watching out for anyone struggling in the water or caught in riptides. They provided first aid for cuts and jellyfish stings and performed CPR on the rare cases of near drowning. They spotted for sharks and, when fins were sighted, blew loud whistles, and yelled in bullhorns, alerting us to rush out of the water. In later years, we heard small planes buzzing low overhead as they patrolled along the Sydney beach expanse, radioing the lifeguards if they spotted any shark activity nearby. I never worried about getting eaten by a shark. The few reported attacks occurred on remote, unpatrolled beaches outside the metropolitan areas.

These brawny men who volunteered their time to patrol the beaches had to complete a vigorous training program. Every Sydney beach boasted its own lifeguard troop, each with a distinctive colored uniform consisting of tiny, sexy Speedo trunks and chinstrap plastic caps. There was both camaraderie and competitiveness among the troops, and teams sparred with each other in elaborate competitions staged throughout the summer. As a doe-eyed teenager, I admired these bronzed hunks as they flexed and performed drills hauling "victims" out of the water, maneuvering canoes through choppy surf, and marching in perfect formation along the beach.

§

Over time, the beach became more than an exhilarating play place for me. It became a sacred space as well, a place where I felt profoundly connected to spirit. I was fourteen the first time it happened. Usually, I would stay with my family in the grassy area above the sandy beach. This particular day, for some reason, I felt otherwise. Perhaps I wanted to hang out with the younger hip crowd, or to escape some family member's teasing remark. I don't recall. But I remember grabbing my towel, finding a spot amidst hundreds of others, and sandwiching myself into a small space in the sand.

I dozed as a cacophony of sounds roiled around me: the ocean roared, transistor radios blared, and kids yelled and laughed and hooted. The sun warmed me. The breeze kissed my skin and cooled my burning back. I welcomed the brief shade each time a wispy cloud skimmed over the sun. The hot sand radiated underneath and around me, and was occasionally flicked on me as thoughtless types scurried about. The scent of coconut Coppertone oil was everywhere. The tang of salt and sea tickled my tongue.

That glut of heightened senses catapulted me into a transformed state. My boundaries loosened. My skin no longer contained me. I became the sun, the sand, the breeze, the ocean roar, the Elvis song, the dim and the strident voices. An inexpressible joy swelled in my chest and throat. A glittering thrum and glow pulsed through every cell in my body. The beach welcomed and caressed me. My tears flowed as I silently sobbed into my beach towel.

People nearby were not privy to my sensuous dance with the beach. I looked like just another pudgy Aussie teenager sprawled out on a towel sunbathing. At first, I had no idea what to make of my experience. I thought my brush with the ocean might have been a fluky sensory rush, but it felt like so much more. I couldn't dismiss it. It wasn't trivial. Quite the contrary, it felt really important. I wondered if it might be a spiritual experience, but my only context of God was what I'd learned in my religious indoctrination from the Catholic Church – that of God as Father, Son, and Holy Ghost. The possibility of God as nature was not on my radar.

As with so much of my life, I kept this experience to myself, sharing it with no one. I feared what anyone would say if I told them. I could imagine my brothers' scornful reactions. "You're nuts, you're soft in the head. Yeah, yeah, and cows do fly. Hah, hah, you're one for the funny farm." Telling my parents was completely beyond the realm of possibility. I feared their judgment and their disdain. And tell one of the nuns or priests? Good heavens, no! They would surely think me a heretic. Weren't spiritual experiences limited to Jesus and Mary and maybe the saints? So I kept the experience hidden, deep inside the closet of my psyche.

On the occasions when I would later recall my beach encounter, my body responded with a similar glow and the reliving became a secret pleasure and a calming resource. It wasn't until years later that I learned the true significance of what I had experienced: nature in the form of beaches and oceans were one of my sacred portals, a way for me to access the holy and the divine. I have since begun to visit the ocean regularly to commune and to find counsel and consolation.

While I didn't recognize this as a child, I had two other sacred portals opening to me in my youth – dance and music.

CHAPTER 6 – TINY DANCER, BALLERINA

Me posing *en attitude*, wearing the regulation tunic required for the Royal Ballet examinations.

"Hit the pill dill, I mean ball girl," Mr. Swan yelled when I missed a stroke. He loved his inane pun – better suited for boys. He, like the other tennis instructors, wore a crisp white polo shirt and pressed cream slacks. His face and arms were darkly tanned and looked like beef jerky. His lips were sun crusted and his hair "a little dab'll do you" slicked with Brylcreem. The girls around me snickered at Mr. Swan's humor but there was some truth to his joke. When it came to tennis, I floundered and when flustered, I fumbled even more.

I loved the rigor of the tennis lessons, though. For an hour a week, we Loreto girls received excellent instruction from the coaches of the Victor Edwards Tennis School. Vic was a highly respected coach who mentored Wimbledon champion Evonne Goolagong. At the start of each lesson, before we ever began hitting a ball, the instructors had us break down and practice the steps of each stroke in slo-mo: forehand, backhand, serve, and volley. But I never capitalized on the exceptional instruction for I hardly ever practiced outside our weekly lessons.

Years later, in the 1990s, I took my kids to buy racquets at a sports store in Seattle. I asked to be directed to the tennis section. When the clerk led me to a rack of metal racquets, I announced, "No, I don't want a racquetball racquet, I want a tennis racquet." I felt so sure I was right. After all, I had learned to play tennis from a world famous coach who had instructed a Wimbledon champion! "These *are* tennis racquets, Ma'am," he replied with a puzzled look. My thirteen-year-old son tugged on my arm, wanting to whisk me away, aching to be invisible. My daughter, three years younger than her brother and not quite as instantly mortified by *anything* a parent might do, grinned in disbelief. Slowly, it dawned on me that larger headed metal frames had replaced my ancient Stan Smith endorsed wooden racket. I'd embarrassed my kids, and later, they delighted in ribbing me about my ignorance. My arrogance and pride had taken yet another fall. I felt humbled.

§

In contrast to my miserable tennis performances, I became the star of the Physical Culture program at Loreto. This half hour a week class consisted of rhythmic arm movements and steps. We weren't allowed hops or jumps, nor were we permitted to lift our legs above the knee as then our thighs – and god forbid – our underpants might be exposed. The physical culture classes weren't aerobic – they hardly worked up a sweat. I found the structure simple, the instructions clear and I knew exactly what was expected of me. I didn't have to second-guess how to please as I did at home where I constantly struggled to find ways to get my parents' attention. Because of my ballet training – I began lessons at age five – I coasted through physical culture, winning the first prize medal every year. Several of my classmates, including the girls on the tennis team, wondered how I did it. It was a snap for me to follow the rudimentary steps connecting my arm and leg movements and I moved with a thoughtless ease. I wondered why such basic coordination steps stymied them, especially tennis team members who I envied for their flow and grace on the court.

At Loreto, my classmates and I were constantly admonished to act ladylike and urged to become "Loreto ladies." This need for decorum precluded most competitive athletic activity except running and tennis. The Loreto program wasn't strong enough to suit my mother who came from an entirely different perspective. In addition to high school math and science, she taught gymnastics at the all-girls private school in Hungary. Like most European educators, she believed in the importance of physical culture and so she made sure that all her children took rigorous exercise classes. For my three brothers, that meant acrobatics training with Tibor Rudas who later became internationally known for producing the enormously successful Three Tenors Concert in 1994 starring Luciano Pavarotti, Plácido Domingo, and José Carreras. For my older sister and me, it was ballet lessons.

I loved ballet. Fortunately, my parents chose an excellent classical school for me to attend – The Frances Scully Borovansky School of Dancing, which was an outpost of the London Royal Ballet. Representatives made the long trek from London every two years to the "hinterland colonies," as they were wont to say with thinly disguised disdain, to examine the dancers studying in Sydney.

The ballet school was housed in the funky old Palings building off George Street by the Wynyard train station. The dilapidated building's elevator worked on a manual pulley system. The elevator operator, wearing heavy suede leather gloves, pulled the thick rope cord that ran through a hole in the lift floor. He had to tug it just right to land the elevator at the same level as the floor. He didn't always hit the mark. Many a time after he opened the creaky metal accordion doors, I had to step up or down several inches to get off the elevator. The ride was sometimes amusing, sometimes hair-raising, but I loved it and invariably chose the lift over the stairs.

Miss Daintree, tall and skinny, directed the ballet school. Miss Potts, short and plug-like, assisted her. Both were gray-haired and thick around the middle; but they both had retained their slim dancer legs and grotesque bunions, residuals from their ballerina days at Sadler Wells. These British grand dames demanded respect by their very demeanor.

When I first started, I attended Saturday morning classes taught by Miss Daintree. She was strict, emphasizing technique from the very first *plié* knee bend. Directing each step in a specified order, Miss Daintree assessed and corrected each student's leg and arm placement. She expected maturity and didn't suffer childish behavior. As with the regimented tennis practice at Loreto, I reveled in the rigor of the ballet training. I adored the repetition, the order of the practice, and enthusiastically adopted the time-honored system of classical ballet: *pliés* first, *battement tendus, grand battements, developés, pas de jambes.* As we progressed came *relevées* – rises on tippy toes – and then *frappé* – beats with the balls of the feet – and other advanced steps. We completed these steps at the railing, the *barre*, first on our left side and then our right, then shifted to the room center for the graceful *port de bras* arm movement, the gliding run of the *bourrée*, the graceful *arabesques*, with one leg poised up ninety degrees behind, and the more advanced *penchée*, where the leg lifts as high as the dancer's extension allows – up to 180 degrees in seasoned ballerinas. Center work included *changements*, jumps with leg changes and, as we got stronger and more skilled, soaring leaps called *grand jetés*.

As I progressed, I also danced the advanced repertoire of *pirouettes* and *posé pirouettes.* What a thrill to begin these spins! Each new step in the higher grades added complexity and difficulty. Last of all, I attempted *fouettés,* the famed one-legged spins *en place*, the *pièce de résistance* of the ballet repertoire. Though I came to wobble through eight *fouettés* with some semblance of technique, I never mastered them, and never could complete any of the spins *en pointe* – in point shoes.

Two pianists provided the musical accompaniment to our dance lessons. I thought Miss Blondie to be the epitome of an old maid with her grim face, her grey hair captured in a tight bun, and her tall spindly figure. She played simple tunes, and banged out the rhythms for our steps without any dynamics and little feeling.

In contrast, Miss Esther – a voluptuous, pretty brunette with rouged cheeks, red lipstick, mascara, and a bouffant hairstyle – always had a smile on her face. She sometimes had to look away to hide her amusement when the instructors chewed us out. Her fingers flew effortlessly as she played such timeless classics as Mozart's *Alla Turca* and Burgmüller's *La Styrienne.* Her soulful brilliance infused not only the music, but my body's every twist and turn as well. I am forever grateful to Miss Esther for teaching me the difference between artless and soul-filled music and how to allow music to permeate and express itself in my body.

§

There were no performances in my early dancing years. Instead, Miss Daintree conducted a formal lesson in front of parents at the end of the year – and it was just that, a lesson. I was surprised and delighted that both my parents attended my first demo lesson. For once, I was getting the attention I craved. I, along with the other youngsters, wore the same uniform as for my first grade examination: a short white linen tunic trimmed with a stiff belt, slit on the sides with matching linen panties. My uniform looked like the ones girls wore in my beloved dog-eared ballet books and I felt proud to look like a real dancer.

"Torso posture is terribly important for a dancer," Miss Daintree announced to the parents sitting at the front of the studio. She demonstrated by stepping up to a student. "Suck your tummy in, Margaret," she said, putting her hand on her abdomen. "Tuck your tail under." She continued placing her other hand on the child's bottom. "That's right," she said with a smile. "Now drop your shoulders down and lift up high. Good." I instinctively followed her every direction, straightening my body and stretching taller.

While at the *barre,* she walked up to another student. "Katherine here is rolling her ankles. The turnout in fifth position is difficult to achieve but the ankles must be straight for maximum balance and to avoid injuries." Miss Daintree leaned down and pushed the girl's ankles up. "That's right, Katherine." I glanced at my feet. I had far from perfect turnout in fifth position but at least my ankles didn't seem to be rolling forward.

"Okay now children, *battement tendus* please and hold the point *en avant.*" She paraded down the line of girls, glancing at my leg, then moving on. "Oh, was that good or bad that she went by me?" I thought to myself anxiously. She stopped by the girl in front of me and leaned down. Looking at the parents, she addressed them with, "Notice how the point on this foot is veering inward. This is known as 'sickling.' It's important for the line of the leg to be straight along its whole length. A straight foot will also be a must for maximum stability in point work later on."

Miss Daintree continued with the class, adjusting sagging arms in second position, correcting the timing to out of step students by clapping her hands, all the while with an ongoing commentary to the parents describing every movement, its purpose and its pitfalls.

"We finish every class with a curtsy." Miss Daintree smiled. I took my step, placed my arms out, moved my other leg behind and took my bow, a tentative smile on my face. I was relieved that Miss Daintree hadn't singled me out in the demo lesson with any technique flaws. As I came up from my curtsy, I sneaked a peak at my parents. Were they watching me? They were speaking to each other. What were they saying? My face fell a little. Did they approve? Did they think I'd done a good enough job? I didn't know for sure, but hoped that they thought that I did. Apu smiled at me afterwards and put his arm around my shoulder, then turned his attention to Anyu – something about work in the knitwear factory. "Enough," I thought to myself. "It's enough that they came and that he put his arm around my shoulder and that he smiled."

§

Years later, as an adult and parent myself, I was appalled to find how unstructured the ballet programs I encountered in Seattle were compared to my ballet training in Sydney. These American studios emphasized fun and free spirited running around with precious little attention to technique. The yearend performances also contrasted sharply: they were the antithesis of the serious and rigorous lesson demonstrations of my Sydney school. The American youngsters, outfitted in gaudy, sequined costumes, pranced around the stage in routines choreographed for cuteness and executed with atrocious technique in front of gushing parents.

§

I had been studying ballet for nearly six years when Miss Daintree invited me to join the Saturday morning Theatre Class. I was only eleven at the time and I was elated that my teachers deemed me competent enough to advance to point work. Delighting in the class's title, I dreamt that this would be another important step towards my becoming a well-rounded actress. Perhaps I could even sing and dance in a musical. By this time, I'd increased my ballet class commitment from once a week to three nights and Saturday morning – and I enjoyed every minute of it.

My ballet buddy was Kerry. Her smile – an orthodontist's delight – lit up her freckle-speckled face. When she laughed, which was often, her unruly brown curls bounced about.

I loved hanging out with Kerry. She lived in the other end of town, but apart from the distance we shared similarities: we both came from big Catholic families and attended private Catholic girls' schools. Kerry had a wonderful spring in her ballet work and a wicked sense of humor. She did crazy impressions of Miss Daintree's British accent, parodying her walk: her head in the air, her hands in preparatory position by her side, and her feet turned out. Once, when beginning the fourth ballet grade, our teacher, Miss Yvonne – beautiful, young and pregnant and much talked about since in ballet circles having babies ruined your figure, and therefore ruined any ballet career you might hope to have – left us for a moment to collect our exam reports in the office.

All of us were nervous and excited as we sat under the *barre* awaiting her return. Kerry and I began to act out getting a bad result. We pantomimed fake wails of despondence at receiving a poor grade, slurping our snot, making huge arm swings to wipe our noses, and swiping our snotty hands on the sides of our leotards. We had the class in stitches. When Miss Yvonne returned, Kerry and I were relieved and delighted to receive our report cards: we were both awarded the highest grade of "Honors."

My favorite times with Kerry occurred after the Saturday morning theatre class. We'd stroll to the milk bar opposite the Wynyard train station where they sold "American style thick shakes." These were way more substantial than the usual Aussie watery milk shakes and I thought they were quite American, though hardly of the sludge consistency I later relished in the United States. Of course, we thought the thick shakes decadent and we slurped and savored every gulp. A tiny cafe that cornered the alley of the Palings building became another favorite, our spot to share an enormously gooey banana split. "Miss Daintree roared at me one time when she caught me eating donuts in the studio dressing room." I giggled, wiping a dab of ice cream from my chin and glancing out the window to see if the stately ballet instructor might be hovering. The coast was clear and I relaxed. "Think how shocked she would be if she came by right now and saw us with this huge banana split," I added. Kerry spluttered with glee. I smiled.

"Please, could you come home with me and spend the day?" I pleaded, not for the first time.

"I want to, but my parents won't let me," Kerry replied, turning away from my gaze, doodling some melted ice cream with her spoon.

"Well, would you ask them again?"

"I'll try," she answered, "But don't get your hopes up." She motioned to the last bite of ice cream. I nodded for her to finish it. My stomach was full and gurgled with disappointment.

"I've got to get home." She sighed. We walked in silence to the Wynyard train station and parted – she to her eastbound train platform, I to the one headed for the north shore. I felt let down and sad.

Kerry never came to my house and I never got an invitation to hers either. I figured it must have something to do with my being a "bloody new Australian" – that her parents thought they needed to protect Kerry from skanky immigrants. I never knew for sure and invented all kinds of stories about why they might refuse to let her visit me at home. Whatever their reasons, I was sorely disappointed to not be able to spend more time with her.

§

As I grew older, it became clear to me that I didn't have a ballet dancer's body. I lacked the extension, the turn out, and the skinny legs. My instructors sometimes asked me to demonstrate *port de bras* and character dancing such as my native Hungarian *csárdás* or the Italian *tarantella*. I received compliments for my flow of movement and characterization and I loved that they noticed my soulful expression, but it hurt that I was never singled out for any technical excellence. They asked other girls to demonstrate hip turn-out in the *pliés* or leg extension with the *arabesques*. When competitions were initiated, my teachers didn't ask me to apply. I felt this to be another indication that I wasn't good enough, or perhaps that I and my parents didn't launch any promotional efforts. With sadness and resentment, I noticed how several other parents volunteered at the ballet studio and lobbied for their daughters. My parents never did that for me.

The ballet school held its first major gala in a city theatre and included performances by the various competitors, chosen by the teachers, as well as group dances for those of us who were not competing. I wore my first and only tutu: pink satin with a circlet of petals over the netting. I was thrilled to dance in a real theatre, to wear real stage makeup, complete with the red dot on the inner eye canthus, an old-fashioned theatrical technique to make eyes sparkle. On stage, my face glowed and my body soared. I felt like I had hit the big time and my dream of becoming a performer had begun to materialize.

Even though I did not compete, I observed and studied the girls who did, and I learned a great deal about myself from their performances. After my group dance, I quickly changed and rushed to sit with the audience to watch Jane's performance. She was my idol, excelling in every aspect of dance: she had impeccable turnout and placement, beautiful extension, and effortless gazelle-like leaps. I thought her to be by far the most expressive and naturally talented dancer at my ballet school. I awaited her dance with a big grin on my face and my fingers crossed. I wanted her to win so badly.

But oh my, Jane missed her first cue. I groaned inwardly. Even from the uppermost tier I could see how her hands started to shake and how her face became frozen in a glassy stare. And then she forgot some of the steps to her routine! I broke out in an embarrassed flush. When she stumbled out of a pirouette and fell, my heart ached and I lay my head in my hands. I couldn't watch any longer. Jane had fallen apart in the competition – literally!

Jane quit ballet soon after the competition. I mourned the waste of what I felt to be her God-given talent. As I mused about her botched performance and her dropping out, I began to realize how important it was to have self-confidence and grit under pressure. I began to comprehend how critical self-confidence is in one's ability to showcase one's talents. I resonated with Jane's lack of self-assurance, and noticed how I too held back, how I feared fully expressing myself. Was I as talented as Jane in some artistic area I had yet to discover? Was I, like her, lacking the courage to follow through?

Sandra was the next dancer in the competition and she, in contrast, possessed the confidence Jane lacked. She epitomized the slim long-legged ideal dancer body and demonstrated flawless technique. "She lacks expression," I thought to myself as I watched her competition performance, still reeling from Jane's debacle. "She dances like a robot and her smile looks like it's pasted on," I scoffed, so wishing that Jane's showing could have been as flawless. Sandra's routine ended in a flourish and I had to admire how she spun around in a seemingly endless set of perfect *fouettés*. I was jealous of her impeccable technique, yet scorned her lack of expressive soulful interpretation. "If only I had her ballet body," I pined, my stomach souring with envy. "I'd be a so much better dancer because I have the expression, the soul."

Next on the stage came Penny: big-boned and heavy-footed. I thought her performance passable; she had the routine down pat. But darn, she just wasn't a dancer! "She's more suited to weight lifting or wrestling," I thought to myself uncharitably. I hated that Penny's presence dominated the dance school. Her mother, ever present and pushy, assisted the teachers with office work. Penny was entered into the competition. Penny was lauded. She trekked to London to the Royal Academy, the requisite odyssey and ultimate testing ground for aspiring colonial ballerinas, most of whom returned without making it in the extraordinarily competitive environment of the Royal Academy. Penny suffered that fate. She soon returned from overseas under a hush-hush cloud of mystery. The exposure of the emperor with no clothes surfaced when the Royal Academy visiting examiners failed Penny. Even though I silently scorned Penny for her lack of ability and detested all the attention she received, I had to admire how she weathered the storm of her exam failure with grace, staying on at the studio as an assistant instructor.

Penny's experience also fueled my lack of confidence, but in a different way than Jane's downfall had. I wondered: was I overestimating my abilities? Did I have delusions of grandeur like Penny had? Was I making a fool of myself, kidding myself that I had talent? Did I look as awkward as she did? Was I as big a girl lumbering around like a "heffalump," the disparaging term some of us dancers coined to poke fun at awkward dancers? I though it more prudent to hide in the background than to display myself like Penny, especially as my body plumped up with puberty. I didn't want to be scorned. I didn't want to be labeled a heffalump. I hung back.

In my final year at the ballet studio, the instructors added modern dance to the classical core. Miss Daintree encouraged me to sign up. I was horribly disappointed as she only recommended the class to the less talented students. Clearly, she thought I was one of them. Even though I knew I wasn't a great dancer, Miss Daintree's recommendation felt like a putdown, and it stung. I tried the class without much enthusiasm and a sinking heart. It consisted of more toning exercises than it did actual modern dance and included core and leg strengthening reps for "the burn." The young and beatnicky instructor gossiped about her boyfriend and boasted about her rock hard abs. For me, the modern dance class didn't hold the magic and lacked the magnificence of ballet. I had become a ballet snob.

So although I had the style and the heart, I did not have the technique or the body for ballet. In Australia, you could legally quit school at age thirteen and this marked the decision point at the ballet school when dancers either went full-time or fizzled out – like me. Academics were too important to my parents and to me. I became one of the ballet hangers-on remaining only in the Saturday Theatre Class and later, even that went by the wayside. As if it mourned my loss to the ballet world, the old, decrepit Palings building which had housed my ballet classes for eight years was finally condemned, shut down, and then razed. The studio moved to new quarters by the Town Hall.

I ventured to one class at the new site after several months away from dancing. I missed ballet and wanted to give it one more try. Maybe I could recapture some of the joy I'd experienced earlier. Perhaps I had some hidden dance talent and I could explore it now that I was more mature. Maybe I could be a great ballerina after all. I also wanted to get back into shape and lose some of the teenage puppy fat I'd gained.

I nervously walked up the steps of the new studio. I didn't recognize many of the students – and the ones that looked familiar didn't remember or acknowledge me. New teachers had replaced Miss Daintree and Miss Potts. The whole environment was foreign and I felt horribly awkward and out of place. I silently dressed in my faded leotards, which felt as ill fitting as the whole scene and then stepped into my cracked, scuffed ballet slippers.

In class, I cramped up at the *barre*, wobbled in the spins, and stumbled as I tried to keep up with the complex choreography. I tensed, tightened, and tripped. My technique had suffered with disuse. I didn't have the heart to continue after that lesson. I gave ballet up for good.

CHAPTER 7 – I GOT THE MUSIC IN ME

Striking a pose in our Wollstonecraft living room. My first place Eistedffod trophy sits on the piano behind me.

Late at night, alone, my father would play his violin, keeping it a private affair. He bowed with hesitant strokes, the mute fork permanently stuck on the instrument's bridge like a gag, as if he feared to unleash his soul, as if terrified to uncage a too big desire. His songs were whispers, barely audible – his tunes, long remembered Hungarian or classic melodies.

To his lasting regret, he'd only had a handful of lessons as a child. Later, while attending the Hungarian Ludovika Military Academy, he played third violin in the orchestra. I have a photo of him sitting proudly in the back row of the orchestra, erect in his dress uniform, his chest puffed out with the slightest hint of a smile on his chiseled face.

Apu listened to 2BL and 2FC radio, the Sydney classical music stations. He loved classical music and his passion for it rubbed off on all five of us kids. But with rare exceptions, such as Perry Como and Danny Kaye, Apu looked down on popular music with intellectual disdain, finding no merit in it – calling it "noise." His criticism really annoyed us as we, like all kids, really grooved on the pop music of the day. We dismissed our father's distaste for rock 'n' roll as old fashioned. Our mother's tastes in music leaned more toward English pop and Hungarian *sláger* (pop) songs. She'd had no musical training of any kind. She loved to sing, but couldn't carry a tune, much to my father's chagrin. That, however, never stopped her from crowing when she felt like it.

Music was a blessing though. It served as a binding force in our family, which was otherwise pretty bereft of sensuality and any overt expressions of caring connections. I acknowledge and give thanks that one of the greatest legacies and gifts my family bestowed on me were the joys of music.

§

When I was nine, my father purchased a state of the art stereo, a big step up in quality from the previous single channel mono record players. The console was about the size of a dining room hutch and its fancy wood paneling housed a large speaker at each end – hence the stereo designation. A record player, AM radio – FM broadcasts weren't to come for years – and a slot to store music albums comprised the space between. The record player had a spindle with an automatic feed mechanism that allowed us to stack several vinyl albums on it at once. The machine would then automatically drop one album at a time onto the platter and then move the stylus arm over and down, so that the needle made contact to play the record. When it reached the end of the track, the arm would move back to its holder and then wait for the next album in the stack to drop and the process would repeat. It sounds so antiquated as I describe it now, but back then, I thought it magnificent, the absolute latest in audio gear. And for the first time, I was able to play a piece of music on demand – and even over and over if I wanted to. What heaven!

In preparation for its inauguration, Apu took me to the central Sydney Palings Music Store (in the creaky building where I took my ballet lessons) to buy our first records. I felt over the moon to share some rare father-daughter time. We browsed the classical stacks and Apu pointed out some of the classics. He chose our very first 33 rpm LP (long play) album: Tchaikovsky's 6th *Pathétique* symphony. To that he added a small 45 disc of Mozart's *Eine Kleine Nacht Musik*. "This is such a beloved, well known piece. We must get it," he said and smiled. When I espied the ballet excerpts from Delibes' *Les Sylphides,* I gave Apu an imploring look. He grinned and added it to our purchase.

At the first official demo of the stereo, my father ceremonially gathered all the family in the living room. "Everyone sit down around the stereo and pay attention." Proudly, he announced, "I'm going to play one of Tchaikovky's best known symphonies, the *Pathétique.*"

I could tell how serious he was about wanting to orchestrate an auspicious learning event, for his hands trembled a little as he placed the vinyl album on the turntable. When the opening mournful minor strains of the first movement floated into the room, my father's face softened with a rapt glow. I looked around nervously at the rest of the family, most of them gazing into space and also lost in the music – except for little Tom who met my gaze and grinned. As the music sped up with a dramatic crescendo, he winked and began to conduct furtively, making micro-movements with his fingers. By the time the orchestra introduced the melodic theme we were both giggling.

Apu silenced us with a cold stare – but then we broke out in another fit when the music strains accelerated and climaxed yet again. My father now placed a finger to his lips, his eyes flashing. I felt badly as I adored my father and shared his love of music. I knew he was attempting to inculcate his love of its majestic and mystical beauty and Tom and I were reacting to the gravity of the occasion with uncontrolled titters.

My outbursts were in large part due to nerves. This was such an unusual activity for my family that I found myself feeling prickly and fidgety. I couldn't stop cracking up and there came a point where my father had had enough of our antics. "Go to your rooms," he thundered. I felt awful. My father's record album shopping buddy had let him down, disappointed him terribly and had ruined the family event. I hung my head as Tom and I were unceremoniously banished. The humor of the situation had rapidly dissipated.

§

My brother Paul demonstrated his love of music with gusto. He'd come home from Uni lectures and head straight for the stereo, loading up a stack of albums and turning the volume so high that the music reverberated through the entire house – and beyond. None of us ever asked him to lower the volume. We basked in his pleasure – and our own – as we listened. I never turned the volume anywhere near so high when I played records. Unlike Paul, I was afraid of annoying my older siblings. I never wanted to call attention to myself because it often resulted in me getting taunted and ribbed.

Paul played all kinds of music: the gamut of Beethoven, including his violin concertos and those of Tchaikovsky, Mendelssohn, and Bruch. His favorite violinist was David Oistrakh – Paul unabashedly claimed he was the best virtuoso, superior even to Yehudi Menhuin. My brother listened to the Liszt piano concertos, his rhapsodies and orchestral poems such as *Les Préludes*. He played Brahms Hungarian dances, Rachmaninoff, Grieg, and Mozart. It was like having our own private DJ in the house and each album etched into me a love of classical music.

Then there were times when Paul was in the mood for pop and country music – Johnny Cash, Buddy Holly, Gus Orbison, Johnny Horton and the Everly Brothers. He played them with the same high volume abandon as his beloved classics. Winifred Atwell's twinkling keyboard honky-tonk rags, and Duane Eddy's plunking acoustic guitar strummings were also among his favorites.

§

Apu's delight in playing music made him want to see to it that all his children had the opportunity to learn to play an instrument well – to know the joys, the solaces, the passion, the emotional release that listening to music and playing music provides. I learned to play the violin but I hardly ever played with my father. He remained too self-conscious and self-deprecating about his ability.

My sibs all learned to play an instrument. Paul and Irene played piano, Tom the violin, and Geza the cello, then later the trumpet when he joined the cadets in high school. Paul had the most musical talent of all us kids. He could bang out a tune such as "In the Mood" by ear and his recall of any music he heard was exceptional. His music teacher was shocked to discover a year into his lessons that Paul couldn't read music. My brother would listen to his teacher play a new piece, recall it by ear, and then play it for his next lesson.

I began violin lessons at age five. My first teacher, Miss Lane, was a pretty, young, soft-spoken redhead. She wore her long flaming titian hair loosely gathered in a bun. I felt instantly at ease with her – not something I felt very often as a child. I thought her rather elegant and wonderful. Miss Lane taught at the Sydney Conservatory of Music, an imposing medieval castle structure, replete with classic crenellations. My feet crackled over roof tar as I walked over the ramparts to her music room.

Miss Lane encouraged me to enter the regional Eisteddfod. These competitions were held annually for music students and the categories included voice and all kinds of classical instruments. I wanted so much to please her, to make her proud of me as her student. I practiced hard, and came to my first event well prepared.

At the conservatorium, Apu picked up a program and led me to seats at the front of the tiered music room. I glanced at the other contestants. Most of them were about my age, a couple looked older. I felt both calm and excited at the same time. I tuned my violin, and then peeked at the program. Perfect, I thought. I'm to play third.

When my name was called, I stood up with confidence and moved into a zone. My violin sang, my bow flowed smoothly, my intonation landed spot on, and my feelings reverberated in the melody. Completely unselfconscious, I became one with the music I was making.

I reveled in my performance as I returned to my seat. Apu smiled and patted me on the back. I knew I had done well, and wasn't at all surprised when the judges announced my name in first place. "Congratulations! Brava, brava." My father beamed as he led me outside. "Let's take a walk."

We strolled through the Botanical Gardens adjacent to the Music Conservatorium, basking in the sunshine and in my success. Apu strutted proudly. "No one played nearly as well as you."

I touched the soft magenta blooms of a bottlebrush tree and reflected, "I did notice how some of the players hit notes off key and others had squeaky bowing."

"You had none of that. You were perfect," he beamed.

Yes, I was, I mused to myself and I smiled up at him. I reveled in the rare opportunity to bond with my father, and the even rarer opportunity of receiving his unconditional approval.

I never again duplicated the magic of that performance. In other competition sections that same year, I placed third – and came in third the following year. That first and only win was a thrill. I felt the joy of acing my performance, of being competent, of being more than competent – I was in the flow.

My father had me take lessons from another violin teacher soon after Miss Lane had her baby. He thought the new teacher was a better fit, and would help to enhance my growing musical skills, but I was sorely disappointed to leave Miss Lane.

Mrs. Muller, the new teacher, lived in the neighborhood of Castlecrag. Maria Néni, a Hungarian friend of ours, also lived in Castlecrag and my parents arranged for her to pick me up at school after collecting her son at the neighboring St Aloysius boys' school and drop me off for my violin lessons. Maria Néni had been an opera singer of some repute in Hungary. She looked the part of the Wagnerian Brunhilde with her bulging torso and her loud, flamboyant personality. She could barely squeeze her bulk behind the wheel of her matchbox Mini Minor. Having only recently passed her driving test, she lacked driving skills, but her inexperience didn't deter her from getting distracted as she peered around to the back chatting loudly and gesticulating madly. The car swerved left and right, jolted forward and backward, and the gears screamed and ground as she shifted. I whispered a prayer of gratitude every time we arrived unscathed at her house. Maria Néni gave voice and piano lessons in her home. When I later showed interest in learning to play piano in addition to the violin, my parents signed me up to take lessons from her.

Mrs. Muller lived a couple of blocks from Maria Néni in a musty, dingy, dark house. An elderly, chunky, sooty haired creature, always serious and dour, she rarely complimented my playing. I cringed in her presence, mentally and emotionally. My desire to play waned, becoming as stale as her house. I wasn't long with Mrs. Muller. My father couldn't help but notice my languor and orchestrated another switch.

My next and final violin teacher was Tibor Bácsi, a quite well known virtuoso in music circles in Hungary and revered by the Hungarian community in Australia. A rotund man with a balding head and a gap between his front teeth, he had the uncanny knack of emitting both the minty fragrance of the gum he chewed and bad breath at the same time. I spent more time having "father-daughter" talks with Tibor Bácsi than I did learning to play the violin. He spent my lesson time bragging about what a good job he'd done raising two daughters. His oldest was a law student at Sydney University. The younger had just matriculated with honors from high school.

Anxious to avoid playing for him as I'd hardly practiced at all, I often complained about my problems – in true teenage fashion. I lounged in the chair and moaned, "Irene got invited to the (Hungarian) White Rose Ball again and nobody asks me out at all."

He smiled. "My girls both have dates for the ball. Your time may come later, you never know." He wasn't that encouraging.

On another occasion when I hadn't practiced, I dodged again. "Oh, I don't know what subjects to take in school next year. It's impossible to decide. Do I focus on the rigorous sciences track or the less strenuous humanities one?" Tibor Bácsi puffed out his chest.

"Well, I had my daughters take the hardest classes every time. They are very smart. You must go full speed ahead with your academics."

When I had told my parents that I had to choose my courses and asked for their advice, their reply was "Oh, you can figure it out." They didn't know much about the new system with its designated "full" track compared to the less stringent one and, as usual, they failed to pick up on the anxiety I was feeling. Partly due to Tibor Bácsi's views but more to follow in the science and math footsteps of my older siblings, I decided on the full classes.

Though some of his advice made sense and it felt good to have an adult to talk to, I also felt like Tibor Bácsi was trying to squish me into the same mold as his daughters – but that he saw me as a poorer, duller replica compared to his own shining stars. Nevertheless, the lengthy chats did serve to allow less time for the violin lesson. Some days I didn't get to pick up my fiddle until the last minutes of our allotted time. Those times I would hide my grin. My diversionary tactics had succeeded yet again! By then I'd lost interest in the violin and so I coasted, as happy to chew the fat as to play.

Tibor Bácsi participated in various local symphonies and performed as a soloist. My family attended his performance of Beethoven's Violin Concerto. In the middle of a rapid *con brio* flurry, the chin rest detached from his violin and the whole instrument dropped to the floor with a solid *thunk*. The audience held its breath. The strains of the orchestra petered out. The seconds stretched. Tibor Bácsi's lack of svelte didn't hinder his agility and speed in scooping up the violin and he fumbled to reattach the chin rest. To his credit, he carried on as only someone of his caliber and experience could, and brilliantly finished the concerto. I was floored! We met him backstage afterwards. Red faced and blustering, he repeated over and over again, "Zees has never happened to me before . . . zees is unbeeleeveble, unbeeleeveble!"

Tibor Bácsi was a heavy smoker and he had a heart attack soon after his performance. With his illness, my violin lessons ended forever. I had reached my violin playing pinnacle years before when taking lessons from Miss Lane. I couldn't sustain that initial drive. I believed I didn't have the talent, and I knew I didn't have the discipline. I had no wish to continue.

§

Growing up, I warbled around the house and, much to my parents' amusement, often sang myself to sleep. I longed to perform as a singer (and dance and act), but I never took any voice lessons. I was reluctant, due, in part, to some early reactions to my singing efforts.

The first happened when I was standing in the knitting factory area of our house in North Sydney. I couldn't have been more than six then and, in a fit of youthful exuberance, I sang my heart out to an audience of two – my mother and one of her Hungarian employees. I sang with gusto, performing "Baa Baa

Black Sheep" with complete abandon as only a child can do. My mother and her worker burst out laughing. I cringed and clammed up, a flush of shame spread to my cheeks, and I stood there with a frozen smile on my face. Their sudden outburst jolted me like an electric shock. I had no warning, no way to protect myself. The only reason I could come up with for their boisterous response was that my singing was terrible. Why else would they laugh so hard? My confidence was shattered and I slinked away.

Some time later, my mother orchestrated a talent show at our North Sydney house. The machines in the factory front room were moved to the sides to make room for performers and their families. Our Hungarian friend Rosa tap-danced to the tune of "Red Red Robin," which my brother Paul plonked out on the piano. My sister danced a traditional Hungarian peasant dance, then she and I performed another Hungarian dance to the song, *Nincsen pénzem* "I have no money but will soon get some…"

My mother had taught me a Hungarian pop song *Meg Untam az Életemet*. The lyrics go:

I'm fed up with my life, I'm going up to Budapest
I'll walk along the main Boulevard every Saturday night
I'll rouge myself up and hold my head up high
Someone is sure to fall in love with me
Along the banks of the Danube River.

In addition to the polite applause, family and friends responded to my performance with furtive smiles. At the time, I believed they thought me cute, but I also felt distinctly uncomfortable. I later understood why: the song my mother chose was hardly appropriate for a seven-year-old child. It was rather like the child beauty pageant contestant whose mother garbed her in *Pretty Woman's* whoring outfit. I wondered at my mother's judgment in choosing such a suggestive song for a child and it struck me as rather bizarre.

But the experience that caused me to forever shy away from singing alone in public happened when I was in fourth grade at Loreto and auditioned for a solo in the choir. I had the class reputation for being the best singer and so my mates encouraged me to try out. I was flattered and somewhat surprised by their support. It was rare for me to feel such acceptance and approval from my classmates. I went into choir practice buoyed up by their compliments, but when the male choir director fawned over Anne's voice – she was in the class behind me and took private voice lessons – I was devastated. My eyes filled with tears, my throat tightened, and my stomach plunged low into my belly. Anne was awarded the solo part and I received the consolation prize of singing a verse as a duet with another classmate. I was jealous of Anne, I fumed inwardly at the choir director, and I felt ashamed that I had let my classmates down. When they had complimented me, I thought I'd made some headway towards being accepted. I thought I could become assimilated and not feel like an outsider any more, but with this failure, my hopes were dashed again. I longed to take voice lessons like Anne, but with my mother's laughing response, and this failed audition, I had completely lost all confidence. I didn't have the nerve to ask for voice lessons from Maria Néni, and settled for taking piano lessons from her instead. I lacked the courage to fight for what I really wanted.

§

For years, I had heard my older sibs rave about the Youth Concerts, live symphony performances held in the Sydney Town Hall. I couldn't wait to participate in this musical coming of age event and was finally allowed to go when I turned thirteen. My mouth gaped and my eyes bugged out as I took in the ornate interior columns of the hall and the magnificent regiment of pipes looming behind the stage. The organ was the largest in the world when it was installed in 1890. My older sibs had remarked on how well behaved the young adult audiences were. "You can't hear any rustling or stirring in the audience. It's so quiet," they announced proudly. I therefore took great pains not to make any noise. I didn't dare cross or uncross my legs, tolerated the numbing aches instead, and I didn't dare turn the pages of my program.

I was enthralled. The strains of Mozart's *Haffner* symphony filled the hall and reverberated through my body. I drooled as I gazed at John Painter, the lead cellist, and my brother's music teacher. As he bowed the mellow contrapuntal melodies of the first movement, my heart raced. Blond and slim, with full sensuous lips, I thought him gorgeous. Not only was I in heaven to hear my first live orchestra concert, I had developed my first crush.

When Mr. Painter came to our house to give Geza his cello lesson, I ran to the door to let him in. I all but swooned, but he hardly noticed me. My hopeless crush waned with time and with the harsh reality that he was both a married and a family man.

One time our Loreto class attended a Youth Concert as a field trip. By now, the performances were familiar to me, but most of my classmates had never attended and knew little about classical music. As we walked to the train station in crocodile two-by-two formation, I prattled on to the girls around me. "The concerts are really great, they are so fab, and the pieces they play are really great. You'll love it!" I thought that with my knowledge they would be impressed.

One of the girls who I admired because they were so athletic and on the tennis team snickered, "Oh yeah, we're going to hear some high-brow music. B-o-ring! It's for fuddy-duddies – like you!"

Their teasing hurt and, once again, I was filled with the feelings of being forever a foreigner, for most of the classical music lovers I knew were Hungarian.

Despite the putdowns at school, classical music remained incredibly important to me. Alone in the house one day, I played Liszt's *Les Préludes* on the stereo. As I lay face down on the carpet, listening to the crescendo strains of the orchestra, I began to weep uncontrollably. I didn't know why the tears streamed from my eyes. There were no specific memories or feelings associated with this outpouring of emotion. Rather, they seemed more like a generic and detached groundswell that flooded my being. The young, immature part of me was unclear about what was happening, but I know now that what filled me that day was a deep connection triggered by and resonating with the profoundly powerful collective musical forces. It was my first experience of tapping into the very soul of music. That day in the living room, listening to *Les Préludes*, I connected with the sounds and the instruments from which they emanated. I connected with the musicians whose skills and hearts flowed through their violins and cellos, trumpets and tympani, oboes and flutes. I connected with the conductor whose talent wove together the individual efforts of the musicians into a rich, seamless tapestry of sound; with the technicians who recorded the music; and with the people who manufactured the magical vinyl disc containing the music I played on the stereo that day – music that had brought me to tears. All of them had served to recreate and interpret the original imaginings of the brilliant composer Franz Liszt, my Hungarian compatriot. All participated in stirring the cauldron of my musical soul as the notes rang out. All resonated in my body as sacred.

There is an utmost physicality to my experience of music. It drenches and flows through me. It is no wonder I that I can't relate to the religion-touted image of the sacred as transcendent. I cannot relate to looking for God out there beyond the physical, in heaven, in the next life. Growing up, I struggled with seeing the body as other than what was drummed into me in Catholic school: an impure vessel to be denied, scorned, and scourged. Gradually, however, with my music, ballet, and nature experiences, I came to experience God and the sacred as imminent, an inextricable part of not only my body, but of the world body that surrounded me.

Classical or pop, sacred or secular, music runs through my veins like lifeblood. No matter how often I listen to Mozart's 21st piano concerto, my heart rises and falls and burns in my chest with each up and down arpeggio in the first movement. Gus Orbison's sweetly delicious tenor voice warbling "You Got It" gets me every time: I bang my fist in my palm with each double tympani clap; my mind-of-their-own toes tapping to the beat. I sit in the Seattle Opera's performance of Wagner's *Parsifal,* and bits of my heart and throat and tears float like a misty eminence toward the orchestra pit and stage, toward the musicians and singers, there to mingle with the strains and melodies of the instruments and voices. I am transported to a mystical "opera zone," so much so that I am no longer a spectator, but rather a contributing participant to the magic and majesty of the opera.

Music is a physical, emotional, and spiritual experience for me. It helps me ground awareness in my body. It provides me with emotional release and expression. Music serves as a portal to the sacred, much like my sacred portal to nature through ocean beaches. It's a way for me to resonate with the pulsating mass of creation. Whether I absorb the strains sitting still or dancing, stomping and spinning to my heart's content, music engages every one of my body's cells in its vibrating mystery. I see and feel God in music.

CHAPTER 8 – EVERYTHING IS HOLY NOW

My first communion, standing in front of Our Lady's grotto at Loreto. I loved my dress but not my veil.

My siblings and I were raised Catholic. My parents had us attend parochial schools. They took us to Mass on Sundays and they made sure we said grace before and after meals – in Hungarian. Even so, I never thought either of them to be spiritual. They didn't talk about their faith. They didn't tell us how God worked in their lives. I didn't have religious discussions with my parents, and I was puzzled that my mother seemed more preoccupied with superstition than religious fervor.

"You will not bury me in the ground like the Church requires. You will cremate me," Anyu declared as she settled herself on the sofa in the light strewn verandah of our Wollstonecraft home. She had just returned from the funeral service and interment of a friend. Anyu directed the fearsome gleam in her eye first at my sister who was ironing a blouse, then at me as I knelt on the shag rug, folding socks. Young Tom was plopped on the floor nearby setting up his toy soldiers for yet another battle. When I nervously glanced at him, he rolled his eyes and this helped ease my discomfort. But Anyu hadn't finished. "If I burn in hell, so be it. I'll enjoy its heat, and may well like the fires of hell better than the cold heavenly clouds," she said with a smirk, picking up a *Vogue* magazine and noisily flipping through the pages. My face tensed with a tight smile. Anyu was on a roll now. "If you don't cremate me, I will come back to haunt you," she declared, staring first at my sister, then at me. I held my breath.

My sister broke the tense silence, setting the iron on edge and looking up at Anyu. "Of course we'll do as you wish, Anyu. You know we will."

"Just make sure you do," she threatened.

I rummaged around in the laundry basket, averting my gaze, busily searching for the mate of an unmatched sock. When Anyu finally turned back to her *Vogue* magazine and began to look at the fashions, I breathed a sigh of relief, sat back on my heels and reflected. This wasn't the first time Anyu had made such an adamant pronouncement about wishing to be cremated. As my sticky discomfort wore off, I thought to myself: *Really, would God send you to hell just because you were burned instead of buried*? And a part of me wondered: *Is the Catholic Church really so petty and rigid*? I glanced at my mother's face and could sense some disquiet underneath her bluster. And I began to wonder about my own demise: would I want flames or worms to eat my body? I pushed such gruesome thoughts from my mind.

I later learned that my mother's fear of burials stemmed from a tale, spread around her village when she was a child. A corpse, exhumed for some reason, was found rotated in the coffin. That frightened my mother horribly and she remained terrified for the rest of her life of being buried alive, of waking up in a coffin underground.

§

I received some of my first religious instruction at the summer camps run by the Hungarian priests and nuns. They didn't teach dogma or fire and brimstone as my school did, but rather told interesting stories of our Hungarian saints. Young Saint Elizabeth – my namesake – built a hospital with her dowry and served the sick. Saint Stephen was crowned our very first king. Saint Ladislas miraculously found the cure for a pestilence that plagued the kingdom when he shot an arrow into the air and retrieved a healing herb. King Matthias was my favorite because he advocated for the little guy. He wasn't a saint, but he did have the famous Church on Buda Hill named after him and was known as "Matthias the Just" because he wandered in disguise throughout his realm to deliver justice to his subjects. The Hungarian clerics combined the religious with the secular. In addition to hymns, they taught us to sing camp songs – some of them rather bawdy. They showed us not only pictures of Hungary's beautiful churches, but also photos of graceful bridges, stately buildings and historic squares. I warmed to the gentle, caring attitudes of the Hungarian nuns and priests who made our religious training more attractive and heartfelt. They did a wonderful job of mixing summer fun with ecclesiastical instruction. I learned that religious times could be blended with everyday times and they could be happy times too. They didn't always have to be serious and austere church ceremonies. Unlike the nuns at Loreto, the Hungarian nuns and priests at camp tolerated some boisterousness from us kids and were more comfortable with our unbridled expressions of emotion and exuberance.

Once I got over the initial horrible separation anxiety I felt in leaving my parents for Hungarian summer camp, I really enjoyed the time I spent in the picturesque Blue Mountains of New South Wales, seventy miles east of my Sydney home. I met other Hungarian kids, and was able to spend a whole two weeks with my dear friend, Suzy. We had a pool to swim in, and played splendid, boisterous games like *szám háború* or "numbers war," a complex game where we kids were split into two teams and where opponents were eliminated by reading off their identity numbers. Each of us wore our individual identity on our foreheads – four large numbers written in our team's color, either red or green, on a 7 x 10 inch piece of cardboard which was then tied with strings around our heads. We all raced into the woods and hid our forehead numbers, either behind trees or by dipping our head down when we sped about in the open. I wasn't very clever at hiding as I scurried about attempting to spot and yell out opponents' numbers. Early elimination always seemed to be related to age. The younger kids, like me, were less stealthy and fell out early in the game. The tactically astute older boys climbed trees for protection, espied numbers from above, and were the last to be eliminated. The team that called out all the opponents' numbers first won the battle. Despite my disappointment in having to leave the game early, I delighted in hearing the whoops and groans reverberating from the woods as each number was called out and in the celebrations that followed. I looked forward to the numbers war, a highlight of summer camp each year.

It was fun being with all Hungarian kids. I could relax and enjoy the comraderie. I didn't have to hide who I was or feel anxious about it. Camp was the one place I didn't have to squeeze myself into a different persona. I didn't have to fit into the Aussie mold. I could just be myself.

In fact, camp was a place where my ethnic background was validated. When I was eight and in my third year at the summer camp, there came a day when Mother Clothilde pointed to me in class. "Elizabeth," she said, "please come up here and recite the Hungarian Anthem for us." I got up from my seat, my head abuzz. My ears felt like they were filled with cotton wool. I could barely hear the flip-flop of my thongs as I walked towards Mother Clothilde. I turned towards a sea of grinning faces. Were they cheering me on or waiting for me to mess up?

I faltered as I began: *Isten, áldd meg a Magyart.* Then I remembered my father at Hungarian Masses, his strong baritone voice resounding with the strains of his beloved national anthem and I continued reciting in a clear voice:

O Lord, bless the nation of Hungary
With your grace and bounty
Extend over it your guarding arm
During strife with its enemiesLong torn by ill fate
Bring upon it a time of relief
This nation has suffered for all sins
Of the past and of the future!

I felt the words. I related to *this nation has suffered* because I knew my parents suffered in World War II and in their exile. And in 1956, just two years before this summer camp, the communists had brutally suppressed a Hungarian uprising. The nation continued to suffer. I felt sad and hurt and proud for my parents as I recited this stirring and emotional hymn.

Mother Clothilde smiled at me after I finished. "I asked Elizabeth to recite the anthem because I want you all to hear that she speaks Hungarian with no accent. Some of you speak with an English accent. Listen to her and learn."

I was proud to hear that I spoke like a true Hungarian. I couldn't wait to tell my parents about my performance when they came to pick me up. As I walked back to my seat, I thought about accents and realized that I was also terribly glad that I spoke English without an accent. At my school, I wanted to be seen as an Aussie, not as a Hungarian. I had a foot in two worlds. Here at camp I fit in. For two weeks in the summer, I could simply be Hungarian just like all the other kids there. But in three weeks I would be back at school – and there I didn't fit in so well. I began to worry. As much fun as I was having at camp, I couldn't escape the reality that all my feelings of belonging would evaporate the moment school started again.

The Hungarian class was over and Suzy punched me lightly. "You speak Hungarian without an accent," she said parroting Mother Clothilde. I wondered if she was teasing me, but then she put her arm around me and gave me a big grin and I knew it was all okay.

Suzy and I headed towards the dining room. We'd been looking forward to dinner all day. The cooks had spent hours shaping hundreds of *szilvás gombóc* by hand. I gobbled my potato dough dumplings stuffed with fresh prunes and coated with buttery toasted breadcrumbs, licking my lips to absorb every last juicy morsel. I was in heaven. My best friend beside me, and one of my favorite Hungarian dishes for dinner. I could enjoy being a Hungarian kid for a little longer.

§

At age seven, I grappled with God to bring me Mouseketeer clothes. By then I'd had two years of Christian Doctrine classes in parochial schools, a year or two in Hungarian summer camps, and had listened to a smattering of Sunday sermons at Mass. I had been taught that God could do anything, and that he responded to requests: *Ask and you shall receive, knock and the door will be open to you.* I had taken that very much to heart.

I was a fervent fan of the Mickey Mouse Club. I was in love with Annette and Sharon and Cubby, and more than anything I longed to become a Mouseketeer. I loved how Jimmy performed the "meeska mooska mouseketeer" spell, and how lo and behold wondrous things appeared in the treasure chest! These Disney fantasies fueled my quest to magically produce the Mouseketeer outfit I coveted.

"Meeska mooska mouseketeer" I chanted and gesticulated over my old battered suitcase, just like I'd seen Jimmy do. I looked hopefully into my makeshift treasure chest. It was bare. I tried again, this time with a little more fervor. "Meeska mooska mouseketeer." Nothing. Day after day, attempt after attempt, my supplications went unanswered. I tried variations. I said a Hail Mary before the incantation. "Please, please," I begged God. Still nothing.

As these empty outcomes accumulated, my heart plummeted. Fierce tears stung my eyes. The Mickey Mouse ears, monogrammed sweater and pleated skirt never appeared, and I blamed God. "I hate you, I hate you," I fumed, bashing my fists on the suitcase repeatedly, for He had failed to answer my prayers.

I had no comfort or support in my utter disappointment and frustration. Mine was a solitary obsession. My parents and sibs had no idea what I was doing, shut up in my room trying to materialize a Mouseketeer outfit. No one knew of my secret longing. After several weeks, I gave up, disillusioned and hardened from the unrewarded effort. What I perceived as God's unresponsiveness provided a shaky start to my childhood spiritual explorations and was to remain a lifelong theme.

§

The same year I was attempting to manifest Mouseketeer clothes, I made my first holy communion. I was in second grade. The school chapel was decorated with bunches of white flowers, and the altar was aglow with soft candlelight. Anyu had sewn my dress and I loved it – a white organza affair with puffed sleeves and a tiny Nehru collar. The skirt billowed with layers of ruffles, rustling softly as I walked up the aisle to the communion rail. My veil, however, was another matter. I longed for the stiff-netted, lace-edged creations topped with tiaras that the other girls wore. My limp veil clung to my scalp, held on with a simple headband. I felt dorky and self-conscious. I felt sure my "Hungarian" style veil announced, yet again, that I was different, foreign, alien.

After all the instruction and hype we'd had from the nuns, I had great expectations of receiving the transubstantiated host, the amazing body of Christ. It turned out to be a disappointing, *is that all there is?* experience. The commemorative white engraved candle and the prayer book with a pearly cover that I received made more of an impression than the actual receiving of communion.

It wasn't until a few years later, when I was a teenager and at a school spiritual retreat, that my love of the sacrament began to bloom. The priest who led that day of religious renewal was a tall, charismatic, and ruggedly handsome Franciscan brother, draped in the order's coarse brown hooded garment and wearing "Jesus shoes" sandals. With a grin and a twinkle, he lectured us about chaste relationships and demonstrated (in parody fashion, of course) the ideal distance between boys and girls in order to avoid provocative kisses that led to the mortal sin of premarital sexual intercourse. I tittered along with my classmates as he pantomimed the teenage scene. When he was finished, I wasn't any clearer from his talk on how to proceed with relating to the opposite sex.

His humor and good looks, though, delighted me, and I – along with several of my classmates – developed a little crush on the good brother. This, and the day of prayer, and his exuberant faith as he shared his spiritual journey touched me. At Mass later in the day, when I received the communion host on my tongue, I felt my heart opening. A warm glow spread all over my body, and a sweetness and reverence stayed with me as I retraced my steps to the pew. Mesmerized, on my knees and with my head bowed, I reveled in the sacred presence and closeness with Christ. I didn't want that experience of "communion" to pass, but the Mass ended all too quickly, prematurely. It was like having an impatient waiter whisk away my food-filled plate while I was still chewing and savoring my meal.

That somatic sacred body memory lingered on in me, recreated to varying degrees each time I received communion, and experienced during the Catholic service of Benediction, which was performed at my school every Wednesday afternoon. In this ritual, the priest displayed the consecrated host in a vessel called a monstrance, placing it within a circle of glass that was set within a gorgeous sunburst of gold. The fragrance of sweet burning incense and the tinkling of bells intensified the sensation of awe I felt viewing the holy host.

The sacrament of communion and the ritual of benediction were my first experiences combining the sensual with the religious, and incorporating body sensations. They were pleasurable yet puzzling, and my religious instruction gave no explanation or support for these experiences. I didn't even consider sharing with the nuns my sensuous encounters– none of us girls did. How could I tell them that my heart exploded when I received the holy host, and that my whole body was bathed in pleasure? How could I tell them that a boundless joy erupted from my throat and enveloped my whole being? How could I share that I believed all this to be sacred, that I felt Christ's presence and love? The nuns never referred to any physical sensations occurring with devotions. Yes, they talked about "love," but in a cerebral, abstract way. Moreover, they drummed into our heads that we were not to give into our "prurient," carnal feelings. I heard the nuns use all the terms of the dictionary definition of sensual at various times in my religious training: "pertaining to, inclined to, or preoccupied with the gratification of the senses or appetites; carnal; fleshly; lacking in moral restraints; lewd or unchaste; arousing or exciting the senses or appetites; worldly; materialistic; irreligious."

Unlike the Hungarian nuns at summer camp who were at ease with boisterous children, the Australian nuns who taught us at Loreto were quick to suppress any signs of teenage exuberance, body pleasure or flamboyance we might exhibit. We were considered "unladylike" if we touched our faces, sat with legs apart, ran in the hallways or danced about with our skirts flying up. We were "hussies" if we wore short skirts or low cut tops, if we held hands with boys in public, or God forbid, kissed them. We were admonished to remain chaste and demure.

I couldn't reconcile my bodily responses to receiving communion any more than I understood the sensual experiences I'd had of music and the beach. I had no context for understanding the sacred permeating anything except prayer, the sacraments, the Catholic Church, and holy people. My religious teachings compartmentalized the spiritual into sterile doctrines and rigid rules of behavior. I was at a total loss to understand how the sensual could infuse the spiritual. Nevertheless, I clung to my mysterious somatic experiences.

§

Very little of the teaching I received in my daily Christian Doctrine classes inspired me. In them, I mostly learned the sanguine rules of the Church, and the dire consequences of venial and mortal sins. The nuns seemed to relish recounting how the saints had to suffer, fascinated by the gruesome ways in which they were often martyred. These horrid stories deepened my resolve to remain lukewarm in my Catholic faith. I cringed and wanted no part of asceticism, torture or martyrdom. Every day at school, when we prayed for more of us to join up to become priests and nuns, I prayed just as fervently that I would receive no such vocation. I had no desire to be cloistered and recoiled from the prospects of suffering and grappling with Satan's temptations. Nor did I want to be a martyr like Christ and the saints. I wished to remain laic, away from the rigors and deprivations of a dedicated Christian life.

The nuns allowed no discussion when it came to the commandments and Church doctrine. We were instructed to take "on faith" every rule and dictum without question. The Catholic Church was the one true church. The pope was infallible when making edicts. Like a good little girl, I swallowed and regurgitated the material for exams. So I was stunned when Sister Annunciata, a tiny, young spitball of a novice subbed for our regular Christian Doctrine teacher one day and challenged us to prove the historical validity of Christ's death and resurrection. At first, none of us girls dared say anything. We all feared retribution. Was Sister trying to trick us?

"Come on girls! Where's the proof that Christ was crucified?" she repeated.

"In the bible," someone behind me answered meekly. She kept at us.

"Do we know that the account in the bible is accurate? Maybe the bible is a work of fiction. What is the evidence that the bible story is true?" Dead silence. We'd never considered questioning the validity of the bible. All the gospels were sacrosanct, weren't they?

"Um, maybe there are other historical documents that verify the event?" one of my classmates timidly suggested.

Sister smiled. "Good, good. Now you're thinking. Now you're using your powers of discernment. You must question. You must come to your own conclusions with your faith," she said encouragingly.

This was my first exposure to religious questioning. The shift it created in my attitude was both jarring and abiding. It marked the start of my slow, yet conscious transition to spiritual discernment.

After that awakening in Sister's Christian Doctrine class, I found myself paying closer attention to the lyrics of "It Ain't Necessarily So" on the radio, a popular version of the song from Gershwin's *Porgy and Bess* sung by Aussie Normie Rowe. It hit number one on the pop charts despite being banned from some of the radio stations for being "sacrilegious." The hold of the rigid dogmas drummed into me by the nuns and priests gradually loosened each time I softly sang the lyrics that challenged the Church and preachers. A chink in my religious armor had appeared. Thanks to Sister Annunciata, and spurred on by the rebellious pop hit of the sixties, I had begun to question, to resist.

§

My religious training in Catholic schools both frustrated and inspired me. I grappled with a god who didn't answer my calls, chafed at the rigid doctrines that bound and was terrified when the nuns threatened us with the fires of hell when we misbehaved. Despite all this, some of the nuns and priests inspired me. I began to embrace the sacrament of Communion. But my most enduring spiritual awakenings occurred outside of religion, through my experiences and connections with nature – like that amazing afternoon at the beach – and through music.

It began with classical music and pop hits, and later expanded to include religious repertoire. In fact, my abiding love affair with music has always been quite ecumenical. In school, I learned a version of the twenty-third psalm – *The Lord is My Shepherd* – that contained a glorious descant. I grinned and glowed as I sang the notes that soared over then sank below the melody line. The contrapuntal melody captivated me; I thought it was stunning. This was the first time I sang a harmony other than the more common musical third above or below the dominant tune. I reveled in its beauty, which amplified the already powerful words of the psalm.

I treasured another sacred hymn, one dedicated to the mother Mary. Every May first, the nuns had us process down the school driveway towards the statue of Our Lady, housed in a small stone grotto. Each of us carried a bouquet of flowers and we took turns setting them around her statue as we sang

Oh Mary, we crown thee
With blossoms today
Queen of the angels
And Queen of the May

The lilting strains of the hymn, the fragrant blooms of the flowers that flooded the grotto, and the endless stream of girls kneeling to place their bouquets at the feet of Mary, moved me to tears. This was a rare pageant that celebrated the power of women, for the Catholic Church fiercely upheld its masculine dominance. I felt an ephemeral and ancient connection with Mary, the nuns, and the girls as I took part in this beautiful, touching ceremony. The ritual was my first exposure to the wisdom and the mystery of the feminine.

On my last day at Loreto, I gathered in the school chapel with my schoolmates and the nuns as I had done so many times over my eleven years at the convent school. As we did at the end of every term, we sang "The Holiday Hymn." I, along with many of my classmates, choked up. My emotions on this last day were even more intense. I broke down, barely able to hiccup out the words of the hymn:

Mother of all that is pure and glad,
All that is bright and blest,
As we have taken our toil to thee,
So will we take our rest.
Take thou and bless our Holiday.
O Causa Nostrae Laetitiae. (Oh, Cause of Our Joy)

Smile upon all that is dear to us,
Smile on our school and home,
Smile on the days we are passing now,
Smile on the years to come,
Brighten our work and gladden our play,
O Causa Nostrae Laetitiae.

Not only was I leaving school and my classmates, I would shortly leave everything that was familiar to me, all that I had known. I had never ventured outside of Australia. What would it be like? Would the air smell different? I felt excited to be going to America, the land of my fantasies and dreams. Sure, there were some things, some people, some places in Australia that I would miss, but I'd also endured times of loneliness and unease. I had never really found my place in the world living in Australia. I was hopeful that I'd find that place in the United States.

Like so many immigrants, my father's great desire in moving the family to the United States was to give his children better opportunities in life. My smart, aeronautical engineer oldest brother was capable of far greater and more challenging work than calculating flight load distributions – the work he was stuck doing at Qantas Airlines.

For my middle brother, Geza, it meant a fresh chance at medical school after he frittered his time with friends and in pubs and flunked university in Sydney. My sister, Irene, suffered from severe test anxiety, so much so that she could hardly remember her own name when she entered an exam room, let alone the answers to test questions. The Australian university system conferred course grades based on a single exam at year's end, which was horrific for her. She ended up dropping out of Sydney University. In contrast, U.S. colleges parcel out their curriculums into quarters or semesters – and grades for each course are determined by an aggregate of several factors including homework, quizzes and midterms. This gave my sister an opportunity to defuse her performance anxieties and improve her standing.

As for me, the family joked that moving to the United States would give me my chance at Hollywood stardom. Though I coveted this dream, I was stung by my family's jibes, which felt more like ridicule to me than simple, good-natured teasing.

But before settling in the U.S., I was off on a different adventure – a semester's study in Paris.

CHAPTER 9 – I LOVE PARIS IN THE SPRINGTIME

Pensive at the Eiffel Tower.

My parents figured that since I finished my 5th year of high school at Loreto in December and the school year in the United States didn't begin until September, I could make use of the nine months in between to attend either a finishing school or some language program in Europe. My father contacted a Hungarian military academy classmate who directed a finishing school in Switzerland, but its tuition was outrageously pricy. A Hungarian friend suggested the *Cours de Civilisation Française*, a program at the Sorbonne University in Paris, which his sister had attended and had really liked. This program served foreign students and, in addition to French language classes, provided an opportunity to audit any regular Sorbonne lectures. The fees were quite reasonable compared to the finishing schools and I welcomed the additional benefit – my sibs could no longer tease me about "charm school" and "getting finished."

And so we chose Paris, though I didn't fully commit to, or really decide anything at that stage in my life. I had no idea what I would experience. I merely rolled along with the snowball of planning. The university sent out local housing options and my father chose a nearby pension run by nuns, the Foyer Masabielle located on the tiny Rue Dugay Truouin. My walking route to the Sorbonne passed through the stately Jardin de Luxembourg. I was to live in the heart of the Latin Quarter.

I had five years of high school French under my belt when I arrived in Paris. Hardly fluent, I understood precious more than I could speak. I remained mute, and stuck to my father's side like a barnacle as he communicated in rudimentary French, setting me up at the pension, opening a bank account, and completing my registration at the Sorbonne. He then abandoned me and traveled with my brother Tom to Madrid.

Alone in Paris after their departure, I returned to the room I shared with two French girls. I crawled under the bed covers, faced the wall in a fetal position and broke down. Feeling deserted and alone, I cried for hours. The separation anxiety I'd experienced as a youngster with my friend Suzy and at Hungarian summer camps returned with a vengeance. My current predicament felt even bleaker: I was sixteen, stranded on a foreign continent thousands of miles from my family, totally alone with strangers in a land where I barely understood the language. My roommates came and went, asking me if I was okay, talking amongst themselves in subdued tones. I thought they were talking about what a mess I was, but I couldn't understand the French and in my despair, I hardly cared. After a while, they left me alone. The hours dragged on and I finally ran out of tears. I took stock of where I was and decided to make the best of the situation. I ventured out and about, finally dry eyed and willing, if not completely eager, to engage in a new adventure.

My brother, too, had his challenges in Madrid. My father placed a newspaper advertisement looking for a family for him to stay with – what seemed to me an amazingly gutsy and even foolhardy move. My father knew precious little about the family that housed Tom. The mother worked as a dentist, the dad an engineer, and they had two young daughters. With no knowledge of Spanish, poor Tom at age thirteen was literally dumped with this family. Though they proved to be reliable and pleasant enough, Tom felt miserable for most of his stay. When my father and I came to pick him up four months later, Tom walked out the door of the family's home without saying goodbye. He never looked back and never kept in touch with them.

My Paris experience differed greatly from Tom's in Madrid. I enjoyed meeting and spending time with my Sorbonne classmates who came from all over. I was the only Aussie, but there were several Americans, students from other European countries, and one or two South Americans. Ours was a congenial and pleasant group, pretested and matched in our French language abilities. Our instructor was a petite, soft-spoken, attractive young attorney. She said she taught in the program because she enjoyed being around fun students. "You are so much less staid than my legal colleagues," she said with a smile. She usually wore black and had the French fashion flair as did so many Parisian women: a well tied scarf, understated elegant jewelry, sleek fitted skirts, classic handsome pumps, off-black shaded hose. She was, as the French say, *bien maquillée* – well made up. I admired her elegance and yearned to be like her.

Within two or three weeks of arriving, I became reasonably fluent in French, enough to carry a conversation with my roommates and engage with shopkeepers. It made all the difference that I was the only English-speaking girl in my pension, as it obliged me to speak French most all the time. My American classmates who roomed together had less opportunity to practice and fared less well with their language competency. Learning to speak French boosted my confidence and helped quell my anxiety about living in a foreign city.

For the first time in my life, I began to develop some independence and initiative. My drive to venture out and explore stemmed from several competing inner voices. I heard my father's voice echo in my head. "Go somewhere every day. Visit the museums, go to events, get to know the people. Be a world traveler." In my letters to him and the rest of the family, I was expected to account for all that I'd done and seen and, ever the good daughter, I didn't want to disappoint. My sense of pride and competition urged me on as well. Another part of me, my fearful inner child wanted nothing more than to curl up and stay holed up in the safe cocoon of my pension dorm room. This part of me feared going out alone into alien territory, was anxious about finding my way on the Metro, leery of approaching people, and terrified of being accosted or hurt. My parents' expectations and my competitive pride overrode my fearful child. And another subtle, heretofore nascent part of me began to emerge. My curiosity to explore surfaced, along with an ephemeral inner confidence I hadn't known I had. That courage was intermittent and fleeting at first, but it created an occasional burst of warmth in my chest, enough to support a genuine desire to look for, and experience the new. I began to venture out, exploring the city whose vibrancy surrounded and beckoned me to come look, see, and explore.

There was so much to take in in Paris. I listened to the reverberating organ strains and marveled at the splendid rose window in the Cathedral of Notre Dame. Giddy on the Eiffel Tower, I gazed at the uniform heights of building rooftops, laid out in the nineteenth century by city planner Baron Haussmann like carefully pruned ancient hedges stacked along the radiating avenues leading to the Place de L'étoile. I strolled down the broad L'Avenue de Champs-Élysées, walked through the groomed Jardin des Tuileries, and regularly crossed the Luxembourg gardens as I went to and fro from my classes at the Sorbonne. When I played tennis a couple of times with my roommate on the garden's courts, I almost felt like one of the locals.

I toured the huge and overwhelming Louvre where I got lost – but still managed to find Da Vinci's famous portrait – the enigmatic Mona Lisa. Gazing at her, I didn't see why that tiny painting had created so much hype. I dutifully walked through the military museum of Les Invalides to honor my father's military past. In the Cluny, I marveled at the intricacy of the medieval tapestries depicting the five senses of taste, hearing, sight, smell, and touch. How uniform and tiny the stitches! How perfectly clear every figure and flower! How vibrant the reds and the blues! In that museum began my appreciation and love of needlepointing that I have taken up intermittently since then.

I stood mesmerized by Monet's spectacular water murals hanging in the L'Orangerie. Wow! How did he paint the water so real? It seemed like I could have touched the canvas and felt the wetness. And how could he depict the floating lilies so beautifully with the use of just a few strokes of vibrant reds and pinks? I longed to be alone in the gallery so I could take in the whole panorama, for then I could have imagined myself actually standing in Monet's garden in Giverny. But several other viewers surrounded me, obscuring my full view. It irritated me to have to keep shifting about so I could peek around to see the gorgeous images.

I attended the opera and was delighted by the strains of "Fi-igaro, Fi-igaro, Fi-igaro" in *The Barber of Seville*. I used my dancer's critical eye when I went to see the ballet, *Coppélia*. The prima ballerina made each step look like hard work and the male partner hefted the ballerina as if she were a ton of bricks. The lackluster performance came to a dramatic climax when the male dancer, who was holding the ballerina, staggered and then collapsed with her on top of him on the floor. The audience gasped. A Sorbonne classmate who had accompanied me later quipped, "The sad thing is, I can imagine how good the ballet could have been."

Then I began to do the unthinkable – totally counter to my reserved, mousy demeanor, unveiling a racier side of me. I danced at nightclubs, "*boîtes*," and once stayed out all night with my roommate Juliette and some other girls from the pension. I spent most of the night nursing a drink or two. I was flattered when a couple of boys asked me to dance, but overall the nightclub experience proved a rather noisy, jam-packed and numbing affair—not nearly as exciting as I expected it to be. When the club closed at 5 a.m., we walked to the stinky *Place Pigalle*, watched the grocers and fishmongers unpack and stock their market stalls and drank hot *café au lait* at a tiny kiosk. We returned to the pension bleary-eyed just as the doors were unlocked at eight in the morning. As our alibi, we had told the nuns that we were spending the night at Juliette's uncle's place, but seeing how exhausted we were upon our return the nuns became suspicious and discovered our ruse. I, the youngest, received a summons into the office of Ma Soeur Annunciad. Horrified, she asked, "What would your father think of your uncouth behavior?" I grinned as I told her, "I've already written him about our plans and he wrote back that he was thrilled." That took the wind out of her wimple!

§

I found that Paris was a vibrant and, at times, a hazardous city to navigate. I was so naïve when I first arrived. I strolled leisurely through the city's beautiful gardens, and browsed the shop windows admiring with equal pleasure the haute couture and the everyday chic that French women seemed to sport with such élan. But I soon discovered that anytime I slowed down, invariably a man would sidle up and proposition me. When I complained to my roommates about these lewd guys, they counseled me. "Yes, these incidents are common" Juliette said. "You don't want to attract shady men's attention by dawdling. You must keep moving at all times." I soon adopted a brisk, deliberate walking style, but despite these measures, I was still plagued with unwanted advances.

One night as I quickly strode towards the pension in my newly adopted intentional manner, a car drew up alongside me. The driver reached to open the passenger door and with a repulsive leer, asked for sex. I hurried to the pension gate and buzzed to get in, my heart pounding, relieved when the door flew open. I scampered inside, still shaking. I was only able to relax when I heard the driver slam the door and when the car sped away.

I got savvier, but my emerging self-protective "street smarts" were no insurance that I would not be accosted again. It seemed it hardly mattered whether it was day or night. I was in the Metro one day, on my way to meet my Uncle Zoltán at the Eiffel Tower. I felt eager and happy with anticipation as I strode up the Metro tunnel from the subway to the street, but I became uneasy as the crowd thinned and my steps echoed on the tiled walls. I heard another set of footsteps quicken and approach me from behind. Startled, I felt something butt against the back of my black leather coat. I glanced around and saw a man with an open trench coat, his erection exposed. I was shocked, shaky. Totally unglued, I ran as fast as I could in the direction of the exit. I got away, fortunately unharmed. When I reached our appointed meeting place, I said nothing to my uncle about what had happened, too mortified by it all. In any case, I didn't think he'd understand. I was afraid that he would think less of me to have had something like that happen. I was also afraid he might tell my parents and I didn't want to make waves. I wanted to demonstrate to him how well I was doing in Paris, how world-wise I was. I had become so conditioned to never sharing anything personal or painful with my parents, or anybody else for that matter. I did the same with my uncle that day.

But my scariest encounter of all occurred one spring day. I was browsing along the Rue Montparnasse and spied a crepe blouse that I wanted – the kind very much in vogue at the time – displayed at a good price in a shop window. I stepped into the boutique to get a closer look, but became a bit uncomfortable when the sole male mid-eastern-appearing shopkeeper walked over to serve me. I asked to try on the blouse, but as I approached the dressing cubicle, I smelled chloroform. My apprehension turned to raw fear. I dropped the blouse and bolted out of the store like the hounds of hell were after me. I was still shivering and shaking when I got back to the pension and described the scary incident to my roommates. Later, after I'd calmed down, they told me about the active slave trade around Paris. Girls' abductions were far from rare. Chloroform drugging proved an easy way to subdue a target female. I flinched to think what might have happened to me. I felt incredibly lucky – and I never went again into another boutique alone.

Every city has a seedy side. In Sydney, I had encountered the occasional sot drunkenly weaving his way by me as I stood on the underground platform, waiting to take the train home after my evening ballet lessons, but I'd never encountered so many terrifying moments in such a short period as I had in Paris. Was the city that much more salacious? Was there something about me that attracted such attention? I didn't think I stood out and never considered myself forward or sexy – far from it. I remained withdrawn and avoided flashy, provocative clothes. After all, the nuns had taught me to be a demure "Loreto lady," and I had taken their training to heart. Might it be precisely that demureness that marked me as a target for these perverts? I didn't know.

I was grateful to have a roommate with whom I could share my troubles. Juliette hailed from the South of France from a small border town near Biarritz. She had thick, dark, shoulder length hair, a beautiful olive complexion, and a brilliant grin that she loved to flash, her face jutting forward. Fluent in Spanish as well as French, she spoke a little English as well. She attended a multilingual secretarial school in Paris. Juliette radiated warmth – she said that people from the South of France were friendlier in comparison to Northerners.

My other roommate, Louise, who hailed from Brittany in the north, indeed had a cool, distant manner. Juliette loved to make fun of Louise. She'd pretend to brush waist long hair and with a haughty air would say "Mes cheveux sont degolas!" "My hair looks disgusting!" I'd giggle, for Juliette perfectly captured the tone of Louise's frequent complaint as she'd comb her long muddy tresses, which were indeed oily and stringy towards the end of a week without washing.

Juliette and I hit it off right from the start. I was so glad to have a roommate to gab with, someone who "got it" too. I experienced my first close "sleepover" friend since my childhood Hungarian buddy, Suzy. I felt less reserved and less shy with Juliette than I had with my Aussie schoolmates. I could let go of the fear of being judged as "uncool," for being a foreigner. Even though Juliette, at eighteen, was a couple of years my senior, I felt her equal and I felt her warmth toward me, much different from how I felt around my sister. Irene was more like my other roommate Louise: detached, a little prickly, and more unapproachable.

Juliette and I attended Mass together most Sundays. We played tennis on the courts in the Jardin de Luxembourg. We loved to chat and walked all over Paris.

"I'm always going with you to your school and on your errands. You never come to the Sorbonne with me." I was complaining, and not for the first time.

"Arrête, Elizabeth, mais arrête." Juliette put her hands up and shook her head, her dark eyes flashing and her smile captivating. "I'm in Paris to work. You're here to learn about it, so it's natural that you should want to see and go places at every opportunity."

Juliette was right. She spent many hours writing papers, cramming for her demanding language and business courses. I hardly had to study at all, but I still pouted.

"I'll walk with you to your classes tomorrow. Will that make you feel better?"

I grinned and nodded.

One evening Juliette and I strolled down the Champs-Élysées after seeing the complicated and sobering movie, *Thérèse Desqueyroux*.

"I hate not having English subtitles," I said. "There was so much I didn't understand."

"Well, there's a lot of English I don't understand and that I want to learn," she said with a twinkle in her eye. "Like, how do you say *tais-toi*?"

"Shut up."

"Shuddup, shuddup. That's good," she said brightly. "Now what's *merde*?"

I grinned and sped ahead to avoid answering, but Juliette trotted to catch up. She wanted to know and had the devil in her. She grabbed my arm.

"What's *merde*? What's *merde*? Tell me, tell me."

People were turning to stare. I gave in and whispered in her ear. Delighted, she marched down the avenue crying, "Sheeet Eleezabet, Sheeet!" We burst out laughing and, arm in arm, skipped down the boulevard.

§

I had come to the city of gastronomic finesse, but being on a tight budget I had little opportunity to eat out. Fortunately, I was able to sample the delicious flavors of French cuisine at the pension. For breakfast, the nuns ladled steaming *café au lait* from large pots into our mugs. We bought our own baguettes and jam to go with the coffee. The long baguette lasted a few days becoming dry and crusty by the end, but still tasted delicious when dipped and moistened in the piping hot milky coffee. Lunch and dinner were full hot meals, flavorful country French cooking, roast beef, braised chicken, perfect *al dente* vegetables, all with subtle, flavorful butter sauces.

It was in Paris that I ate my first artichoke. I attacked the whole leaf with gusto, chewed and scraped the inside of my mouth with the sharp spine. My roommates chuckled with amusement at my startled face. "Ah, Elizabeth, tu est si drôle." They taught me how to dip the tender end in the tasty vinaigrette, and how to pull the delicate pulp with my teeth. Delicious! I have loved all things artichoke since my first taste.

As part of my experience, I joined in some of the time honored Parisian traditions. As countless would-be and accomplished authors, artists, and philosophers had done for decades, I spent hours with my Sorbonne mates sitting in Latin Quarter cafés, nursing a single espresso. One time, I met an artist who scribbled an abstract drawing for me. "That'll be worth a fortune in a few years when I'm famous," he vowed. He had a dream, as did I. I still held onto my desire to go to Hollywood, and I would soon be living a step closer than I had been in Sydney, for I would soon be in Seattle, where my family settled after Paul landed an engineering job with Boeing. Just like the wanna-be bohemian artist who had scribbled a sketch for me, I imagined being a movie star, signing autographs. And I dreamed of being in love in Paris, *toujours l'amour*.

In Sydney, I was asked to a couple of dances by classmates' brothers, but I had never been invited on a date to a movie or to eat out. I'd never kissed a boy. I was jealous of my sister who had a series of serious boyfriends, and of classmates who had "steadies" and lots of dates. I thought there was something wrong with me. I invented way, way, way too many reasons why no one was interested in me: I was too fat; I wasn't pretty enough; my hair was too straight; I was immigrant trash; I didn't know how to flirt.

The first date I went on in Paris was set up by a new arrival at the pension. Suzanne hailed from England. She wore gothic garb – mesh stockings, tight mini skirts, all in black. She topped her outfits with a large brimmed black felt hat. Dark lipstick contrasted starkly with her ghostly pale face.

Suzanne kept odd hours, meeting all kinds of men outside the pension gate. She obviously had much more dating experience, so Juliette and I were delighted when she set us up on a double date with a couple of university students. Both boys were Moroccan with dark olive complexions. Jean Pierre was taller, with unruly hair and a serious gaze. Reda gravitated to me. He had thick lips and was more the talker. The guys picked us up in a Volvo and drove down the Champs-Élysées, where lights blazed in a florid procession toward the venerable monument, the Arc de Triomphe. The shimmering sites, traffic honks and blaring radio music enveloped me. My huge smile ached and my body trembled, swept up in the joy of the moment. What bliss! I was young and alive in "Gay Paree," living the good life, the absolute great life. I was sixteen, out with a girlfriend on a date with young men, driving down the romantic heart of the City of Light. It was stunning. I felt privileged. This had to be confirmation: I was meant to be in Paris.

We headed to the *Scotch Club*. Jean Pierre was moody, nursing his drink and refusing to dance, but we couldn't care less. Reda danced with Juliette and me, and so did lots of other boys. I felt the belle of the ball and had a bloody good time. Being with a date made the nightclub experience much more glamorous than when I had gone with girlfriends a few weeks before. At the end of the evening, Jean Pierre hugged Juliette. Reda brushed a kiss on my cheek and asked, "Would you like to go out with us again?" Juliette and I gladly accepted. We got back to the pension at two in the morning. Juliette climbed into my bed and we gabbed and rehashed our date for two more hours. We hardly cared when the next morning, La Soeur Annonciade blew up at us for having gotten in so late.

Juliette and I were excited to go on our second date. This time, the boys took us to a Tunisian cake shop and ordered lamb sandwiches, deliciously seasoned with cumin and garlic. All went well until the MG that they doted on wouldn't start. Jean Pierre kicked the tires, swore using words I'd not heard of, and that made Juliette blush. Reda grabbed his arm, trying to settle him down, but he was fuming too, his eyes narrowed, his fist clenched. They left us at the shop to retrieve their other car, a Volvo. They showed up much later, their hair astray, their shirts sweat and oil stained. I was frantic. Juliette climbed in the front with Jean Pierre, I in the back next to Reda. Without any hesitation, he put his arm around me and drew closer. His lips were wet and he reeked from a pungent aftershave mixed with sweat. His coal eyes flashed. "I've paid for two dates. I now want to have sex with you."

My stomach soured. I recoiled, slid away from him and shook my head. He spat out, "I'm sure your father bedded several women in his day. Why are you so bothered?" I felt totally blindsided and began to shake. I felt disgusted at the thought of him pawing and invading me, and my temper flared: he had insulted my father.

"You don't know what you're talking about. My father was never like that."

Reda smirked. "How would you know?"

I'd had enough. I motioned to Juliette that I wanted to go home. Jean Pierre drove us back to the pension, a stony silence weighting us down. Juliette and I fled from the car with hardly a good-bye. Once inside, I broke down in her arms.

I sobbed, hiccupping, "How dare he say those things about my father. He's a good man and he has morals." The thought of him having sex with other women filled me with horror.

Juliette patted my back. "There, there. Of course, your father is a proper man, and those boys were anything but. It's over now, Elizabeth. We're okay."

I felt personally affronted – roiling with outrage and shame – and utterly confused. Our first date had been heavenly. What on earth had happened since the wonder and charm of the romantic drive down the Champs-Élysées?

I clearly had no idea how to act around boys and no sense of their underlying feelings and motives. I was rattled by the experience. Still, I held out hopes of finding love. He would appear, romantically and magically drawn to me, just like in the song "Some Enchanted Evening" from South Pacific.

And I clung to the Victorian mores I had been taught by the Loreto nuns: that girls had to wait to be asked out by boys; that girls who approached boys were hussies and that those who flaunted their bodies in tight miniskirts were provocatively brazen. The passive stance promoted by the nuns suited my introverted nature; I was comfortable waiting for my prince charming.

§

When Apu picked me up at the end of the semester, I was no longer the naïve, clingy girl he'd dropped off in Paris. I was a young woman now, and ready to conquer the world. Craving independence, I now knew how to spend my money and manage my time. I "parlez vouzed" my father to death on the trip home, making him chuckle. Four months ago, he'd been the communicator as I'd watched with wide eyes. Now I was his translator. I lapped up his approval, beaming with pride and, secure in my newfound competence, I felt ready to embark on the next chapter of my life in the U.S., in Seattle, Washington.

CHAPTER 10 – THE BLUEST SKIES
YOU'VE EVER SEEN ARE IN SEATTLE

While at Seattle Community College, I modeled at Plymouth Pillars Park in Seattle for a photography student.

It was several weeks before I got to see any blue at all in the skies of Seattle. Dreary, gray clouds and drizzle greeted my parents, younger brother, and me as we flew into SeaTac, the Seattle Tacoma International Airport, on the evening of December 23, 1966. Paul, Irene, and Geza, who had relocated to the U.S. several months before, whooped and hollered at the boarding gate and flew into our arms in a rare show of familial affection. I felt welcomed and was delighted to see them after so many months.

"Isn't this freeway great? We can travel so much faster than in Australia." Paul grinned as he accelerated to more than sixty-five miles-per-hour weaving in and out of traffic on the wrong side of the road. I felt unsettled by the traffic configuration, but at the same time, I had to smile. My brother hadn't changed at all: he loved driving and he loved speed. In the mid-sixties, the only freeway in Sydney was a token strip that extended about twenty miles from the northern suburbs of Sydney towards Gosford, hardly the scope of the concrete jungles that crisscrossed the U.S.

"Here's 'downtown' - that's what you must call 'the city' here." Irene smiled, wanting to quickly catch us up with the American lingo.

"And look, there's the Space Needle." Geza pointed enthusiastically to the city's famous landmark. The windshield wipers lazily swept the drizzle drops.

"Does it really rain a lot here?" I timidly asked.

"Well, yeah," replied all three sibs in unison as they burst out laughing.

"But wait till the sun does come out," Paul went on enthusiastically. "It's totally worth all the rain. Mountains surround the city: the Olympics to the West over there . . ." He pointed to the left, "Cascades to the east, Mount Baker to the north and Mount Rainier – that one's amazing – to the south."

"Yes, besides, in the winter you can ski and it only takes an hour to get to the slopes," added Irene. Their liveliness didn't rub off on me. I'd never skied in my life and I wasn't sure I wanted to try. I began to feel an inexplicable, weighty gloom pressing in on all sides. That somber mood was to remain with me on and off for weeks. The dark and wet was far from what I was hoping for in my new adopted country. I'd left warm, subtropical, familiar Sydney far, far behind.

§

My sibs had bought a house for our family in the University District. Built in the 1920s, the three-story house was well worn, but still charming with its painted wood paneling and French doors. My father, in a rare move, actually complimented my sibs on their choice of real estate, noting that a solid older home in a university district was a sound investment and was likely to retain good resale value. Paul and Irene felt proud to receive Apu's approval.

Our first couple of days in Seattle whirled by as we prepared for Christmas. I shopped for the first time in a supermarket. I walked up and down the aisles of the Safeway megastore, gawking with astonishment. I'd never seen such a store before – everything from produce to cleaning products, from dairy to seafood, from beer and wine to flowers – all could be purchased in a single locale. In Sydney, my mother and father traipsed all over the city to forage for the family fare. They drove to a Hungarian butcher on the other side of the city for fresh and prepared meats, to the farmers' Haymarket in the city center for crates of fruits and vegetables, to the continental bakery on Kings Cross for pastries. My mother picked up poultry, fish, and flowers in city shops, and lugged them home in mesh sacks on the train after her day's work in the factory. She sent me down the street to the neighborhood milk bar for sundries we'd run out of like soap, salt, or eggs. Our milk and bread were delivered to our doorstep every day. I just couldn't get over finding every one of these items – and so much more – in a single store.

§

I'd read yuletide tales and heard carols sung about "White Christmas" and sleigh bells ringing, "Walking in A Winter Wonderland." Back in Sydney, we would have been heading to the beach on Christmas day, basking in Sydney's summer heat. I'd be listening to the frolicking strains of "Six White Boomers" (an Aussie term for kangaroos), a Christmas song that local singer Rolf Harris had adapted to the warm climate.

Instead, my first Christmas in Seattle was my first ever Christmas in a cold climate. I had all these romantic images in my head from popular Christmas songs and Hollywood movies. Instead of a bikini, I was bundled up in a heavy coat, scarf, and mittens. Charmed by the winter holiday, I braved the chill, damp, and rain of late December in Seattle.

The festivities were lovely and yet I felt isolated in my new homeland. I knew nobody. I'd left behind everything familiar and comforting. And despite my best efforts of going through the motions of being happy, it didn't take. The cold, dark, gray drizzle mirrored the icy cavern in my gut. My family now represented my sole reference point in a new country and the bleak winter environment brought into stark relief the lack of intimacy I felt with them. My Sydney surroundings, the sunny warmth and my beloved beaches, had begun to fill the void, softening the hunger for love and attention that went unsatisfied by my family relationships. The Aussie physical environment served as community, as ally. In addition, in my last years in school, I had begun to forge some connections with classmates and mentors such as my drama coach

Miss Gandon, and in some ways I felt closer to them than I did my family.

My Sydney life was like soft golden butter spread on thick slabs of fresh bread. I knew warmth and flavor, albeit simple, in every bite. Never mind that there was just butter and no peanut butter or ham or sweet jam, no richness of relationships, even in Sydney. But at least I had bread and butter. In Seattle, it seemed like I had indigestible soggy bread and moldy butter.

The hard reality hit me almost immediately. I was going to have to start all over again, from scratch. How would I ever learn to love this gray town with its gray weather? Where would I make friends? I felt paralyzed. I hardly knew how to begin.

It didn't help that Seattle, itself, came up short in my eyes. And it wasn't just the climate. Seattle in the 1960s was sadly lacking in any metropolitan pizzazz. Back then, the city's downtown had no nightlife; the streets lay deserted after business hours. I scoffed that there wasn't even a good espresso to be had anywhere in the city – hard to imagine that Starbucks would get started in Seattle decades later. I parroted my family's judgments and opinions. Even though they were enamored with the geographic beauty of the city, to them, Seattle was a provincial, "hick town" and it didn't match up to the vibrant, cosmopolitan, and international Sydney we had left behind.

Of all the shortcomings I ticked off on my mental checklist of Seattle's drawbacks, the hardest one for me to bear proved to be its lack of proximity to the ocean. Yes, Seattle sits on the shores of Puget Sound and has an abundance of water surrounding it – Lakes Washington, Union and Sammamish notwithstanding – but it was the sound of the ocean's pounding waves that I longed for, the easy access to the pulsating melodies of warm summer beaches.

Forty years later, I helped my daughter, then in her twenties, drive back to Seattle from San Diego. In that subtropical Southern California landscape, I regained a physical sense of connection. It felt familiar, like Sydney. The pounding ocean waves, the colorful bougainvillea and hibiscus, the whole flavor of the place brought me back home. I felt a kinship, one that I'd almost forgotten in the many years I'd spent in Seattle.

Then, as I drove from San Diego north to Seattle, something phenomenal happened. As the landscape and foliage changed and my daughter and I encountered the first evergreens in Northern California, I felt a physical repulsion, an aversion to the land. I longed to make a U-turn and it was all I could do to keep my hands from turning the wheel of the car around. I'd never had that sense before, not in mind or in body. I yearned to be back in San Diego and even began to weigh options of how I might move there. I felt like a salmon who had the unwavering urge to return to its birthplace, its roots: and just like the migrant fish, some sort of chemical honing substance drove me back to the comfort of my childhood environs. I felt close to tears but didn't share my experience with my daughter. Her home was the Northwest, just as mine was Sydney. I didn't want to let her know that her beloved locale had repulsed me.

The Northwest has been my home base for most of fifty years and it has taken me a long time to acclimate. For years, I felt uprooted from my native habitat, displaced like a tropical plant forced to become a houseplant, struggling to survive and grow, finding it difficult to blossom and near impossible to flourish. In some ways, I was like the frangipanis I attempted to grow indoors: they struggled, failed to thrive, and ultimately withered.

It wasn't until recently that I experienced another evergreen tree "U-turn" encounter. This time, the stately pines were on Ebey's Landing on Whidbey Island in Washington State. I love hiking there and often feel that the locale rends the curtain between my everyday and the sacred. On this occasion, as I sat in quiet contemplation, I gazed at the sparkling waters of Puget Sound, the gorgeous clear blue sky, and the glistening Olympic Mountains in the distance. My attention drifted to the meadow below, and then, the evergreens just beyond it called to me. I had a strong sense, a message from the pine trees that the Northwest was also my home, like Sydney and San Diego. I didn't have to choose one over the other. My tears overflowed and with them came the clear knowing that I had finally, fully come to roost in my adopted home.

§

I began to explore colleges in Seattle for the fall of 1967. Attending the state-run University of Washington wasn't an option because their policy at the time required all foreign high school graduates to have had a year of U.S. college credits before admission. I next looked into Seattle University, a private Catholic institution. I set up an interview with the admissions director before heading on a family road trip to California. When my parents talked of taking some extra time to see the Redwoods, my father, knowing I needed to be back in Seattle for the interview, asked if the side trip was okay with me. I blithely replied of course, that was no problem, and didn't bother to call to postpone my appointment.

I checked in at the Seattle University office three days after my scheduled appointment. Acting every bit the privileged teenager, I didn't even apologize. The admissions administrative assistant cut me off at my first sentence, "You missed your appointment, and you didn't even bother to call to cancel. You're not the kind of student that Seattle U looks for, no matter what your credentials."

She dismissed me with my mouth gaping. I had no comeback. I had burned my bridges at that institution.

I paid the price for acting full of pride. I deemed my Australian education far superior to that in America. That's what I had learned from my older siblings. Paul mocked the American system, scoffing that an Aussie high school degree was equivalent to a U.S. bachelor's degree. He claimed that his Sydney University BS in engineering was equivalent to an American master's degree. "We didn't have to take Mickey Mouse courses outside our field like they do here," he ridiculed. "Humanities! Christ, you can take bloody underwater basket-weaving and have it count towards an engineering degree." He topped off his rant with his usual: "They're all bloody idiots." I took on the familial pride and sense of superiority. I thought I was owed immediate entry into college, but underneath, I roiled with feelings of inadequacy and feared entering a new educational system in a foreign country.

After my Seattle U debacle, I licked my wounded ego and slinked over to Seattle Community College. Based in the old Edison High School stone building on Broadway and Pike, SCC was the first community college established in the Seattle area. The admissions department received me warmly, but had reservations because of my marginal SAT scores. I had done well in math, but my language scores were below average. I attributed this to having taken the test immediately after returning from Paris where I had hardly spoken English for six months. I rationalized to myself and to the admissions director that my language scores reflected my rusty language skills. Deep inside, I feared I just wasn't smart enough. Maybe my Aussie education wasn't as great as my brother Paul thought it was. Maybe I wasn't as intelligent as the others in my family. The college had me take the Washington Pre College Test, similar in format to the SATs and I was relieved to score equally well in the language and math portions of the test. I rationalized that enough time had elapsed for me to re-acclimate to fluent English, but the lingering doubts and lack of confidence persisted.

The admissions director found another deterrent besides my low test scores: I had not matriculated from my Australian high school. I was the first class to go through the Wyndham Report system in Sydney, which increased the high school education from five years to six. I had completed only five years of the new system and therefore lacked matriculation. The college picked up on this discrepancy and required that I complete several credits of high school level classes including English and the requisite Washington State History. A blow to my uppity pride, I had no choice but to submit to the requirements of my new educational system. I completed the requirements for an American high school diploma with straight As and in no time began college level classes.

In my second quarter at SCC, I auditioned for a play and landed a minor part. I turned the role down. With my high school thespian experience, I thought myself to be a seasoned actress, above "bit parts" and deemed them a waste of my precious time. The following quarter I again tried out, this time for Molière's *Two Pretentious Maidens Ridiculed*. I landed one of the two lead roles and I was ecstatic. The director, a bigger person than I, had overlooked my pride and obnoxiousness in turning the previous part down and had given me a second chance. Despite my haughty attitude, I worked hard. I reveled getting lost in my role. I loved the farce of it. I relished being in the theatre limelight again. As in my Australian acting efforts, I felt in the zone when performing, and I was delighted to be acting in America – one step closer to Hollywood. To my chagrin, however, I wasn't "discovered," received no fanfare, no rave revues, and no agents clamored to offer me a major movie contract. That play proved the extent of my drama dream in America – my career a proverbial flash in the pan.

One time on a ride home after a long rehearsal, four of us cast members sang along to Linda Ronstadt's "Beat of a Different Drum" blaring on the car radio. I was young, cocky, and fearless. When I transferred to the University of Washington, I felt intimidated by the robust, high profile drama department that included the on-campus public television station. Rather than risk failure, I shied away and gave up on my acting dream.

§

In the fall of 1968, I began my sophomore year of college as a transfer student at the University of Washington. I had finally graduated to the big leagues of a major university. I enrolled as a "pre-major," but took mainly science classes including the rigorous upper level chemistry series. I relished the orderliness of the elements of the periodic table. With OCD precision, I carefully followed the cooking recipe-like steps in my lab experiments. My zeal was rewarded: I received straight As in both the lecture and lab sections. I declared my major in chemistry and was awarded a departmental scholarship my junior year. I was on a roll, but my college career stuttered and came to an abrupt halt when my relationship with the boy next door heated up.

CHAPTER 11 – HOW CAN I IGNORE THE BOY NEXT DOOR

Snapshot of me taken by Lee, the boy next door, soon after we began dating.

"Island, Snohomish, Whatcom, Thurston . . . dang! What is that dratted county on the peninsula?" I groaned, sick to death of memorizing. What a waste of time to have to spend President's Day holiday cooped up inside, cramming the names of all thirty-nine counties into my spinning head for a stupid Washington State History midterm. How demeaning to have to take these dumb high school courses in the first place. I rubbed my book-weary eyes and gazed out the window . . . and did a double take . . . what on earth were those guys up to?

In the window of the house just a few feet over an oversized laurel hedge, two crazy guys were grinning and waving wildly. I glanced down at my book as a blush and a thrill raced through my body. They couldn't want *my* attention! There must be someone behind me – I turned my head – but of course, there wasn't. I snuck another peak and couldn't resist a smile from breaking out: they were now gesticulating, motioning for me to open my window. I tugged and pulled and finally got the old, swollen, wooden window loose. A puff of icy air breezed over my face. I wrapped my arms around my chest.

"Hi," one of them said, exhaling a plume of smoke and passing the joint to his buddy. "My name is Chuck, what's yours?" Not to be outdone, the other – with dark rimmed glasses – chimed in, "I'm Lee– you look so studious over there. What are you working on?" Just then I heard a distant bell ring and a voice yelled, "Chuck, phone call." With a longing look in my direction, Chuck scurried out of the room.

At that moment my fate was sealed, for it allowed Lee to seize the moment and he quickly blurted out, "Would you go to the Med School dance with me next Saturday?" I gulped. My hand flew up to my face to hide my huge grin. Flattered and floored, I immediately said yes and gave him the phone number he asked for. Now completely overwhelmed with the attention and the invitation, I muttered, "I have to go," and fled downstairs.

Within minutes, the phone rang. "It's for you, Liz," Paul yelled, holding the battered yellow kitchen wall phone in his outstretched arm. I grabbed it tentatively. Who on earth did I know well enough in Seattle that would be calling me?

It was Lee. "I have to apologize," he began sheepishly, "I already have a date for the dance, but I really wanted to get your attention while Chuck was out of the room. I still want to go out with you another time. Please say yes." And fate was further sealed for, instead of brushing him off as a jerk, I again felt flattered. A med student had just asked me for a date, for heaven's sake! I again said yes.

On our first date, Lee took me canoeing on Lake Washington by the languid reedy inlets of the Arboretum. This six-foot, slate blue eyed, bespectacled, lanky guy with dark brown curly hair seemed so world-wise and mature. And he liked me! I wore stretch aqua Bermuda shorts and a boat-necked striped top of the same color made in my parents' Australian knitwear factory. Weeks later, Lee shared how captivated he was by my wiggling ass as I sat rowing in front of him. I loved that he thought my Aussie accent cute, and I was even more flattered that he found me sexy.

Lee didn't have much money to spend on dates. On one of our first get-togethers, we drank coffee at the Hub, the student union building on the University of Washington Campus. "You know, the reason I moved into the house next to yours is because I had a huge row with my dad," he began, hardly touching his coffee. When I took a sip of the bitter, lukewarm brew, I could understand why. I slid the mug away and leaned into Lee to hear him better over the din of the cafeteria conversations.

"He was inebriated, drunk out of his mind, slurring his speech, and weaving around," Lee continued, his eyes flashing, his speech now pressured. "I called him on his drunkenness and he took a wild swing and slammed his fist into my face. I looked a mess with my nose dripping blood and that sobered him a little, but I'd had enough. I yelled at him that I was moving out and that I wouldn't accept any more goddamn financial support from him. I packed my bags and left that night." He looked at me with a little smirk on his face. I sat back, alarmed.

"The next day I marched into the med school financial aid office to ask for a student loan and, hearing my sob story and seeing my swollen and bruised nose, I got the funds no sweat." He grinned.

"Oh, Lee, I'm so sorry about your dad," I said with sympathy but I also felt a little uneasy.

I'd heard my share of family arguments for sure, but there was never any physical violence between my parents, and none between my parents and us kids – except the wooden spoon as punishment for well-deserved mischievous behavior. I did endure passing slaps from my brother, Geza, once his teenage hormones began to rage. I'd cringe every time I walked by him in the hallway expecting – and inevitably receiving – his thumps. I feared being around him and couldn't understand why he persisted in lashing out at me. My only consolation was that I wasn't being singled out: Geza slapped Tom around the same way.

"Hey, no problem!" Lee's voice drew me out of my reverie. "At least I got some distance from my dad and I'm now independent of that asshole."

I smiled tentatively. Yes, that family blow up had serendipitously facilitated my meeting "the boy next door," and I was excited about that, but there was something about Lee's family relationships that niggled at me. The alcoholism and the violence were disturbing for sure, but his story had also triggered some memories of my family's less radiant qualities and that hurt me deeply.

Nevertheless, my attraction to Lee grew. I relished his medical school stories for they re-kindled my attraction for the healing profession, first sparked by a horrendous teenage crush on television's Dr. Kildare. James Kildare embodied the complete fantasy of what I desired in a relationship. The young doctor was caring, attentive, competent, and he flirted with some of his lovely young patients. I felt a surge of sexual attraction towards the gorgeous actor, Richard Chamberlain. Most importantly, I thought the physician he portrayed really saw his patients and I longed for that same kind of attention. I longed to be recognized and heard. I longed to replicate the wonderful acceptance I'd felt for the first time when Mr. Fortnum reflected back my mixed emotions about my dental braces so many years ago. He had cared, and was fully present to me.

Lee, like Dr. Kildare, was in the medical profession and so it was too easy to project all my secret longings onto him. Soon after we started dating, we talked almost daily. How could I not be captivated? As a med student, he was soon to be a professional with social status and he had great income potential. My parents were impressed with that and so was I. Lee was a catch. And since I knew so few people in Seattle, he became my main social contact and support. It was easy for me to gravitate and cling to his company.

Lee's persistence and continued attention flattered me. When the days grew warm that spring, we took advantage of the sunshine and lugged our books and blankets outside.

"You know, my roommates are teasing me about you." Lee grinned at me as we sat in Ravenna Park on a grassy knoll. I looked up from my calculus text and tilted my head.

"What do you mean?"

"They keep reminding me that I'm dating a minor, that I'm robbing the cradle." He smirked.

"Oh," I said, looking down.

"They're even cautioning me that I could be accused of statutory rape," he added with a wicked gleam. I blushed and turned away. "They're just kidding," he said, touching my arm. "You're not yet eighteen, you see, and till you are, you're not considered an adult legally."

"I get it," I murmured, glancing back at him and then away. He thinks I'm too young, I thought to myself, gazing at the tall evergreens swaying in the gentle breeze. Their pine scent wafted towards me, a scent of Seattle, a new scent, a foreign scent. At times, I hadn't felt like I belonged in Australia. Maybe the pattern would be repeated here: maybe I didn't belong in America either. I smoothed the corner of the blanket, attempting to dispel that sense of estrangement. I glanced at my math textbook and tried to focus. My heart flipped. I hated calculus! I had taken it at Loreto and had done so well, but here in the U.S., I had floundered and struggled to keep up. I was barely maintaining a C-minus average. The negative self-images were piling up quickly in my head. Lee pulled me out of my downward spiral reverie.

"You know, you're really mature," he began again. "You've lived in Australia and Europe and you speak three languages. That's pretty impressive. I've hardly been outside the U.S., except to Canada and barely over the Mexican border." I smiled, absorbing every bit of his accolade. Yes, yes, I thought to myself! It's not all bad. I'm not all bad.

"Your family is really cosmopolitan and well educated," he continued. "My dad only did one year of junior college and my mom barely graduated high school. They're really quite provincial." He frowned. My spirits soared. Disaster had been averted! I may be acceptable after all, I thought. Maybe Lee did think I was attractive. Maybe there was a place for me in this new country.

Another time I ventured next-door to Lee's, books in hand, ready to study, but we soon drifted away from our books and began to chat. I had begun rehearsing the Molière play at Seattle Community College.

"We're beginning to block the scenes," I said, excited to tell Lee more about my role, always wanting to impress. "I'm learning a dance as well – it's easy for me as I took ballet for so many years."

"You had a pretty good education going to private schools, taking music and ballet lessons." Lee smiled ruefully.

"Yeah, I did," I answered, filling in the Os and Es on my class notes.

"I grew up going to public schools and never had private lessons," he continued. "In grade and middle school we lived in a rough area of Sacramento. There were gangs and lots of my classmates were delinquents, some of them even spent time in juvie."

I stopped doodling and glanced up at Lee, surprised and somewhat alarmed. Lee had gotten in with a rough crowd. What did that mean? He broke into a crooked smile and shrugged his shoulders. "I had to hide my good grades, otherwise I would have gotten beat up. I could have easily become a hoodlum. My saving grace was that my dad got transferred to Seattle and we moved to Bellevue." Lee got up from the couch and loaded a record on the stereo.

"Simon and Garfunkel's new album. Chuck just bought it and it's great," he announced, handing me the *Scarborough Fair* album cover. He sat back down, shoving his books aside and sidling closer to me as the many-tiered voices of the title song softly serenaded us.

"Anyway, the schools in Bellevue were amazing. It was cool to be smart and the environment of academic excellence buoyed me up. I loved it! Really, Bellevue High is as good as any private school around here. It helped get me into med school and here with you," he whispered, putting his arm around me and drawing me close.

"Hmm, yes," I answered, but couldn't say any more before his lips met mine.

"Wh . . .what if your roommates come in?" I asked with a shiver, pulling away.

"Heck, they've all done this before," he answered. "In fact, it's expected around here."

This world of necking was new to me, but certainly not unwelcome.

§

I felt pleased to influence Lee enough that he decided to venture to Europe for the first time between his junior and senior years of med school. He took out more student loans, bought a Eurail pass, and planned on staying mostly at hostels. I received a single postcard from him for the whole two months he was gone. He wrote: "Sleeping on park benches and stealing fruit from orchards to stretch my funds, but I'm having a marvelous time!"

I spent that summer working as a library assistant at Seattle Community College. I was proud to have my first full-time job, checking out and restacking books and hanging out with the professional librarians, but wondered whether my relationship with Lee would continue after his return. I thought it might be over as the days flew by without any further postcards from him.

"Hey, Lee was on the same plane as me but he didn't recognize me," Geza announced as we drove him home from the airport. My brother had just returned from spending the summer in Munich, learning German so he could complete his college language requirement. My heart sank. Lee didn't say hello to my brother. He was done with me. He had probably found a new girl in Europe. I tried to hide my heartache, slinking away when we arrived home, but the tears began to flow once I reached my room. I closed the door and dropped face down onto my bed, smothering my wails in my pillow. I moped all afternoon for my lost boyfriend.

"Liz, there's someone here for you," Paul yelled up the stairs. I jumped up, startled. Oh, man, could it be? I flew down the stairs and into Lee's outstretched arms.

"I just got back today and I couldn't wait another hour to see you," he murmured breathlessly into my ear. He looked even skinnier that before, if that was possible, but his face shone and he eagerly began to share all his adventures.

Oh, life is good after all, I thought with glee. My boyfriend still wants me. He had come back to me. We took up our relationship where we had left off, Lee even more ardent than before.

As a result of Lee's European experience, I became even more important. He now paid for more formal dates — to The Windjammer piano bar at Shilshole, where we nursed a single white Russian for hours. Though barely eighteen, I looked mature enough that I never got carded. We enjoyed our first dinner date at The Flame restaurant in downtown Kirkland where one of his high school friends served us. Though now defunct, the then-fancy steakhouse was one of the few stylish go-to places on the east side. The cost for our succulent sirloin steak and baked potato overloaded with butter, sour cream and bacon, bit a large chunk out of Lee's budget. Though I enjoyed being wined and dined, I also felt uncomfortable and beholden when he splurged.

For my Christmas gift that year, Lee doled out a small fortune on a set of skis, boots and poles. "Oh, Lee, this is too much." I voiced my unease as the equipment lay splayed out around me. "You can't afford to be this extravagant and really, I don't need such expensive gifts."

"I wanted to do this for you," he said with pride. "I want to take you skiing besides." In accepting, I felt strings beginning to constrict and bind me to him.

Our second spring of dating bloomed in 1969. Lee was close to graduating from medical school. He had to decide where he wanted to apply for medical internship and the deadline for "the match" process was looming. Though his first choice had been Hennepin County Hospital in Minneapolis, he opted at the last minute for Highland Alameda County Hospital in Oakland, California, in order to be closer to me. He had begun to woo me in earnest. He began to talk about us as long term.

Late one evening in May, Lee hesitated at my front door after a long necking session on the worn out, carrot-colored couch in our living room. He gave me one last kiss, then blurted out breathlessly: "I want you to come to Oakland with me, and if you want to take that as a proposal of marriage, you can."

My head began to swim and I sagged a little in his arms. I gently pushed away and leaned against the wall. I was flattered – of course – and yet terribly conflicted and panicky.

"Wow, oh wow," I stuttered. "This is so sudden, I have to think about this. I can't give you an answer right now."

"That's okay," he replied, taking me in his arms again. "I know you're really young but I want you. I'll give you time to think about it." He kissed me lightly, and hopped down the porch steps.

Yes, I was young – barely nineteen. I knew I wanted to graduate from college and have a career, and I didn't want to be pressured into an early marriage. I also wanted to play the field, for I'd had little experience dating.

I'd gone on a couple of dates with Doug, a cute engineering student whom I had met in my chemistry class. Doug belonged to the Psi Upsilon fraternity, the same one Lee had pledged ten years earlier. Doug and I danced the stomp to "Light My Fire" at a Husky social at the campus' Hec Edmundson Pavilion. He also took me to a Husky football game. He was sweet and considerate, and I liked him. I had more history with Lee, though: we'd connected almost daily; our physical relationship had developed more and we had obvious sexual chemistry. Moreover, Lee was older, more mature, and more assertive than Doug. In the end, Lee won out.

I'd also gone on a couple of dates with Julius, a bespectacled, gawky Hungarian immigrant with a barky laugh who had grown up in New Jersey. He had recently moved to Seattle to work at Boeing and had befriended my gregarious brother Paul. Though I had developed some pride in being Hungarian in the U.S. and for the first time saw it as an advantage rather than the bane I'd experienced in Australia, Julius' superior Hungarian attitude rankled me. Maybe that was because he was touting what I'd heard from my parents for years: he bragged about how great Hungarians were and how we needed to "stick together." He tried to insinuate himself ahead of Lee, boasted about how his engineering education was superior, how he was already graduated and earning a good income. He was pretty open about wanting to find himself a wife of good Hungarian stock. The defining moment in our relationship occurred when Julius took me on a skiing date to Crystal Mountain.

As we drove up, I kept reminding him, "You realize that I'm a complete beginner. I've only been skiing a couple of times."

Julius dismissed my concerns. "I'm sure you are underestimating your abilities. You'll do just fine." He egged me on and pressured me to ride the longest chair. I wobbled off the chairlift at the top of the mountain and gazed about. To my horror, the only option down was an advanced black diamond run. I took one look at the steep drop, and balked. I couldn't even see the bottom of the slope! It was so steep that skiers were completely disappearing from view moments after they took off.

"There's no way I'm going down that run," I declared. "I'll break my neck if I do."

"Come on, you can do it no sweat." Julius' gaze flickered. He was a little unnerved.

"No, I can't and I won't," I retorted. "You go ahead. I'm taking the chairlift back down." My stubborn refusal got through to Julius.

"Okay, Okay, I'll ride with you," he muttered in a deflated show of gallantry. As we rode down, he became more uncomfortable and red-faced as skiers coming up shouted, "Chicken!" "Lost your nerve, eh?" I couldn't care less. I just wanted off the mountain in one piece. I did feel a little bad for Julius – he was mortified. That date proved to be our last. Julius returned to New Jersey soon after – wifeless.

§

Lee graduated from medical school in June and moved to Oakland to begin his rotating internship. I still hadn't committed to marry. I still wanted my freedom. I wasn't ready to settle down and I still questioned whether Lee was the one for me. I signed up for summer quarter at the University of Washington. Lee and I wrote letters to each other most every day. Absence actually did make my heart grow fonder. I wistfully sang along to the pop hits, The Happening's "See you In September" and Fifth Dimension's "Marry Me Bill," and I eagerly awaited the daily mail. Lee wrote chatty letters about his long work shifts, all the hippies he'd taken care of with overdoses and STDs. He wrote all about what he wanted to show me in the Bay Area when I came down to visit. He always ended his letters with "love you." I wrote about my Zoology classes, the "oohs and ughs" of having to dissect everything from mice and sea urchins to worms. I ended with "I miss you and love."

After summer school ended, my mother and I drove to Oakland. At age fifty-seven, Anyu had recently received her first ever driver's license and had purchased a sporty yellow Chevy Nova. I was terrified when my mother drove. She had slow reflexes for which she compensated by slamming on the brakes at the last moment. I drove as much as she'd let me, and spent the rest of the ride to California with clenched fists, my feet jammed into the floorboard in a futile attempt to facilitate her braking.

While in the Bay Area, we stayed with Hungarian friends in Albany. The family graciously opened their home to my mother and me. Lörinc Bácsi worked as a draftsman for an architect firm in San Francisco. His wife, Panni Néni worked as a office manager at a real estate office on Shattuck Avenue in the heart of Berkeley. Lörinc Bácsi had been my father's Ludovika Military Academy classmate. He'd spent several years in a Communist prison after World War II. He never spoke of his internment. He loved his red wine and soda water *fröcs*. In the evenings, he was sometimes pleasantly inebriated. I suspected he had much to forget.

That summer in the Bay Area, I felt part of a community again for the first time since Sydney. My family social circle in Australia had been with Hungarian friends and now, in the United States, I felt I belonged to a group. Our Hungarian hosts frequently entertained and on one of these evenings, I received the new title of "sweet-little-two-tone-thing." Lee had somehow referenced my bikini tan lines in the conversation and Lörinc Bácsi endearingly came up with the quaint description. The older Hungarian men joined in with ogles and snickers. Rather than becoming offended, I felt flattered to receive their attention. I smiled and blushed.

Later that night, Anyu called Apu and begged him to join us in California. But my father had already distanced himself from the marriage and refused to come. She railed into the phone calling him every Hungarian dirty word I had ever heard – and some I hadn't. The mistress of high drama and belittlement was at it again. To my horror, she was performing her antics within earshot of our hosts. I sweated, my heart pounding. I wanted to crawl into a hole. I tried to gloss over her abominable behavior – and fortunately, our hosts did too. The outburst had marred the lovely evening with friends. I didn't think I could be part of this community after all.

§

Towards the end of my stay in California, Lee took me to see the live production of the musical *Hair* in San Francisco. The summer of '69 saw the height of hippydom and the demonstrations against the Vietnam War. The Haight-Ashbury and Berkeley drug scenes flourished, and the fight for the Peoples Peace Park in Berkeley gathered momentum. Psychedelic outfits splashed throughout the *Hair* audience and mirrored the gaudy hippy costumes on stage. I loved the music – "Age of Aquarius," "Good Morning Sunshine" – but as a straight-laced and prudish teen, I cringed when I heard the graphic lyrics of "Sodomy." At the end of the first act when the whole cast stripped naked, my face drained of color. I felt light-headed and nearly fainted when I stood up for the intermission.

After the musical, Lee stalled as we sat in his old beat-up VW bug. He didn't start the engine.

"Did you like the dinner?" he asked.

"Oh, yes, the Mexican restaurant was delicious."

"And the show was pretty great, huh?"

"Amazing," I replied, "Thank you so much for a lovely evening." I began to squirm a little.

I knew Lee had gone all out, spending a bunch to make the evening special. I suspected he had an agenda and he finally turned and looked me directly in the eye.

"I wanted to make this a special night to show you how much I care for you. I also want you to know that I won't wait for you any longer. I'm getting older and I am ready to settle down. If you don't agree to marry me, I'm going to start dating again. You must give me a decision one way or another – now."

I couldn't hold his gaze and turned away, my heart pounding. I studied the sidewalk, the passersby. I wished I were one of them – outside – anywhere but here in the car. I was young and immature. I didn't feel hopelessly in love or swept off my feet. Sure, Lee's ease of conversation, maturity, and intelligence attracted me and I liked that he turned me on. I also liked that he'd had more life experiences and was established in a profession. I feared that if I refused him I wouldn't find as good a catch. But I was already lassoed by his dominant ways. With some reluctance, I took a deep breath and turned to him.

"All right," I whispered.

He put his arms around me and kissed me. As he started the car, I kept repeating to myself that it would be okay.

The following day we announced our engagement to my mother and our hosts. They were happy for us. Lee and I looked for a ring at an Albany strip mall jewelry store. After much deliberation, I settled on an engagement and wedding ring set I liked well enough, but which had black antiquing. This style was popular at the time, but I didn't care for it. The jeweler agreed to remove the antiquing but the black in the wedding ring seemed to be an omen of the shadows in our betrothal. Even scraped from the setting, the darkness lingered as a cloud in the unconscious of our relationship and I felt its gloom glomming onto me.

Lee was pleased. With my acceptance of his proposal, he had achieved what he wanted. I continued to vacillate but didn't voice my hesitation. We agreed to wed in December, around Christmas. I returned to Seattle for fall quarter at the University of Washington. As the wedding day loomed I became more anxious, more resistant to following through with the ceremony. This was my life's first major discernment, and I railed in torment.

I went for long walks trying to figure things out. I cried, muttered rants and raves. I felt pressured into marrying too early. *I still have dreams of becoming a movie star*, I whined to myself as I crossed under the Montlake Bridge. I quickly sped past a college couple groping each other on the concrete bench, averting my gaze with embarrassment. In reality, though, I had already set that dream aside: I never even looked into trying out for plays at the University of Washington and I hadn't signed up for any acting classes either. My drama dream had faded fast. I wondered what other dreams would fade if I married Lee. What doors of opportunity would close forever? And on the flipside, I agonized: what doors might slam shut if I don't marry Lee? I glanced back at the happily necking couple and pondered: would I be throwing away the opportunity of a lifetime if I didn't marry Lee?

I continued to deliberate over the pros and cons of the marriage as I sat down on a bench below the Health Sciences Complex, on the shores of Portage Bay. I was grateful that there were no other people around – and no boats came through from the Montlake cut. The dreary weather had settled in for the winter, and it was far too cold to be puttering about in a cruiser. I dropped my head into my hands. I was at my wit's end, nauseated: the decision to go ahead with the wedding just didn't feel right. I wasn't sure I was in love, but then I had no idea what love was – not really. Lee was my first boyfriend, for Christ's sake! I never thought my parents were in love, and hell, they hardly even talked now. Apu mostly stayed away and barely said a word to anyone when he was in the house.

I had no one to confide in: not my parents, not my brothers or sister. I had never let on to them about personal issues, and it didn't enter my mind to begin doing so now. *I don't even have any close friends*, I moaned, shivering as the wind picked up. I buttoned my coat and plunged my fists into the pockets, staring at the water lapping against the mossy stone wall. I felt completely alone. I called out in a silent prayer. *Help me God, help me figure this out; tell me what to do.* There was no answer. I repeated my entreaty in a heated whisper, glancing around me to make sure I was still alone. Still no answer. As in my childhood when I pined for the Mouseketeer clothes, and prayed for them to appear magically in that battered suitcase, I again felt abandoned by God. In complete frustration, I growled, *I hate you, God!* He had dared to defeat me yet again.

I felt like Job, commiserating with how the Almighty had clobbered the biblical figure over and over. Though Job responded with amazement and shock, he – unlike me – remained faithful to God. I expected and perversely reveled in His silence. "You are infamous and callous," I muttered. I had begun to lose what little faith I had in divine intervention. Darkness loomed in my heart and in the skies. I got up and trudged home completely deflated, no closer to resolving my crushing dilemma.

Finally, in early December, unable to bear the pain alone any longer, I telephoned Lee and voiced my hesitation in going through with the marriage. He caught the next flight to Seattle.

"What the hell's going on with you?" he exclaimed, once we were left alone in the living room.

"I'm just not sure about this whole thing," I muttered, glancing out the window at the gray skies. "It's all happening so fast. I think I need more time."

"You promised to marry me," he declared, looming up into my face. "You said yes. You have to go through with it." He poked at his glasses that had slipped down his nose. "Christ, the invitations are out, I've made plans to get time off. I've put money down for the honeymoon trip. All my family's coming to Seattle for the wedding."

"But, what about – "

"You have to go through with it," he said, a cold gleam in his eye.

For the first time, Lee turned me off. I hated the way he pursed his lips when he was angry. I thought that really unsexy. I became enraged at his lack of understanding, but I kept the ire inside.

I shivered, encircling my arms around me, wanting to shield myself in a makeshift cocoon. The rain had begun to fall and I stared at the tiny drops collecting on the windowpane that mirrored the tears dribbling down my cheeks. I felt cornered and unheard. Lee didn't explore my feelings, my concerns, or what I was up against. I wanted to tell him how I had wandered about Seattle for hours trying to figure things out: the agony I had gone through, all the angst, the buckets of tears I had shed. I desperately needed for him to understand. But Lee didn't want to understand. He was all about what he needed and expected. I slumped and surrendered. He was the victor. He had won the battle.

"All right," I whispered. I had again caved in and agreed to go through with the marriage. Lee unhooked my arms from around me and wrapped them around him. He lifted my chin and smiled. I smiled back hesitantly.

With my doubts and Lee's dominance, I realized our life together was off to a rocky start. But as I gazed into Lee's eyes in that moment, I made a clear decision. I resolved to put my reservations aside. I vowed to give our marriage my best shot. I leaned forward and kissed him.

CHAPTER 12 – GOING TO THE CHAPEL
AND WE'RE GONNA GET MARRIED

Wedding day. A shy tilt of the head and a hopeful smile.

As a teenager, I dressed like a prude. Yes, I wore miniskirts – but only once the barely-covering-butt fashions had gone completely mainstream. Yes, I finally wore a string bikini, when at age sixteen my father insisted and purchased one on our Tahiti stopover on route to the U.S. Two years earlier, I had bought a prim black-and-white, plaid, one-piece swimsuit that my father immediately dismissed. "You look like an old-lady. You need to show off your beautiful young figure." I felt uncomfortable. Weren't fathers supposed to say exactly the opposite? Weren't they the ones to put the brakes on any revealing attire their teenage daughters postage-stamped on their bodies? His urging to expose more struck me as bizarre.

For my wedding, I chose a demure gown with a Nehru collar and long sleeves, fashioned of thick brocade and edged in lace. The non-revealing dress reflected my conservative traditionalism. I wore no pearls as those – according to my mother – signified bad luck for the marriage. The lack of pearls didn't help her marriage – nor did it keep mine out of trouble.

My December wedding day, three years almost to the day of my arrival in Seattle, dawned dreary and drizzly. On the eve of the wedding, the house filled with my Hungarian bridesmaids: Kati from Vancouver BC and Ildi from California. Both were daughters of Apu's military academy buddies, and I barely knew either of them. They were all we could think of to pad the wedding party, as I hadn't made any girlfriends in Seattle. My acquaintances slept in my bedroom while I crashed on an extra mattress in my parents' room.

"You must stop the wedding," my mother hissed to my father. I lay paralyzed a few feet away, afraid to make any noise at all. "You'll leave me if she marries," Anyu continued; her voice now with a frantic edge.

"You're talking crazy nonsense," my father whispered. "Her wedding has nothing to do with us."

"Yes, it does," she wailed. "You know it does. You're going to leave me."

"Shh! Settle down," he fumed in an undertone. "You'll wake everybody."

I couldn't sleep. I had heard their every word. My parents' troubles added to my own angst. I was committed to marrying Lee, yet I still sensed a malaise and the dullness that permeated my body weighted me down even more. I lay frozen and numb through the night.

This wasn't my mother's first attempt to stop my wedding. After we announced our engagement, she had been upbeat enough and professed her approval. "You got a good catch," she said with a crooked grin. "He's a doctor and a professional – a man of status and a good provider." But as the reality of my marriage dawned, her acceptance began to wane. "Are you sure you want to marry him?" she questioned. Then came the jabs: "Why must you leave me? I'll be all alone," she'd whine. Her questioning added to my own doubts, but she was voicing her needs and so I could hardly expect any unbiased counsel from her.

Even more confusing was her contrasting delight in the glitz of the wedding preparations. Her fashion sense bubbled over as she helped choose my wedding gown, going away outfit and bridesmaid dresses and as she fawned over the flower arrangements. I appreciated her help but grew wary at the same time, for I had experienced Anyu's barbs and biting ways in the past – and her persistence.

Two weeks before the wedding, Anyu stormed into my room as I was making my bed. She grabbed my shoulder and spun me around. "I need for you to stay with me," she demanded. The fearsome gleam in her eye stunned me. "You are your father's favorite. If you stay, then he will stay as well," she continued. I sidled away from her angry reach.

"I can't do that Anyu. I'm marrying Lee," I replied, but my voice wobbled. I didn't sound nearly as determined as I wanted it to be.

Anyu stepped closer and thrust her face up to mine, spitting out, "I condemn you to hell!"

I tottered back. She turned with a whirl and marched away.

This phrase in Hungarian grabbed like a vice. Horrified, I couldn't believe my mother – how any mother – could utter such a vehement curse on a daughter. And so, what I thought a rare blessing in my life – the occasional sweet times as my father's favorite – had come to haunt me. My mother used my favored status to attempt to manipulate my father into staying with her. Anyu also used it as a wedge between her and me: I would be the cause of my parents' break-up because I was to follow through with the wedding, and so allow Apu to leave. I was the glue that bound them together. Though I knew it to be an absurd accusation, it smarted nonetheless. In subsequent years, Anyu continued to lash out, accusing me of this "betrayal."

§

On the morning of the ceremony, all the wedding party ladies had early hair appointments at a nearby salon. I wanted all of us in up-dos, and had my heart set on a soft-around-the-face loose chignon. The stylist created a severely pulled back, concrete structure with every single hair lacquered into place. I smiled outwardly but I was seething inside. It was just like the time when I had asked for curls as a seven-year-old and had ended up with that horrid "golligwog" frizz. I had – yet again – failed to get what I wanted.

I felt at ease though hardly elated as I walked down the aisle on the arm of my silent and somber father. Lee's tight smile didn't seem so comforting. For some mindless reason I had decided to include a Mass in the wedding ceremony, even though Lee and most of the guests weren't Catholic. I realized my folly as the ceremony dragged on and only a timid voice or two echoed the liturgical responses. Hardly anyone besides my family came up for communion. The reception in the church hall was a simple fare consisting of cake, champagne and candied almonds. No speeches, no entertainment or dancing warmed the celebration. The guests didn't linger.

Lee and I flew to San Francisco that evening and he surprised me with the location of our nuptial night. He had traded an on-call shift with a fellow intern in return for using his place for a day. His unabashed bachelor pad was a stunning A-frame structure in Sausalito with a sweeping view from the master bedroom of the San Francisco Bay and Golden Gate Bridge. My virginal king size bed was fitted with black floral sheets. I felt uncomfortable and awkward in the playboy pad, especially after Lee regaled me with tales of the racy parties the intern had hosted there. The stories did little to help boost my wedding night jitters and glaringly highlighted my sexual inexperience.

I was able to relax a little more on the second night of our honeymoon. Lee had booked us for a night at a stylish boutique hotel in Sausalito. I loved the ritz and the elegance and wanted to stay longer, but Lee had planned to continue our honeymoon at Lake Tahoe. There we stayed at a ski cabin along with a bunch of other people.

"I don't want to share my honeymoon with strangers," I pouted as I pulled up the covers our first night there. We had just spent the evening cooking and eating dinner with the other renters.

"My finances are limited," Lee shot back as he lay down beside me. "I've splurged as much as I could afford for the wedding and the honeymoon." He put his arms around me. "Don't be so ungrateful," he needled.

Yes, I was ungrateful. I sulked, turning away from him. The bubble of the elegant honeymoon fantasy that I had hoped for had burst.

§

We settled into our Oakland apartment, close to the hospital. A few evenings later, Lee announced, "I'm going out for a beer with the guys."

"What do you mean? It's your first night off. I want to be with you."

"Tough titties." Lee snickered. Tough titties? Who even says that?

My rage bubbled up. "But Lee, what about me?"

He sniffed and puffed himself up. "I refuse to be pussy whipped. Deal with it." He headed for the door.

"Oooh!" I stomped after him, fists clenched. He shut the door in my fiery-red face, laughing.

"Damn you," I yelled, grabbing the nearest object and hurling a textbook against the wall.

"Damn you, damn you." I burst into tears. I paced around the apartment, sulking and seething. *How dare he take off and leave me alone? How dare he not include me? I'll make him pay, he'll be sorry.*

When Lee slipped into bed a few hours later and tried to cuddle, I could smell the beer on his breath. I flipped his arm away, slithered to the edge of the bed, and yanked the covers over me.

I refused to speak to him for over a week. I'd learned how to do the silent treatment from my mother and sister. I knew how to hold a grudge. I threw his meals on the table and answered in monosyllables – and only if I absolutely had to. Lee hardly cared, as he was mostly gone, working his eighteen-hour shifts. Besides, he'd gotten his way. With a slinky grin on his face, he acted as if nothing was wrong. That fueled my anger even more but I had to give in eventually. Slowly, gradually, I thawed, for underneath the hurt, I desperately wanted Lee to honor, cherish and to hear me.

§

I enrolled for a semester at UC Berkeley. Lee remained true to his commitment to support my continued education and helped wrangle not only in-state status, but a student loan for the tuition as well. I was grateful to him for keeping his promise and that helped to ease my resentment.

During that spring of 1970, the Vietnam War escalated. Berkeley, along with several other areas in the country, heated up with demonstrations and riots. As violence erupted, the Berkeley campus authorities shut the university down.

At the time, I hadn't formed a clear opinion about the Vietnam War. I had little political savvy. I was raised in a family in which the military attitudes that my father had learned in the Hungarian army ruled. My Catholic schooling discouraged questioning authority. I complied with my superiors in most ways, always wanting to please. I had little experience in resisting and felt threatened by any form of rebellion. Though somewhat skeptical about the U.S. involvement in an undeclared war, I hesitated to question the government and I kept up an insouciant detachment towards politics. I was ignorant, having little interest in reading or watching news reports.

Moreover, I looked down on the hippies and was critical of their drug use and sexual promiscuity. Their flagrant permissiveness contrasted sharply with my rigid "good girl" persona and I felt deeply threatened. I feared what I might learn if I lost control of my tightly held-in feelings by using drugs. I fit exactly the uptight mold that the hippies delighted in ridiculing. I couldn't imagine joining the demonstrators for I feared the exposure and possible danger – even arrest. I stayed safe in my conservative cocoon of ignorance and denial, limiting my involvement in the Berkeley demonstrations to spinning animated tales of how I zigzagged through the campus riots, evading teargas. My rebellion was to come years later, and it proved to be mostly an internal and a solitary one.

§

Lee and I did entertain some, when his crazy intern schedule permitted. One time we took Lőrinc Bácsi, who has so graciously welcomed my mother and me into his home the summer before, to a San Francisco symphony concert. I knew he was an ardent Beethoven fan, for he had shown me his extensive collection of classical LPs. The concert season of our first year of marriage was Joseph Kripps's last year as conductor and the series was all Beethoven. The evening we treated Lőrinc Bácsi, the orchestra played the *Emperor (5th) Piano Concerto* and the *Seventh Symphony*. These were among Lőrinc Bácsi's favorite compositions and they were certainly among mine. It was fitting that the concert took place in the venerable War Memorial Opera House. The old soldier's eyes were moist during the whole performance. I felt touched and honored to provide this gift for him. He showered his thanks afterwards as we walked outside and down the steps. I glanced back at Lee silhouetted against the columned façade of the beautiful building and smiled. I felt love and gratitude for him that he had provided this wonderful gift to our family friend.

§

Lee had joined the Navy ROTC in college and the call to active duty loomed after he finished his internship in June. "I've signed up for naval flight surgeon training," he announced one day in May. I was fixing *rakot káposzta*, a casserole dish that my mother had sent the recipe for soon after we wed. Lee loved it.

"What do you mean?" I looked up from stirring the bubbling mixture of ground beef, onions and pepperoni. I was stunned. I had no clue that he would take such steps.

"I don't want to continue with a residency right now – I don't know what specialty I want – so that means I'd get drafted in to the navy right away."

"Oh," I muttered, sliding the pan from the hot burner, a flush of anger on my face. "You might have told me." I deliberately bumped his shoulder as I marched by him to get to the fridge. He had left me out of the decision-making process and I felt hurt, affronted and outraged.

"Quit being a bitch, Liz." I cringed at his now all too familiar insult. "It's my decision and not yours. There's no way I'm going into the navy as a general medical officer 'cause they're getting assigned to the front lines with the marines. Do you want me crippled or carted home in a body bag?"

"Of course I don't," I answered, a shudder of fear climbing up my spine as I carried the sour cream back to the stove. "I just want us to make decisions as a couple," I continued, adding a huge dollop of sour cream to the meat mixture with a snap.

"Well, tough titties. It's my life," he fumed.

"I know it is, Lee, and I want you to be safe." I poured the meat mixture over a bed of cooked rice and began to layer sauerkraut on top.

"You're making rocket kapoosta, my favorite." He smiled, coming up behind me and putting his hands on my shoulders. "It's only an extra six months in the navy, Liz. I thought it was worth it, and the training is in Pensacola, Florida, so we'll get to travel and see the country." He reached over my shoulder and poked his finger in the casserole. I slapped his hand away.

"Hey, keep outta there. I'm not done,"

Lee had made good points about his safety and I did relish the thought of traveling cross-country, but I still held resentment that he'd made his decision without my input.

"My tour of duty begins in the fall," he added grabbing the paper on the kitchen table and heading for the couch. "When do we eat?" he asked as I popped the dish in the oven. I rolled my eyes. I again held onto the hurt. I was mostly silent during dinner and for the next four days.

§

We returned to Seattle for the summer before Lee began flight surgeon training. He insisted I keep up with my studies and so I reenrolled at the University of Washington for summer quarter. We lived in an empty unit in my mother's apartment building by Seattle Pacific College. My father had invested her portion of the initial and only proceeds of the Sydney knitwear factory into the twelve-unit structure. The couple that had purchased the factory on contract had declared bankruptcy soon after the initial down payment.

Lee and I enjoyed our bohemian lifestyle in the bare bones apartment. All we had was a mattress, a few utensils, and a tiny hibachi grill. That summer, fresh salmon sold for rock bottom prices and we ate lots of it prepared with a little butter and lemon juice and cooked on the tiny barbeque. Coupled with fresh corn on the cob, it made for delicious eating. I joined in Lee's enthusiastic cost saving measures and I quite enjoyed roughing it – for a time.

A few years later, my parents sold that apartment complex at a huge loss, just as the Seattle economy was tanking. Boeing lost the government supersonic transport contract and huge layoffs decimated the real estate market. The empty city rattled and a cryptic billboard appeared south of the city: "Will the last person leaving SEATTLE – Turn out the lights."

My parents' financial woes continued to haunt them: they had lived off my mother's teaching income during the war when my father's military salary dried up; they had started over from nothing in Australia and had weathered several down seasons in their knitwear factory; the sale of the factory netted them with nothing but the initial down payment. Now they were struggling with yet another huge financial loss. This, coupled with their failing marriage, shook them to their core. We kids didn't know how to help. My father moved out and completely withdrew. My mother's way of dealing with the separation and financial downturn was to complain, berate, and manipulate. In observing Anyu's antics that summer, I realized that I emulated her in more ways than I cared to admit, directing my bitchy ways mostly towards my husband.

§

After my finals, we had a free month before Lee reported for duty in Florida. By now, we were really low on funds. Because of the prickly relationship with his dad, Lee was reluctant to ask his parents for a short-term loan, but ask he did and they came through. We were thus able to finance a road trip through Canada and across the U.S. to Pensacola. We first drove to Banff, to gorgeous knife-edged icy mountains reflected in stunning blue-green glacial lakes. The astonishing scenery filled me with awe. My every expectation of the grandeur of alpine vistas was finally met. In stark contrast, my trip to the tallest peak in Australia had sorely disappointed. Mount Kosciuszko, the highest mountain in the continent, rose to a mere 7,310 feet. When my family drove to the top of the peak, all I found was an ugly, bald hilltop with a few clomps of dirty snow. I felt shortchanged. In Banff, the alpine magnificence was redemptive and took my breath away.

I longed to stay at the stately, elegant Banff and Lake Louise Lodges, but their splendor was way beyond our budget. "Quit looking at me with those longing gazes, Liz. We can't even afford to stay in a motel in this town," Lee said. "We can't afford to eat out either," he added when I glanced at the menu posted in the hotel restaurant window. I sulked as I stomped through the elegant lobby.

Before leaving Seattle, Lee had purchased cases of canned food at the Sandpoint Naval Air Station PX. His motto was: when you buy, buy in bulk as it's "a good deal." In the evenings at the campgrounds, he dismissed my traditional cooking suggestions.

"I know how to cook camp food. Let me handle this," he insisted as he stirred some ground beef on the Coleman stove. "Help me open these cans," he ordered, gathering an armful of them from the trunk of the car: stewed tomatoes, corn, beans, peas, and cream of mushroom soup.

"We don't need all of this stuff. It's too much and it'll taste gross," I whined.

"No way." He grinned, "You'll see how delicious it'll be. Keep on opening."

I muttered under my breath: "What crap . . . what shit . . ." with every twist of the can opener. My arm was aching and my emotions were getting out of control.

"Cut it out, Liz, quit being a bitch." Lee dumped the contents of the cans into the pan, mixing them into the ground beef and then, to my horror, began adding large squirts of ketchup, Worcestershire sauce and A-1 steak sauce.

"Whoa, Lee, this is totally ridiculous. That mess is inedible." My stomach was grumbling but the hodgepodge in the pan didn't look appetizing at all.

"Damn it, Liz! I know what I'm doing," Lee shot back and slammed the pan on the campsite's worn down picnic table. We had no plates and only two forks. Lee threw one on the table for me, grabbed the other, leaned over the pan, and dug in. I took a bite and was grateful I didn't gag. The concoction tasted weird, but at least it was edible. The huge pile of slop had to be eaten for dinner and breakfast, as we had nothing to store leftovers in as we travelled. There wasn't any variety to our menu and with each passing day, I became more and more bad-tempered, but I mostly held my irritation inside.

Our route meandered through the fertile Okanagan Valley and into Penticton, the heart of fruit growing country. There we bought a crate of succulent peaches, thinking we could munch on them as we wound our way down through Montana and Utah. "Sorry folks, no fruit allowed into the U.S.," the border guard declared. "I have to confiscate your peaches." Much to his amusement, Lee and I slurped as many peaches as we could before handing over the rest.

"Purchasing a whole crate wasn't such a *good deal* after all," I said as we crossed the border.

"Zip it, Liz. You're a royal pain in the ass."

I leaned into the car window, drew my arms around me and sulked. I grew tired of Lee's "good deals" and I hated everything about camping. I hated the tiny, flimsy pup tent and the gritty, muddy campsites. I longed for a soft bed with fresh sheets, a clean floor and a hot shower. I hated Lee's meal concoctions and hungered for a good sit down meal. I was fed up with the vagabond existence I'd endured all summer, first in my mother's apartment house and now camping. Roughing it had completely lost its charm. I became more and more irritable.

"Why can't we stay in a motel?" I moaned as we headed south of the border and darkness was approaching. I punctuated my displeasure in true princess bitch fashion by stomping my foot on the car floor. I ramped up with an angry show of tears as I shouted, "Look, there's a Motel 6."

"Stop it," Lee shot back. "We're camping tonight."

This time, I refused to give in, shifting my tactic and pleading.

"It'll only cost $6 to stay there. What's the difference between paying $2 for a campsite or $6 for a motel?"

"No way!" Lee sneered, but I wouldn't let it go.

"You're about to hit the big time in the navy. You'll make $15,000 a year, more than your dad ever made in all the years he worked as a manager for Kress stores. What difference does it make if we are twenty or thirty more dollars in debt at the end of this trip?"

"Yeah, that's right, honey. It's my salary, my money, so pipe down," he growled. I pouted but my tears and pleas were to no avail. Lee wanted to scrimp, and his wishes prevailed.

I didn't agree with Lee's stinting. My parents had gone through several economic downturns, and they had survived. I didn't believe in holding on to money so tightly, as my parents had showed how it could disappear in a flash. I wanted to enjoy what I had. But I could not influence Lee and I had no recourse because I wasn't earning any money. He could be as frugal as he liked and he didn't fail to remind me of that. He had the upper hand and I felt trapped.

§

The gorgeous country we saw helped to soften my irritation over the scrimping and camping discomforts. We drove through the Glacier-Waterton Peace Park on the U.S. Canadian border and passed by a stunning shrine of nature's fury, which stirred my senses. It was a similar and yet different feeling to what had moved me so deeply as a teenager at the Sydney beach. Here, I felt the awesome presence of the sacredness of nature, but its quality felt more powerful than the gentle presence I'd experienced at the seashore. As I gazed at a hillside of trees that had been uprooted like toothpicks and arranged in parallel array on the ground like soldiers lined up in strict formation, I felt mesmerized, and my body stilled and hummed. I sensed the magnificent violence that nature was capable of wielding. I had learned about the destructive powers of God in the Old Testament stories, but what moved me at that moment was how my body resonated with those tumultuous forces. I recognized that I harbored these turbulent capacities inside of me and that I expressed them in my life – mostly in my anger towards Lee. The association of my ire and the sacred power of nature felt mysterious and murky, but my body experience riveted me, and I began to wonder what it all might mean.

Later that night the park ranger at the campground gave us the explanation for the meteorological phenomenon we had just seen. The trees had been uniformly leveled by an implosion, a most unusual weather pattern consisting of a single forceful gust that uni-directionally hit the mountainside and toppled the trees in exact parallel lines. Fascinating! In the same talk, the ranger also warned us that grizzly bears had been sighted nearby and cautioned us to carefully pack and dispose of all our food scraps.

That night Lee and I lay awake in our pup tent. A modest breeze blew.

"What was that?" Lee whispered with alarm.

"I don't know," I answered, a little unsettled.

"Damn, it could be one of the grizzlies the park ranger was warning us about. Did you leave any food out, Liz?"

"No, I didn't," I huffed. "I may not be a seasoned camper like you, but I ain't stupid."

"Gees, there it goes again. The bugger is scratching our tent, ready to rip into it and pounce. Where's the flashlight?" he hissed, reaching around the sleeping bags.

"Do you really want to annoy the bear by flashing a light in his eyes?" I hissed back. I was angry at the whole damn camping situation but I was pretty scared as well.

"No, stupid, I want something in my hand to clobber him with." His putdown rankled. Why did he always have to belittle me?

We settled into an irritated, frightened silence. As the minutes passed, the noise became less ominous.

"Hell, it's just a breeze that rustling a branch against the tent," Lee finally admitted with a shaky laugh. Perhaps that night, even he would have preferred staying in a sheltered Motel 6 room.

The following day, we continued south to Salt Lake City to visit Lee's aunt and cousins, and we then drove on to the tiny town of Fairview, Utah, to spend a day with his grandmother. Mabel still lived in the humble stone house in which she, as a single parent, had raised Lee's mother and her two older sisters after her husband was killed in a mining accident in the nearby Wabash Mountains. Lee's grandma was a white-haired, well-padded, and wizened old lady who welcomed us warmly, baking scones and grilling pancakes on her ancient wood-burning stove.

"I can still carry wood," she said, pushing Lee away from the pile and hefting a log in her plump arms. "I may have had to give up chopping wood, but I can still run circles around you, boy."

Lee laughed. "You're scary, Gramma, a force to be reckoned with."

She chuckled. "Darn tootin' I am." She beamed at Lee, relishing our company.

I experienced an extended family for the first time when I visited Lee's relatives in Utah. I never knew my own grandparents and grew up with only my parents and siblings in Sydney. All my aunts, uncles and cousins resided back in Hungary. I felt touched to be part of a large clan that welcomed me so warmly. I loved Lee for giving me this gift and I softened and finally stopped griping about our roughing-it trip.

From Utah we traveled south to Tucson and stayed overnight with a childhood friend of Lee's. After venturing into Mexico to briefly check out the dilapidated border town of Nogales, Lee and I headed nonstop to Pensacola, a 1600-mile driving marathon across Texas and Louisiana. By then Lee was really fretting about finances and he refused to shell out money for either a motel or a campsite.

We coasted into Pensacola twenty-four hours later, grubby, bleary-eyed, and irritable, ready for a hot shower and a soft bed. We were apprehensive and anxious, yet ready to embark on a new commission in the navy.

CHAPTER 13 – ANCHORS AWEIGH

In the clinical lab, training as a Medical Technologist.

As Lee and I sped along through Louisiana, I mused, "Wow, how luxurious that ground cover is! It's growing right up to the edge of the highway pavement and it's more impressively green than Washington – and that's supposed to be the 'Evergreen State.'" My first impression of the South floated in my foggy, dog-tired brain as Lee and I rode along in silence – sweaty, smelly, and punchy from hours of driving. I was delighted with the lush vegetation, but not so much the lush bugs that I later encountered and that also flourished in the florid humidity of the Deep South.

I loved our brick-faced, stately apartment complex. We rented a practically brand new one-bedroom unit, by far the nicest living space we'd lived in so far.

"Lee, help, help!" I shrieked. I had just opened the dresser drawer and there, sitting on top of one of Lee's white t-shirts, lay a huge black cockroach the size of a fist. I dropped the folded laundry I was holding and stumbled backwards. In true damsel in distress fashion, I ran into Lee's arms. He winced at the dreadful site, but did manage to gingerly dispose of the creature.

I was even more disturbed when I met the giant cockroach's smaller cousins. In the evenings when I turned on the lights in the kitchen, I saw a flurry of black dots the size of chocolate chips scurry into the cracks and cabinets. At first it was a dot or two and I even thought I might be seeing things, but as the army grew, I became alarmed.

One night, thoroughly disgusted with seeing a hoard of cockroaches scurrying for cover when I ventured into the kitchen for a glass of water, I marched to the apartment manager's unit and banged on the door. As soon as it opened I blurted out, "We have cockroaches in our kitchen." The bleary eyed manager fumbled as he tied his threadbare dressing gown.

"That's impossible," he muttered.

"I assure you it is not." He straightened up with indignation.

"The apartment complex is brand new, and we fumigate regularly."

"I beg to disagree and invite you to view our kitchen convocation." I swirled around and headed to my apartment. He followed, his slippers slapping behind me. I led him into the darkened kitchen and switched on the light. His mouth gaped at the spectacle. The fumigators arrived the following day and I had the disgusting task of disposing of hundreds of dead cockroaches. Gagging and heaving, I filled two vacuum bags with their carcasses.

§

Apart from the repellent bug encounters, I felt for the first time since I had married Lee that I had a taste of the good life. He was a lieutenant in the navy – and his rank as an officer came with perks that I, too, could enjoy. I no longer had to swallow Lee's camping swills. Instead, we dined at the elegant officers' club. For pennies, we feasted on sumptuous steak dinners, sipped white Russians, and danced away the night. Long ago, my mother had taught me to play bridge, and I now delighted in playing with other naval wives at the officers' club. I was living her dream and I could hear her voice in my head, see her sly smile as she counseled me before I married: "Don't work, live a life of leisure, and have your husband generously provide. Lie on the couch all day in a silk robe. Eat bonbons." She gave this advice partly out of bitterness, for she was describing the life she had hoped for when she married my father. That was before the terrifying war and arduous immigration completely squashed her dream. What she ended up with was years of disruption, danger, dirty diapers, and work drudgery. Though she wanted me to have the luxuries she wasn't able to garner for herself, she also wished to live vicariously through me and wanted to hear my stories. When she came to visit in Pensacola, she absorbed every perk that we enjoyed: the fancy meals, the dancing, and the bridge parties. I wanted that for her, for I knew how hard her life had been. When I took her to the officers' club and saw the glow on her face, I thought she must be reminiscing about the good times she had had long ago as an officer's wife in Hungary. I was glad to give her this gift. I also wanted to show off to her, to let her know how well I was doing, how well Lee and I were doing. I avoided spats with Lee and held in my snide remarks.

I was like my mother for I, too, craved the luxuries that Anyu advocated. I wanted Lee to provide them, for I harbored a desperate need to be taken care of. Yet, even in the short time I had known Lee, I knew my life would never be a bed of roses, for he continually voiced his expectation that I provide financial support for the partnership. I felt torn between the need to have a career and to contribute, and the desire to be pampered and to have a family. My resentment grew as I came to realize that Lee would give me little choice.

Yes, I longed for a life of leisure, but yet another saying of my mother's echoed in my head: "My university years were the best years of my life." Because of her happy experience, she wanted all of us kids to get a college education and this expectation rubbed off on me. I wanted to have fun in college. I wanted to flaunt a degree and I wanted to showcase my intelligence. Lee continued to fully support my college career and for this, I was grateful. While in Pensacola, I attended classes for a quarter at the University of West Florida.

§

While I loved the perks of dining in the officers' club, Lee preferred all the other good deals to be had on base – and there were opportunities galore. The purchasing power of his salary expanded at the base PX where groceries and all sorts of goods were sold at deeply discounted prices. We carted boxes of Dinty Moore beef stew, cans of peas, beans, corn and tomato paste. Lee bought a fancy Pentax camera and a Seth Thomas ship's clock. He grew even more excited when he discovered the Quonset hut that had been converted to a hobby hanger.

"Look at this huge space, Liz" he cried with glee, his voice echoing through the cavernous structure. "Look at all these tools we can use. Table saws, drills, wrenches . . . they have everything," Lee was like a kid in a toy store. "We can make all our furniture here." Although I was charmed to see his delight, I became apprehensive when he referred to "we" when he talked about doing projects. I supported him getting involved in hobbies, but I had no interest in joining in.

Right away, Lee came up with an idea for a scheme: he became enthused about hatch-covers. The craze to salvage oak plank hatch-covers from old wooden ships, refurbish them, and display them as coffee tables had just begun. Whereas our Pensacola friends refinished a single hatch-cover table as a conversation piece, Lee's eagerness knew no bounds. "It's a cheap way to furnish our apartment. They'll look great," he promised. Wanting to please him, I went along with the grandiose project – initially.

We trolled shipyards along the Gulf shores and purchased a dozen hatch-covers. We lugged each grimy 30 by 60 inch, iron-strapped piece of dead weight to and from the car and into the hobby hanger. We spent hours sanding cruddy oily goop – highly toxic creosote – off the oaken hatch-covers. Though our friends used a more easily and quickly applied urethane finish, Lee wanted more resilience and shine. He chose the toxic and arduous chore of using a fiberglass resin finish. We applied gallons of liquid fiberglass, layer by wearisome layer. The fumes overwhelmed. Each pouring had to be timed just right after the hardening catalyst was added, for it gelled quickly. We labored for days. Lee was a ruthless taskmaster, insisting we return each day to apply yet another dratted coat.

After all the coats of fiberglass, came the painstaking sanding process that required hours of elbow grease to bring about a lustrous shine. It took two grades of sandpaper, coarse and fine, and several applications of liquid sander to achieve the high gloss finish that Lee wanted. The scope of the project so overwhelmed me that I dreaded the thought of trudging yet again to the hobby hanger to work on yet another phase of the burdensome project. I resented all the time I spent doing "dirty work." I felt indignant that Lee had drawn me into such a hateful and undignified project, one that I thought was below me.

"I don't want to go to the damned hanger this afternoon." I bitched and balked, stamping my foot as I stood by the sink in the kitchen.

"Damn it, Liz, this is the only time I have to do this, and you have to help me," Lee fumed pacing back and forth. "I do everything around here. I'm earning our keep. I'm studying at all hours." I remained stubborn, slapping the tea towel on the counter.

"But why can't we go out to the officers' club? We haven't been out all week because of this dratted project." My tone was strident.

"Jesus, Liz, all you want to do is go out and spend money. You're not earning a damn thing – in fact, you're a financial drain because you're a student. You're an economic liability." His accusation hit home and I slouched a little but I wasn't ready to surrender.

"I cook and clean for you – that counts for something – and when I graduate I'll be making money too." I pouted, my nose in the air, hands on my hips, looking him straight in the eye.

"Your income will never make up for the opportunity cost of your time in college. I am losing a bunch by your not working. The least you can do is to help make this cheap furniture with me. You owe me." He stopped pacing and planted himself, his red face up against mine.

I was livid too. "Ooh, you . . ." I didn't have a comeback. Instead, I turned away from his harsh gaze and threw a just dried pan into the cupboard with a thunderous clatter. I growled. Completely unglued, I stomped into the bedroom, threw my purse over my shoulder, stomped out to the car and slammed the door.

I did Lee's bidding, but I felt cornered and caged. He had played the guilt ace card yet again. I pummeled the sanding liquid into the fiberglass finish with a forceful mixture of guilt and rage. Lee attempted a time or two to make small talk. I responded with a withering glare. He gave up, ducking his head over another hatch-cover and busily sanded away. I sulked and kept up the silent treatment for three whole days.

In the end, the only saving grace to the whole project was that Lee finally tired of the work as well and ceded the construction of the furniture bases. He commissioned heavy wrought iron legs to be forged and mounted for each piece.

So where other couples had bought into the hatch-cover fad and quickly fashioned a single conversation piece, Lee's aggressive and toxic approach created a houseful of heavy clunky, chunky, bruise creating, impossible-to-budge hatch-cover décor. For weeks, we had mucked around in that horrid hobby hanger – all that for four coffee tables, two end tables, and a dining room table with two matching benches. Each time I eyed the stuff, it reminded me of the physical, emotional, and marital turmoil forged into its creation.

§

Our first year of marriage was flying by. Despite our arguments and differences, I enjoyed the companionship of a new relationship, appreciated the financial support that Lee offered, loved the stimulation of what I was learning in my college courses, and soaked up the perks of military life. At the same time, I began to resent Lee's demanding ways and his tight fisted budgeting.

One of the few things that loosened Lee's hold on money was peer influence. When his classmates raved about trips they planned to take to New Orleans and the Bayou country, Lee joined in the excitement. That led to a New Orleans weekend with Lee's flight surgeon classmate John and his wife, Patty, both from small town Kansas, wide eyed and eager to explore a vibrant city. Having company around provided a shield: Lee couldn't scrimp and so we stayed in a nice hotel in the French Quarter.

I smiled as I looked up at the Bourbon Street sign, humming the theme to the TV series, *Bourbon Street Beat,* and remembering how I had enjoyed watching it as a teenager in Sydney. I thought the starring actor, Richard Long quite a hunk.

"Look, here's an oyster bar," Patty said. Her freckled fair face lit up as she tugged at her husband's sleeve. "They're supposed to be fabulous in this town. Please can we go in and try them?" John frowned, his eyes shifting behind his dark rimmed glasses, his close-cropped crew-cut seeming to stand even more on end. He was less of a culinary adventurer than his wife, especially when it came to seafood.

Lee cocked his head at John with amusement. "I'm game, Patty" he said, and strolled into the bar. I followed. I wasn't so sure about oysters either. The only one I had tried was back in Australia when my dad's friend had pried some oysters off a reef by the Sydney suburb of Sans Souci, shucked them and invited Apu and I to sample them. It had tasted fishy and slimy. Nevertheless, I was game to give oysters another try. I followed Lee into the bar and perched on a stool.

The tall, lanky bartender grinned at us. He had long unruly curly hair, a days-old beard and wore a stained white apron.

"We want to try the oysters," Patty said.

"Wanna start with a dozen?"

"Yep," Lee replied.

The server pulled a bunch of shells from a bed of ice, cracked each one open with a single thrust of his stubby knife.

"Have you ever cut yourself?" I asked, admiring his skill.

"More times than I can count." He chuckled. "Comes with the shucking territory. Here," he added, setting a bowl of hot sauce in front of us. "Dip the oyster in this sauce. It's what makes it special." The oysters were huge and I marveled that they had none of the fishy tang like the one I'd eaten in Australia.

"Hmm, this oyster has a sweet, subtle, nutty taste." I glanced at the bartender with a surprised look.

"Well, yeah, we've the best oysters anywhere!"

"And this cocktail sauce is delectable, just spicy enough." Patty brushed sauce off her lip with her finger and licked it with a smack. John was the last to sample the delicacy and we watched as he tentatively took a bite. He broke into a grin.

"This is great! Bring us another dozen." He laughed.

"Comin' right up." The bartender grinned.

To my delight, we had even more culinary pleasures to enjoy the following morning. Lee had splurged for the first time ever and taken me to a truly elegant restaurant: we had reservations for the famed Breakfast at Brennan's. I nearly swooned as I walked into the elegant, chandeliered dining room.

"Oh, my." Patty sighed. "This place is over the top."

"I'll say," I said, as I took in the pristine white linen tablecloths, the fresh rosebud spray centerpieces.

We were seated in velvet-cushioned seats by a stream of starched waiters who pulled out chairs and placed linen napkins on our laps. They continued to hover throughout the meal, pouring juice, champagne and coffee, presenting each dish with an explanation and a flourish: everything from baked apples, delicate crêpes, and bread pudding to spicy filé gumbo and eggs Sardou: poached eggs on a bed of artichoke bottoms with creamed spinach and Hollandaise sauce.

"I am stuffed," Lee moaned after a couple of hours of feasting. We groaned in agreement but the banquet had yet to show its crowning glory. The waiters wheeled a delicate trolley to our table and proceeded to prepare Bananas Foster. They sautéed the fruit quarters in brown sugar and spices, then flambéed them. As the flames shot up Patty exclaimed, "Oh wow, this is really elegant. I'm so full but I have to at least have a taste." She grinned as the server dished the bananas over individual servings of vanilla ice cream.

"Hmmm, that is so good," I moaned. Licking my lips I added, "We have to get this recipe, Patty."

I felt so rich and elegant and oh, how I wanted – and thought I deserved – that sort of entitlement! The lovely spell broke as Lee signed for the bill and muttered under his breath, "This cost a damned fortune! Don't get used to this expensive lifestyle, Liz. It ain't happening."

We parted from our friends in the parking lot and headed back to Pensacola. I pouted and seethed in silence the whole way home. Why did he have to ruin such a lovely meal? Why couldn't we have such luxuries – at least once in a while? Why did Lee have to count pennies every time – all the time?

After our New Orleans weekend, we still went on outings, but nothing like the elegance of that Big Easy weekend. We made another side trip, this time to Mobile, Alabama, for the Azalea Festival. We toured around and saw many gracious, stately homes. Their gardens were splashed with blooms in brilliant yellows and pinks, and peaches. My heart warmed and I felt a little more at home remembering the similarly colored riot of azaleas that bloomed every spring in our front yard in Sydney. Large oak trees festooned with moss framed the charming tableau of these gracious southern neighborhoods. My eyes spun from side to side, front to back, striving to take in the whole spectacle, and a persistent grin lit up my face.

We explored the bayou country and discovered a family-style restaurant, housed in a rustic shack along the water's edge under moss-draped trees. The servers seated us at a large wooden table, shared with complete strangers, and we passed around generous portions of southern soul food: gumbo – the best ever – jambalaya, collard greens, fried fish and chicken, black-eyed peas, corn bread, pecan and peach pies. We relished the mouth-watering creole cuisine.

§

Lee's flight surgeon training was coming to an end. He had studied hard for every exam because the stakes were really high. The class rankings determined the billet assignments – where each person was to be stationed. The top students snapped up the cushiest billets: San Diego, San Francisco, and Hawaii. The lowest ranked were awarded the dreaded leftovers: the dangerous deployable billets to the battlefronts in Viet Nam, or adrift on aircraft carriers, or at remote outposts such as Adak, Alaska. I got caught up in Lee's angst and feared that we might be separated or even worse, that he might be wounded or killed in Vietnam. We both breathed a huge sigh of relief when he finished high enough in his class and landed an assignment at the Willow Grove Naval Air Station just north of Philadelphia – a non-deployable and non-combat billet.

In March of 1971, I proudly pinned the tiny wings onto Lee's uniform lapel at the graduation ceremony. The movers came and packed all our stuff – groaning and moaning as they hoisted all the leaden hatch-covers. We had a few free days before needing to report for duty in Willow Grove and decided to drive around the Florida peninsula. Lee wanted to save on motels and so we drove all night.

We arrived in Miami in the wee hours and found an upscale neighborhood in which to park while we waited to check into a motel. We began to make out. Unfortunately, the posh area had regular patrols and a cop found us *in flagrante delicto*. I blushed and quickly yanked my top down. Lee had enough presence of mind to whip out his medical license. The cop got into the humor of the situation and theatrically growled at us to "get the hell out of Dodge." We drove, no longer daring to stop, until we checked into a motel later in the day. That evening, we celebrated my twenty-first birthday. I ordered my first officially sanctioned brandy Alexander. It was an anticlimax as, due to my mature looks, I had always dodged the ID scrutiny of bartenders. Now that I had come of age, I hoped that Lee would treat me with more deference.

§

Lee and I quickly settled into our new life in Pennsylvania. We had learned to adapt to change for we had already weathered three moves and even more road trips our first year of married life. At the Willow Grove Naval Air Station, Lee soon realized that his work was more as a general medical officer than a flight surgeon. In the small clinic, he treated the aches and pains of sailors and their dependents with just a few navy pilot physicals scheduled here and there to break the pattern.

The commanding officer of the medical facility towed the military line with a mean streak. He wasn't well liked by his underlings. Lee fortunately had an ally and buddy at the clinic, another young doctor who had just finished his internship and who joined the navy as a general medical officer. Harry grew up in a small North Carolina town and had the charm, blond hair, chiseled handsome face – and the Southern drawl – to prove it. An avid golfer, his dream was to play a round at St. Andrews in Scotland and this he realized some years later. His other dream was to become a neurosurgeon and this, too, he successfully accomplished after his tour of duty. Harry, like Lee, remained skeptical of all things regimented and military. They commiserated and bolstered each other up through the travails of military life and especially life with their callous commanding officer. They became firm friends.

I idolized Bill's wife, Rose, a gentle, charming, blonde Southern belle, who was trained as a nurse. She hired on at Abington Memorial Hospital where I had just begun a yearlong training program as a medical technologist (MT ASCP.) Abington served a large upper class suburban area north of Philly. John Eiman, a prepossessing, no-nonsense physician, ran the first rate clinical and pathologic lab. On the first day of our training, he gazed at our little group of eight-brand-new-white-uniform-clad students. After his welcome and opening remarks, he grew quite serious. I squirmed in my seat and wondered what he was about to say. Was he going to outline the dire consequences if our work wasn't up to snuff?

"I want you all to remember something and remember it well." He pointed his finger at each one of us in turn. "Everyone who passes through the doors of this hospital, whether patients or families – even the staff at times – are dys-eased. Do you know what that means?" We nodded. "Good. These people are anxious, apprehensive, and in pain. They are dealing with chronic or acute illnesses. Some of them are receiving terrifying news. I want you to be aware that they are dys-eased every day you are here and I expect you to treat everyone, everyone with deference and great care." I was impressed with his insight and I held onto his wise counsel not only over the course of my training year, but throughout the many years of my medical career as well.

I threw myself into the med tech training. At last I was learning biology, physiology and biochemistry – no longer esoteric, but relevant to saving lives. I eagerly soaked up clinical chemistry, microbiology, hematology, blood bank technology, and rheumatologic lab studies. I delighted that Lee and I now had a common medical language. I desperately wanted his admiration and acceptance. I felt proud anytime I could upstage his medical knowledge with some lab medicine trivia. Finally, I thought, I am on my way to being an equal partner. But even though I passed the MT ASCP certification exam with ease, Lee still didn't treat me with any more deference. I was determined to win his approval and I began to entertain dreams of becoming a physician myself. Surely if I succeeded in becoming a doctor, Lee would have to treat me as an equal.

For the remainder of the time Lee was stationed in Pennsylvania, I worked at a small community hospital in nearby Ambler. I kept in touch with my med tech friends and made new friends at my workplace. I warmed to big, burly Charlie, the lab clinical director. I loved his bear hugs and admired him for how tenderly he talked of his wife and family. I envied Donna, the senior lab tech, because she had met Paul Newman through her husband who drove in the same racing car league as the actor. I was still holding onto a wisp of a dream, that of becoming an actress.

I settled into the lab work life, proud to contribute financially to our marriage for the first time. But my additional salary wasn't enough for Lee. He craved even more economic security and began to moonlight in emergency rooms. He signed on with two hospital emergency rooms to cover weekend shifts, working forty-eight hours at a stretch – this in addition to his full time military duties. He was chronically tired.

"Lee, I'm worried that you are running yourself into the ground with these marathon weekend ER shifts." I handed him a steaming cup of honey-lemon tea and sat at his bedside. He broke into a fit of coughing and blew his nose into a towel. I persisted: "I'm working fulltime now as well. I'm contributing financially so why can't you relax and spend more time at home? I miss you," I said, touching his arm. Lee moved away from me, took a sip of the tea and stared at me.

"I have to make up for lost financial opportunity costs on my medical education, and your lack of earning any income." In between bouts of coughing, he spluttered, "Damn it Liz, my high school and college classmates are six years ahead of me in earnings. I've got to catch up. I don't want to work forever as a doctor. I plan to retire from medicine in ten years, you know. Mark my words!"

"But look at you, Lee! You're exhausted. You're sick. How can you keep this up?" I urged, raising my arms in frustration. Lee took another sip. I softened. "You're never around and I need you."

"You have my fat paychecks, Liz." He smirked. "Christ, can't you see I'm building a financial base for both of us?"

"But at what cost?" I cried. "Your work at the base will suffer and then where will you be?"

"Hell, that clinic is like having R and R compared to the ball busting ER shifts," he boasted. "I can treat snotty noses and backaches with my eyes closed."

I tried one last tactic: "Harry only moonlights once every couple of months. Why can't you be like him?" I whined.

"Quit being a harpy," he snapped back. "I need to sleep." He handed back the mug and turned to the wall. I walked out, frustrated and unheard. I had made no headway.

I was yet again unable to influence Lee. He had yet again refused to listen to me, refused to lighten his schedule in any way. He finally had a taste of financial control in his life and had the satisfaction of more money rolling in than he'd ever had in his life. He was loath to give up the bounty for any reason. He tolerated the long hours and reveled in the exhaustion and adrenaline rushes of ER work. He wore fatigue like a merit badge. And all of this was more important to him than to me. I spent long hours alone and unsupported. My needs for a close partnership remained unmet. After our latest argument, Lee stayed away from home even more.

§

Despite Lee's horrendous work schedule, we did manage to take some lovely trips, again mostly coordinated with, and inspired by friends. With Harry and Rose, we ventured to Vermont for a wonderful week of skiing at Mad River

Glen where I schussed down intermediate slopes, making sort of proficient Stem Christie turns.

Lee and I drove to New York City a couple of times. We stayed with some of his high school and medical school friends. We also visited Hungarian friends of my parents in Mount Vernon. On another trip, Lee invited his mother for a tour to see the gorgeous fall colors in the northeast. Autumn was Fern's favorite season and the foliage hues matched her rusty, red hair and fair complexion. We met her at the airport. "Oh, Lee, you are so good to invite me." She smiled, hugged us both and then smoothed her stylish camel suit. "I hope I brought the right clothes for this trip."

"You look lovely," I said.

"You'll be fine, Mom." Lee looked back as he headed to baggage claim. "I have a great trip planned. It'll be the best, you'll see."

Fern settled in with pleasure, riding in the front seat alongside her son, soaking up his doting attention, oohing at the fall colors and aahing at the picturesque towns in the Berkshires. I was glad she was enjoying her visit, her first ever to the East Coast. We stayed in quaint inns and B and Bs that we'd read about in the newly published *Country Inns and Back Roads* tour book.

"Oh, my . . . this is so darling," my mother-in-law whispered as we hauled her luggage into the antique filled bedroom. "Look at the matching drapes and bedspread . . . oh, and the cute dried flower wreath over the bed. It's perfect, don't you think?" She clapped her hands. "Oh, Lee, you are so good to me."

I smiled. She was like a little girl, but I also felt a little resentful. Lee didn't splurge nearly as much with fancy inns when it was just the two of us. Nevertheless, I soaked up the extravagances when we travelled with others and I felt happy to see Lee more relaxed. His boyish enthusiasm exploring new areas helped to ease my discontent.

Getting away on trips helped distract Lee from the military stresses and helped to keep our relationship on a – sort of – even keel. The moonlighting ER jobs were other ways that helped him escape the constraints of the military. I supported his outside work in this regard, for Lee did not do well with regimentation and rebelled against blind authority, just as he had done with his father. I worried when I saw him bristle over the military's "asinine rules," fearing that he would act out, be reprimanded or – even worse – get court-martialed.

The early seventies saw the height of the Viet Nam War, and Lee opposed it. I admired him for helping several war-torn sailors get medical discharges. Though post-traumatic stress disorder – PTSD – was yet an unrecognized clinical entity, several of these sailors were badly scarred from the craziness of war, and Lee was passionate in his drive to help them get out from under the cogs of the military machine. His advocacy for these psychologically and physically damaged personnel, along with his disregard for military regimentation made him some enemies, among them his commanding officer.

It didn't help that Lee flaunted many of the military rules. He was less than attentive when it came to spit shining his shoes or getting the clinic spruced up for inspections. But I became most worried when he bought into the military underground "cumshaw" system, absconding with some surplus materials. "Everybody does it," was his response to my growing concerns of the possible repercussions of his outspokenness and his edgy and flagrant behaviors. But Lee, too, became anxious and lost his bravado when some goods on the base were reported missing. "I'm in deep shit trouble, Liz. They're onto some of the stuff that we've taken. This could be bad, really bad." He trembled. I'd not ever seen Lee so scared. He quickly and secretly replaced the items he had pilfered. He and I were both relieved and thankful that, in the end, he managed to get himself honorably discharged after his tour of duty in the spring of 1973.

CHAPTER 14 – TROUBLE IN PARADISE

Me in front of our Salem rental, displaying fifty pounds of strawberries that I had picked. I froze and made jam out of the lot.

"We're in the Northwest, Lee, back where you want to be," I exclaimed as we drove north towards Salem, Oregon, for another emergency room position interview.

"Yeah, but it's not the same as Seattle. Seattle has evergreen trees. This is hick farm country," Lee griped. I changed the subject, hoping to get him in a better mood.

"The ER interview in Albany went pretty well, don't you think?"

"It did. That doc sure gave us the VIP treatment – took us out to that fancy lunch, drove us around and all, but it's a small ER. They don't see many patients and I'd be bored stiff. I need a higher volume trauma center. I need to build my resume."

"How does this Salem ER job look for volume?" I asked, eager to keep him flushing out his desires and keeping him upbeat about the upcoming interview.

"Their volume is much higher and the department chief I spoke to on the phone said it was the designated trauma center for the whole Willamette Valley." He was conceding grudgingly and glanced out the side window, away from me.

"Well, that sounds great. It's what you want, right?" I smiled at him.

"You don't get it, Liz." He looked at me with disdain. "I want to be in Seattle, not in this hick town. But there's nothing available in Seattle. It's such a damn desirable place to live that all the ER jobs have been snapped up. I missed out on that dream and I'll never ever get to work there," he sulked. I wasn't about to give up.

"If you feel so strongly about Seattle, why don't we go up there and you can work piecemeal and wait for a good job to open up."

"No way!" He gave me a long dirty look. I feared he'd run off the road and motioned for him to look straight ahead. "I have to keep working, Liz. I have to take a job right now. I can't wait around looking for the ideal job to open up in the ideal location. I'm not a dreamer like you. Besides, I have a bunch of catching up to do with my classmates who have been in the work force six years longer than I have. Look at Rick– he owns a house in Bellevue and has two kids already. I'm way behind with my education and starting a family – let alone the fact that you with your education needs are a liability as well."

I sank into the passenger seat. "I guess you're right about that."

"Damn right I am," he exploded. "You have no idea what you're talking about – waiting for a job to show up. Hah! Show's how naïve and uneducated you are about economics." I turned and looked out the side window, musing after this – Lee's latest and now almost predictable – tirade.

The cultivated fields and orchards were green and gorgeously luxuriant in the early summer. I felt warm all over to see this agricultural bounty. The Cascade foothills provided a lovely backdrop to frame the scene. How could Lee not warm to such a beautiful landscape? As we were nearing Salem, clusters of evergreen trees popped up here and there.

"Look, Lee, there are evergreen trees here too. That's like Seattle, right?" I was excited.

"There's only a few of 'em. It's just not the same. You don't get it, Liz, and they don't have Puget Sound here. They don't have all the water." He glowered.

"They have the Willamette River," I ventured timidly.

"Quit trying to get me to like this place, Liz. There's no way I'll like where I live until I'm back in Seattle. There's nothing like Seattle."

I let out a deep breath. "I only hope you don't let on to your feelings in the interview, Lee. I imagine that the people here really like where they live. It is gorgeous country after all."

"I'm not stupid, Liz. I know how to butter people up. Just get out of my face. You don't know anything." I cringed at his put-down.

I looked out the window again, hoping he would be able to butter up the docs in the Salem emergency department. I also hoped he could learn to love where we ended up living – even if it wasn't his beloved Seattle. I had such great hopes for our life together now that he was out from under the regimentation of the military. I thought that at last we could really begin to enjoy a happy marriage: Lee would get a great job; I'd finish college and begin to contribute financially; we'd be back in the Northwest where he always wanted to settle. Oh, how I wanted that wonderful relationship. I dreamed of that Eden, that paradise.

When Lee set about looking for an emergency room position in 1973, these jobs were hard to come by. Emergency medicine was a fledgling specialty and board exams in the field were years away from being established. Lee's extensive ER experience in Pennsylvania did give him a marketing edge and he did land the job in Salem, Oregon. He joined three partners, tried and true Oregonian outdoorsmen, fishermen and huntsmen, who loved where they lived. But for Lee, nothing could compare to the Puget Sound region and he lost no time boasting about Seattle and bashing Oregon. Needless to say he was not welcomed with open arms by either his partners or the nursing staff, for they had imprinted on their luxuriant farming and outdoor paradise. My professional aspirations didn't help either, for I didn't fit into the mold of the stay-at-home wife with children. We were definitely the odd couple and try as I might to get Lee to soften his views and silence his displeasure at having landed – for him – a poor, second best Northwest locale, I was yet again the young and inexperienced spouse, unworthy to give him counsel. My frustration grew as I imagined the wrecks that might well be looming ahead of us.

§

I loved the luscious beauty of the fertile farmlands of Oregon and the bounty of fruits and vegetables that it yielded. I adopted the local lifestyle with zeal. I drove to farms and picked boxes of fruits and vegetables. I used the recipes from the pamphlets that the Oregon State University Farm Program put out to can and freeze berries, peaches, peas and green beans. One spring morning, I u-picked fifty pounds of strawberries and spent the rest of the afternoon and evening freezing whole berries and sugar packed berries and making my very favorite – freezer strawberry jam. Not all of my food preparations turned out well – my attempt to make pickles proved an inedible, rancid disaster.

Learning about the farming culture was not only fun, it was a way to connect with my husband and the people he worked with. Lee enjoyed finding out about the best local farms for produce – he loved a good deal after all – but along with these half-hearted attempts to fit in, he continued to boast about how much better Seattle was.

One of my greatest delights in living in Oregon was that we lived only an hour away from the ocean. Lee and I sometimes drove to the beach to take in the sunset. I loved gazing at the pounding waves, listening to their call and their counsel. As I walked and dipped my toes into the sand and salty brine, my heart settled. I was with "Mother Ocean" and my irritations at myself and with Lee slowly melted away. My feelings of self-doubt and inferiority lessened their grip around my chest. For a few moments, I could forget that I wasn't a good enough wife. I could let go of Lee's criticisms that echoed in my head: you are immature; you are not contributing financially. I could release the anger I held towards Lee and myself. I felt the strain on my face melt in the ocean breeze and I'd break into a smile. Grabbing a bowl of delicious clam chowder at the nearby rustic Mo's cafe was a lovely end to our time by the ocean. These moments of being together with Lee proved to be precious connections that gave me hope.

§

During our first year in Oregon, I completed requirements for a BS in Zoology at Oregon State in Corvallis. Lee and I rented a dilapidated bungalow a block from campus and he commuted forty miles to his work in Salem. After my graduation, we moved to a more stylish 1930's rental house close to Lee's workplace. While we were living in Salem, the retail business that Lee's parents owned in California failed. His father, Gus, had devoted his working life to retail, climbing up the ranks of the five-and-dime Kress Company. When he was forced into early retirement after managing their Seattle store for more than ten years, he invested in a Rasco Tempo store, a Kmart-type business in Sacramento. Though quite brilliant, Gus was a deeply troubled man who drank to cover up his disappointments and sorrows.

I helped Lee's parents drive their moving truck up from California and my in-laws stayed with us for several weeks in our tiny one-bedroom Salem rental. My father-in-law had an outward *belle indifference* attitude, oiled by gin, that covered the anguish and bitter disappointment he felt as a businessman and a provider.

"I'm off to bed," Gus slurred as he slapped his mystery paperback on the side table and drew himself up from the couch. His blue eyes were glazed over, his jowls were slack and red, his usually slicked-back, thin strands of hair now a jumbled mess, his shirttail hanging over his paunch. He lurched and stumbled. Fern grabbed for his arm but he shoved it away. "Get the hell away, Fern. I'm fine." Fern shot an anguished glance at me. I looked away, trying to ignore what was happening. I didn't know how to deal with it.

The next evening, when Lee arrived home after a grueling work shift, Gus was tottering about bleary eyed. "Christ Dad, you can't even stand up straight. You're plastered!" My husband began to throw open kitchen cabinet doors and drawers, his face flushed, his mouth pursed in a tense, thin line. "Where the hell are you hiding the booze?"

"None of your goddamn business, Lee," he muttered, his words smeared.

"Damn right it's my business, you're in my house and I'm fuckin' sick of your boozing."

"Oh, Lee, please don't." Fern broke down in tears, wringing her hands.

"He's a goddamn alcoholic, Mom. He's a drunk and I'm sick of it . . . and I'm sick of you covering for him." Gus attempted to stalk off, but managed only to weave from side to side. Fern hovered right behind. Lee slapped his hand on the table. "Fuck-in-a!" I startled, terrified.

From then on Gus only drank hard on the days Lee worked, but most every evening, he drank furtively to the point of numbed out inebriation. I steered clear of him. I had no idea how to deal with a mean drunk and he scared me. Besides, my relationship with Gus had never gone past sharing superficial pleasantries.

Despite his drinking, Gus and Fern initially seemed on a sort of even keel. Every morning, when more sober, he and Fern strolled from our rental to the

Dunkin Donut shop down the hill. There they sipped coffee, dipping a donut while they read the newspaper and engaged in light, superficial conversation with the locals.

One evening, Lee confided in me after his parents had gone to bed. "I'm thinking Mom and Dad should live with us," he said. "They've practically no money and Dad's in a bad way. He's going to drink himself to death if I'm not around." I took his hand. "We can do that, Lee. Of course we can. I want to help them any way I can."

Though I felt rather aloof from Gus, I had become fond of my mother-in-law. It was the little things I noticed, like how often she took time to write letters. "You're good to correspond with people," I said.

Fern smiled as she licked the pink envelope flap and added her latest letter to a small pile. "I think it's important to keep up with friends. This letter is to Ruth. She and I grew up in Fairview, you know. Her family was well off, and we were dirt poor." She frowned and sighed, and then continued. "But she's been my friend despite that, and we've stayed in touch through the years. What about you, Liz? Do you write to your Australian friends?"

"Not very much." I turned away, pretending to pick lint off my jeans. I felt guilty.

"Well, do it. You'll be glad you did." She got up and headed to the kitchen. "I'm ready for a cup of coffee. My Mormon friends would be upset to hear me say that, but I enjoy my vice." Her hazel eyes twinkled. "Will you join me?"

Fern, ever one to cling to etiquette, carefully folded paper napkins and set mugs and teaspoons out while I brewed a pot in the kitchen. As we sat and sipped, Fern looked around the tiny living area. "You know, if you lowered those pictures, they would look a lot better."

"I don't know anything about decorating," I said, embarrassed, clasping my mug and gazing about the willy-nilly spaced pieces on the wall.

Fern had a faraway look in her eye. "If I'd had the chance, I would've loved to have become an interior decorator." She shrugged and smiled at me. "I can show you a little – if you want."

I looked up at her. "Would you, really?"

She nodded. "Let's get to work. Do you have a hammer, pencil, and a tape measure?"

My mother-in-law carefully measured and grouped plaques of New Orleans recipes on the wall over the dining room table. While in Pensacola, I had joined some navy wives in a decoupage project, and had mounted and brushed layer after layer of shellac over colorfully illustrated recipes of eggs Sardou, bananas Foster, shrimp Creole, and oysters Rockefeller.

She then positioned the large photo of me at age three sitting accordion style with Paul, Irene and Geza, and nestled it just a few inches above the old red velvet couch.

"Wow, this looks great!" I was amazed to see how much better the room appeared, how "decorated" my house had become, but Fern wasn't finished. She took in the room, one arm crossed on her plump stomach, her other propped on top with her hand alongside her cheek. "You know, if you angled those chairs around the couch, you'd have a cozier seating area." She began to shove.

"Let me do it, Mom." I pushed and turned the chairs, just as she directed. When she was satisfied, we stopped to admire our work.

"You're really good at this, Mom. Thank you so much."

"Oh, I'm not very good at this at all," she said, but she was beaming.

I looked up to my mother-in-law and clung to her advice. I soon developed a closer relationship with her than I'd ever felt with my own mother. I finally had a maternal figure who was teaching me mother/daughter things. And it felt wonderful.

Fern was instrumental in helping Lee and I purchase our first home in Oregon. She came along when I toured for-sale houses with agents and advised me step by step. She had purchased several homes over the years and I eagerly soaked up her expertise. The home we ended up buying was brand new. Fern helped me select the finishing decorating touches: paint color, wallpaper, carpet, lighting and plumbing fixtures. My mother-in-law was in her element and loved to live vicariously by assisting me. She had never purchased a brand new home and she would have loved the experience of decorating a home from scratch. She was a decorator at heart, had great fashion sense and I appreciated her help.

We purchased a large enough home for Lee's parents to live with us, but that was not to be. As the weeks passed, Gus's despair grew. He had no work and no purpose and his ego was bruised to be dependent on his son's hospitality. He drank more and more.

One day, Gus disappeared. Fern leaped at Lee when he came home from work. I had just walked in from running errands.

"Your dad blew up again. He's been gone for hours," she wailed.

"Jesus H Christ," Lee fumed. I shivered. "I'll go look for him. You stay here in case the asshole comes back."

"Oh, Lee, don't be that way," Fern cried.

"You know I'm right, Mom. Dad is a drunken asshole." Fern sank into the couch and I sat beside her, putting my arm around her trembling shoulder. Lee grabbed his keys and bound out, slamming the door.

"I'm so sorry, Liz." Fern moaned. "You have been so good to us. You don't deserve to go through all this."

"It's Okay, Mom. I'm family. I just hope Dad's all right."

We settled into an uneasy, seemingly interminable wait, fixing coffee, trying to make small talk. A couple of hours later, the phone rang out. I jumped.

"Well, I drove around and finally found him holed up in a motel." Lee's voice was pressured and shrill on the speakerphone. "He was drunk, almost senseless, splayed out on the bed. He had a loaded gun by his side for Christ's sake!"

"Oh my God!" Fern screamed, collapsing on the chair.

"It's Okay now, Mom. I took the damn gun away and made him promise he wouldn't try anything like this again. I'm bringing the sod home."

A silent pall descended on our household. I was new to the drunken family dramas and I, too, was shocked into silence. Gus mostly kept to himself and remained sober enough that Lee couldn't call him out on any backsliding. The détente between them was tenuous at best and the loaded atmosphere in the house was uncomfortable.

Soon after Gus's suicide attempt, Lee's parents turned down our offer to live with them. Even though their finances were tenuous, they chose a more independent life and returned to Seattle. Gus had little in the way of retirement income despite his thirty years with Kress Company. He resented being forced into such a meager retirement. He began drawing on Social Security and this added to his rancor. My in-laws rented a small apartment in downtown Bellevue, across the street from the shopping mall. There, Fern began work at the Frederick & Nelson department store as a salesperson in housewares, where she braved the hard floors that wreaked havoc on her bunions and her lumbar arthritis. Gus mostly drank, but managed to pull some night shifts at the 7-Eleven a few blocks away on Main Street. When he had to serve old acquaintances that dropped in to buy sundries, it became clear to Gus just how far his status had plummeted from when he had managed and owned large retail stores.

While my in-laws were living in their own hell, Lee and I settled into our brand-new, 2,600 square feel, split level home in a showy suburb of Portland and I embarked on an odyssey into the man's world of medicine.

CHAPTER 15 – IT'S A MAN'S WORLD

The Deans donning the physician's cape at my medical school graduation 1979.

My journey to get accepted into medical school began while we were still living in Corvallis and I was attending Oregon State University.

I quipped as I luxuriated in the rusty claw-foot bathtub of our dilapidated bungalow. "Ain't this the fanciest house you've ever seen?"

Lee cracked up and almost fell off his perch on the edge of the tub. I continued between guffaws: "Here we have this elegant lumpy, carved up linoleum floor – sloping, mind you – and that decorative touch is hard to find these days. And don't forget these mildew-speckled bathroom walls – and there's no extra cost for the op art." I chuckled.

"Wasn't it hilarious to see my partner's reaction when he and his wife came to dinner?" Lee slapped his knee. "Their eyes grew wide and their smiles froze on their faces – and oh, the dead silence."

"I guess we made an impression," I mused. "They deemed our tiny rental shack completely unsuitable for the status of a physician. I don't think it helped your situation at work, I fear."

"Hell, they can't do anything to me. There's no way they can get me to leave if I don't want to."

That, I wasn't so sure of, but I didn't say anything. I sank lower into the bath water.

Our conversation shifted. "Well, they didn't like the idea of you wanting a career either," Lee said. "You're not the sweet, supportive wife type that tends the home and the kids."

"No, I guess I'm not . . . at least not yet."

Lee brushed absently at imaginary lint on his jeans "You've almost graduated and you've aced your last year with a straight four point. You could do whatever you wanted. What's your thinking about med school?"

The possibility of my attending medical school was not a new consideration for us. We had bandied the idea about for some months. I took a deep breath.

"I would like to go for it. What do you think?"

"It's a hell of a grind and you have to be up for it. You're certainly smart enough – smarter than me, in fact."

"That's not true," I shot back. "I think you are way smart."

"No, I know I'm not. Listen, Liz. If you want to do this, I think you should go for it. Take the MCATs, and apply. I'm not one for fitting into any goddamn social mold and I sure as hell don't give a rat's ass what my partners think."

"You mean it, Lee?" I looked into his eyes, wanting to know what he really thought.

"Go for it!" he replied but he didn't hold my gaze, got up, and walked away.

The intoxicating pressure of my desire bubbled in my belly and rose to my head. I became giddy, chuckled, and splashed around the tub grinning like a fool. A crazy, mindless joy overtook me and I resolved to do whatever it took to get accepted into those hallowed medical halls. And I had Lee's permission.

§

There were multiple, complex reasons for my wanting to go into medicine, some of them unconscious at the time of my bathtub resolve. Though I had trained as a medical technologist and loved the exposure to pathophysiology, lab diagnoses, and hands-on patient care, I found the med tech experience isolating, repetitive, and somewhat boring. As in my drama gig as an undergraduate at Seattle Community College, I coveted the leading role – this time that of the physician. Bit parts, relegated to supporting roles in a clinical or research lab were not for me.

Medicine attracted me because it was an established discipline. It's curriculum and expectations were clear, albeit rigorous, arduous, and fraught with challenging milestones and hazardous rites of passage. I knew some of the hardships imposed by the profession. As a new bride, I had witnessed Lee's exhaustion as an intern. He took call every third night and slogged through grueling thirty-six hour shifts. As newlyweds we hungered for each other's company, so on occasion, he would – in an eloquent cloak and dagger routine – secret me into his call room overnight. We hoped to share some amorous moments, but he rarely made it back to the room from his ward duties.

Despite the hardships, I embraced the daunting training steps: the first two years of basic sciences, last two years of clinical clerkships, the ball-busting – chauvinist pun intended – internship and residency, to finally emerge in a lucrative, rewarding and secure practice. The clarity of the training scope and its regimentation appealed to me. I didn't need to forge my own path. I merely had to follow and successfully complete each meted level. It wasn't until I left my medical practice thirty years later and embarked on the quicksand terrain of coaching, consulting and spiritual direction that I experienced fuzzy and porous work scope boundaries – and unpredictable cash flow. It was only then that I woke up to the scary new world of marketing and networking.

Another reason I wanted medicine was because I strongly desired the intimacy of relationships that the profession offered. I had had a hopeless crush on TV's Dr. Kildare when I was thirteen, not just the character's brilliance and actor's gorgeous looks but, more importantly and influentially, his caring and compassion. I yearned for these kinds of close relationships.

In the 1990s, I had the pleasure of meeting the actor, Richard Chamberlain, at a spiritual conference that he led with his friend David Spangler. Then in his sixties, Richard's handsome presence still made me blush. His warm baritone voice, even in quiet conversation, resonated across the open spaces of the retreat grounds and stirred my heart. Sitting next to him on a lunch break, I shared how his role as Dr. Kildare had influenced and inspired me to go into medicine. He acknowledged that medical school applications had indeed increased significantly after Dr. Kildare aired. Despite his awareness of this fact, Richard had no personal sense of his impact on viewers and was quite bewildered, humbled and touched by my story.

Another attraction to the field of medicine was that it gave me the opportunity to use my intellect. I had a good brain and I was prepared for the ultimate challenge of immersing myself in the expansive scope and complexity of medicine. I didn't want to let my mind go to mush.

Security was a determinant in my discernment process as well and it won out over my second passion – that of acting. I opted for professional status and income stability. I finally let go of my acting dream, turning in my drama mask in exchange for a stethoscope and a white coat. And that decision came with consequences: I squelched my creativity and dampened my inner fire – but only for a time.

Other drawbacks to a career in medicine loomed. Not only was I letting go of my acting aspirations, I had to postpone starting a family – for several years. Combining pregnancy and parenting with medical training was too daunting to consider. At the time, I felt the sacrifice of waiting to have kids a worthwhile compromise.

Finally, there was the women's lib factor in determining my resolve to enter medicine. The sixties and seventies – along with civil rights, Vietnam demonstrations, flower power, drugs, and free love – ushered in the bra burning women's libbers: Gloria Steinem and the like. The then popular poster of a woman pictured from behind in thigh high boots and a miniskirt astride a urinal symbolized the equality women yearned for – and began to demand. Lee supported women's lib. He encouraged me to pursue a career and to take advantage of the increasing opportunities the women's movement afforded. I appreciated his support. His paradoxical attitudes, however, confused and took me a long time to decipher and overcome. While he wanted me to be a women's libber, he consistently dismissed my opinions and rejected my counsel.

In the end, I wanted to become a physician so I could be Lee's equal, salvage the costs of my education, and provide a significant financial contribution. Entering his profession was a way to even the marital playing field. I longed to bridge the gap of what he perceived to be my inexperience and youthful naiveté. I desperately wanted a cooperative partnership and I was competitive enough to do whatever it took to create it.

§

I applied to the University of Oregon Medical School in 1974. I was not accepted. Undaunted and with encouragement from the school's director of admissions, I reapplied the following year. The gauntlet had been thrown and I resolved to do whatever it took to succeed. I expanded my application pool to several other medical schools and I received interviews at both Oregon and Tufts in Boston.

I flew to Boston, terrified to be travelling alone for the first time. I spent the night before my Tufts interview over the toilet, retching and with diarrhea. The next morning, I stepped off the bus and walked briskly past barbwire-topped, rusted chain fences that surrounded scruffy weeded concrete lots reeking of urine and sour garbage. Boarded up, lifeless cement hulks adorned with crude graffiti loomed above me. I was sweating despite the January cold. My breath caught and my queasy stomach lurched. My eyes darted left and right, straining, alert for any sudden movements. My heart pounded when I saw no one; it pounded just the same when people – mostly blacks – walked by; it pounded the whole time.

"What on earth made me think I was cut out for inner city life." I groaned inwardly. "Do I have the guts to withstand the grueling medical training? Do I have what it takes to care for down-and-out, indigent patients? I'm really scared. I don't think I can do this."

After the arduous solo flight, the night spent retching and the morning slum trek, I'd lost most of my confidence and nearly all my resolve, so when I received a warm welcome at Tufts, I was quite bewildered. The admissions committee members – unlike those at Oregon – were non-threatening, pleasant, and engaging. They treated me with respect as if I were already a colleague. The interview process went smoothly, and I received reassurance that I was a highly competitive applicant. I was most impressed with the school and I flew home encouraged.

Two weeks later, I received my acceptance letter from Tufts. At the same time, I received word that I was on the waiting list for Oregon. Armed with my Tufts success, I marched back to the director of admissions and pled my case.

"I am going to med school for sure. My preference, though, is to stay in Oregon where my husband is established in an ER job, and where I have in-state tuition." The director grinned at my persistence. "Hold on a sec and let me make a call." A minute later, he returned. "Dr. Bacon is on the admissions committee. I just talked to him and he's willing to see you right now."

I trotted up to Dr. Bacon's office and gulped nervously as I tapped on the door. A soft, mellow voice called out "Come on in, Elizabeth." Dr. Bacon was already up on his feet and reached out to shake my hand. A tall, slim man with twinkly eyes and a grey beard, he motioned me to take a seat.

"I hear you already have an offer from Tufts," he began. "I'm not surprised as you have really strong credentials. You have a broad background – I love that you grew up in Australia. My wife and I would love to go there sometime. What city did you live in?" And so began a pleasant conversation where he asked me about my Hungarian background – "Ah, Budapest, I loved that city" – and my musical experience – "wonderful, wonderful, you are a classical music buff. So am I." Then he leaned forward, placing his elbows on the desk, clasping his hands together, gazing at them as he did so. Then he looked up at me with a smile. "You know you have nothing to worry about."

"Really?" I blurted out.

"Really." he nodded his head. "I can almost guarantee your admission and I think you can expect a letter from us before too long."

My acceptance letter arrived later that week. I ripped open the envelope at the mailbox and whooped and hollered with joy as I tore back into the house to tell Lee.

§

My University of Oregon freshman medical school class consisted of one hundred and some odd students. Fifteen of us were women, part of the first jump in the percentage of entering females nationwide. In previous years, six percent or less of the entering classes were women. Those in our class were the pioneers of a new wave in medicine: the rise of the feminine into the tightly held masculine enclave. Ours was a slow but inexorable invasion. Our MCAT scores and grade points were significantly higher than our male peers. We had to fight harder to edge into the paternal, chauvinistic medical bastions. We paved the way for our younger sisters and I'm gratified to see that today, women comprise over fifty percent of med school admissions.

In September 1975, I joined my classmates in the main auditorium of the Basic Sciences Building atop the Markham Hill Health Sciences complex in Portland. I took in the daunting lecture hall with its multiple tiered seating, the huge counter that separated faculty from students, and movie theatre-sized screens behind them. I listened to the welcomes, the orientation speeches, the admonitions and myriad expectations, the reminders of the hallowed profession we were about to enter. We recited the venerable Hippocratic oath, vowing to "above all, do no harm."

As I relished the splendor and the expectancy of what lay ahead of me, I felt my heart swell and its warmth spread throughout my chest and belly. My body expanded beyond my skin and vibrated with joy. The auditorium appeared brighter, sharper. I sensed my surroundings smiling and a clear message came to me: "Welcome, you are meant to be here." I knew in my body that I had found my calling. A radiance of unequivocal assurance swept through me. This awareness sustained and consoled me throughout my medical career. It served to rekindle my resolve whenever I quavered and faltered during medical school, training, and practice.

§

As I settled into my freshman classes, Lee became more and more distant. He hated the formaldehyde smell that I came home with from anatomy class and I could hardly blame him. Despite using gloves and no matter how hard I scrubbed, I could not get rid of the horrible stink of the preserved cadaver I painstakingly dissected every day for a whole year. Lee didn't join in my enthusiasm for what I was learning. He wanted nothing to do with "reliving" med school. I was surprised and hurt. I had looked forward to sharing my newfound knowledge. I thought being part of his profession would bring us closer, would increase my worth in his eyes. But Lee stayed away, kept busy working long ER shifts and took on extra shifts to pad his growing financial nest egg. He wandered home from the Salem hospital on back roads, often showing up hours after I expected him home. When the roads turned icy, I worried that, exhausted from his long shift, he had slid off the road in a dazed state.

One time I met him at the door, furious, my eyes moist with misery. "You're three hours late. Why didn't you call me?"

"Quit harping, Liz, you're a royal pain in the ass." He pushed past me. I brushed away the tears that plopped onto my cheeks and stayed out of his way the rest of the day.

I finally came to realize that my worry didn't affect his safety one way or the other and I was able to let go of it. I also recognized that I didn't need to alienate him any more than I already had.

§

My social life centered on my classmates. We gathered at the tavern a block from the medical center every Friday and, like ardent sports fans, animated and on fire, gave a blow by blow of the latest exam, the latest foible of one prof or another. We laughed about the escapades of our classmates, one of whom – a technical climber— scaled the outside of the several-story Basic Sciences Building. We shared a camaraderie bound by our intense learning experience and our just as intense insecurities of ever becoming competent physicians.

Unlike other spouses and partners who often joined in our social activities, Lee didn't spend time with my med school friends. My classmates never met him and they jokingly came to refer to him as my "ghost husband." Their teasing was good-natured and underneath, I knew they were concerned about Lee's lack of participation in my life. I was touched. Their caring confirmed what I felt inside – that Lee didn't care enough for me.

§

My sophomore year we started pathophysiology, shifting from the normal physical anatomy, physiology, and histology to the study of diseases in all their gory detail. Along with pathophysiology, we embarked on our first clinical work: that of the physical exam. At first, we practiced the exam elements on each other. I was partnered with my friend Meg, a no-nonsense, short-cropped brunette with soft brown eyes and a quick tongue.

"Gad, you have earwax. I can't see your drum," she complained as she tugged on my earlobe, and poked the otoscope in.

"Ouch, ease up," I responded, trying to mask the embarrassment I felt about what I thought to be poor hygiene. Memories of my childhood came flooding back – my Hungarian friend's mother criticizing me for not washing my face. I flushed with embarrassment. Meg made nothing of the wax other than her frustration with not being able to see my eardrum and gratefully, I relaxed a little.

But the anxiety didn't stay away for long, for then I had to approach an actual patient at the Veterans Administration Hospital, clumsily performing my first *bona fide* exam. I entered the hospital room filled with trepidation and was met with the sickly sweet odor of sweat mixed with tobacco. The vet I was assigned to examine was a long time patient who was used to having awkward med students around. My tension eased a little when he grinned as I came into the room, and introduced myself. His teeth were yellowed and the arm he held out for me to shake had an anchor tattooed on it. He had a barrel chest that puffed out, but the rest of him was emaciated and barely made a dent in the bedclothes. His skin was wrinkled and sallow. Even though I was a newbie in the art of the clinical exam, I knew he was a really sick man.

"I have a heart murmur, make sure you listen to that… and my liver is large, you can easily feel that," he grinned, pulling me out of my empathetic reverie.

"Thanks for letting me know," I murmured, my hands shaking as I tapped my stethoscope to make sure it was turned to the diaphragm side so I could listen to his lungs. "Breathe in and out through your mouth, please," I said, my voice trembling.

"Sure thing, ma'am," he said with a chuckle. I felt even more nervous because the old tar was so obviously amused with my inexperience. I managed to get through the exam and reported my findings to my attending physician, relieved that I was able to do so without any major gaffes.

The more time I spent in the veterans' hospital the more overwhelmed I became. I struggled to take in the sight of all the old soldiers lined up in wheelchairs up and down the hospital halls. They looked so terribly ill: scrawny, sallow, bent over and short of breath. In addition to the physical and psychological injuries related to their wartime service, many of them battled end-stage lung disease and multi-organ failure from the ravages of heavy tobacco, drug, and alcohol addictions. In those days, patients were still allowed to smoke on the wards and I gagged in the fog of tobacco fumes that filled the hallways and hospital rooms. The stalwart vets even smoked beside their oxygen tanks. The nurses couldn't snatch their cigs away quickly enough, or often enough.

Though I joined in with my classmates, joking about the smoking soldiers and the many boneheaded mistakes we'd made in our first patient encounters, my lightness covered a deep disturbance within me. Mingled with the newness of the medical encounter and the tragic conditions of these vets – their loneliness and end-stage medical conditions – came an inexpressible abyss. I didn't know how to be with them, how to communicate with them. I didn't know how to deal with the pain and the illness and the death that surrounded me.

This realization, though acute for all of us students, became a cause for my audacious friend Meg. At first, she started mewing and then began to bellow at the faculty.

"We're not prepared to deal with the humanistic side of medicine," she announced at one of our physical exam lectures.

"That's not what we are covering in this class," the prof interjected. Meg refused to be quiet.

"Our whole training revolves around the *science* of treating illness. We learn technical skills, but no attention is paid to how to communicate caringly with patients."

"You are out of line, girl." The prof stepped around the huge counter and moved closer to us.

Meg raised her voice. "Professor, how are we to cope with the horror of illness and death? How are we to maintain our integrity and sanity in the midst of dealing with life threatening situations 24/7?" I joined in with the sporadic clapping that broke out amongst some of our classmates. I felt relief that Meg had articulated what I felt inside. At the same time I, like a turtle, drew back into a shell and trembled, for I lacked her courage.

"That's enough," the prof roared. Meg finally quieted down, but she had voiced what many of us felt.

Later that afternoon at our nearby tavern hangout, several of us sat around with a pitcher of beer.

"You blew that prof's gasket," Mike said, grinning as he took a swig of his beer, his blonde hair sticking up, his blue eyes flashing with mischief.

"No duh." Meg made a face and thumped Mike on the arm.

"I'm glad you spoke up," I said. "You voiced what I was feeling, for sure." I sank down a little and said to myself, *and what you were too chicken to say out loud back there in the classroom.*

"You're making a mountain out of a molehill," Mike said. "Medicine isn't that touchy-feely. It's a science and you just do your job."

"I don't agree." Meg drew her chair in closer. "I did a physical exam last week on a vet who has liver cancer and is dying. His daughter was freakin' out. I had no idea how to deal with the situation. All I could do was act like a robot in front of them." She looked away. "Afterwards, I broke down in the janitor closet."

"You just gotta be tough as a doc," Mike said, taking another swig, staring into space. "You can't react emotionally. You just hafta take it." He shuffled in his chair and turned back to us with a lopsided grin.

"No way." Meg leaned over the table. "I don't want to be a robot. I want to feel. I want to have compassion and be prepared – as much as you can be prepared – to handle tough situations. I've seen too many asinine docs as a med tech, docs who have turned a cold shoulder to patients that were begging for understanding." Meg's face was red and her knuckles white as she grasped her glass stein.

"Meg has a point there," Jeff said. His tall lanky figure was sprawled out on a beat-up Boling chair that seemed too small for him. "I had a cold fish of a doc treat my mom when she was hospitalized with pneumonia. I could have kicked him for how he put her down, not letting her talk, insisting that he knew it all. He treated her like a lab rat." His eyes narrowed with the pain of remembering.

"Yeah, that's the kinda stuff I mean." Meg gave Jeff a grateful smile. "I don't want to be like that."

"Well, that may be, but I still don't think we need shit therapy or encounter groups to talk about our feelings." Mike poured himself the last of the pitcher and took another huge swig.

"You won't have to worry, Mikey, since you want to go into anesthesiology or pathology – or radiology." Meg had an edge to her voice. "You can distance yourself. You won't have to deal with *feelings.*" Meg stared at him and refused to break eye contact.

Mike looked downcast into his beer. "Well, you may think I'm a jerk but the money's good in those specialties and I have huge student loans to repay."

Meg softened immediately. "I do, too . . . I'm sorry, Mike. I didn't mean to give you a hard – "

"No worries." Mike flung his arm out. "I'm cool." The alcohol was getting to him.

I was glad he lived a short walk up the hill and didn't have to drive.

"I'm maxed out, too," Jeff said. "And not just with loans. I'm going under with studying all this shit and all I can do is bottle the emotions."

"I'm having trouble as well. It's too much." I looked around at our stressed bunch. "I'm just glad Meg has begun to rattle some cages. I think getting some information and having a forum to voice our concerns will help us deal with all this crap."

Meg was persistent. She received pushback from most of the faculty as they were uncomfortable with her forthrightness and viewed her as a rabble-rouser. We found an ally in our quest for a humanistic medicine program in Dr. Labby, one of the faculty psychiatrists who informally counseled and advised many of the stressed students at the medical complex. He accepted the role of advisor for our fledgling program. Meg organized a bare-bones, brown-bag lunch lecture series that introduced such topics as how to cope with death and dying, how to deal with patients' sexual advances, and how to communicate difficult diagnoses. Ways to reach out for help with personal issues such as stress, addiction, and clinical mistakes were also covered topics. These lectures helped us to at least start to think about and work through some of the issues that we were beginning to face.

Meg paved the way and persevered. By our senior year, the humanistic program was on its way to becoming an integral part of the curriculum and Meg was honored with a special award for her groundbreaking and courageous work. She was a pioneer and a true champion. The male bastion of medicine was at last receiving a much-needed infusion of the feminine.

§

Even with the support of my med school friends and Meg's humanistic medicine program, I struggled with the stresses, not only of my medical training, but with my growing marital discord. The stresses soon manifested in my body. My sophomore year, I developed thyroid problems. On a routine physical, I was found to have an enlarged thyroid and a subsequent T4 blood test showed that my metabolic rate was, as my physician informed me, "hotter than a firecracker." I had no idea that my metabolism was so revved up. Only after I received the lab result did I notice that my pulse rate consistently thrummed over 100, and realized that some of my anxiety may have been due to my over-functioning thyroid gland. I wasn't tuned in to my body sensations at all. My somatic education wasn't to come for several years.

As part of the workup, I had a thyroid scan. I drank the radioactive iodine and, as instructed, lay down on the cold, hard scanning table. I was uncomfortable, scared, and anxious. I began to cry. The radiologist blurted out, "Oh, I know what's going on with you. Your hyper-emotionality is just a part of the thyrotoxic symptomatology." I recoiled at his insensitive bedside manner and cried even harder. Some of the tears may indeed have come from my hyperthyroid state, but I also felt terrified and alone. This was my first scrape with serious illness and I was hurt that Lee did not support me enough to accompany me to the scan.

I was diagnosed with Graves disease and referred to an endocrinologist, a thyroid specialist who happened to be conducting a study on thyrotoxicosis. He was measuring the disease's response to anti-thyroid medications as compared to radioactive iodine ablation, the treatment standard for hyperthyroidism. He hypothesized that the use of anti-thyroid medications resulted in a disease remission for an indefinite time and thereby the necessity of lifelong thyroid replacement – the uniform aftermath of ablation therapy— could be avoided. I was all for this option as I did not want any permanent complication, and I was fortunate to be one of the many successful participants in his study. My thyroid level returned to normal on medication and stayed that way for years after the medication was discontinued.

Soon after my thyroid disease came under control, I went through a relationship crisis of faith. Frustrated with our growing disharmony, I started thinking of leaving Lee. I confided in Dr. Labby, silver-haired mentor and confidant extraordinaire for several of us stressed out medical students. He listened to my angst with a calmness that I didn't feel. Later, I approached Lee who reacted with alarm and disbelief, peppered with a litany of expletives. He agreed to accompany me to a session with Dr. Labby who gently suggested, "Why don't you both just live with the issue for a while, see what might come of it."

As we drove away from our counseling session, an ominously charged static enveloped us. I cowered against the window of the passenger seat far away from Lee. He burst into the strained silence with, "Christ, Liz. What the hell is going on with you? You couldn't have chosen a worse time to go berserk. Jesus, I'm under scrutiny at work. I need to look for a new job and then you go and freak out – about us!"

"I'm so sorry, Lee. I had no idea that your work situation had soured so quickly." A wave of guilt jolted me.

"Yeah, sorry doesn't cut it, Liz. I now have to get my shit together for a job interview and on top of all that, I have your crap to deal with – your immaturity, your selfishness, your just plain craziness. For Christ's sake, Liz, get your fucking shit together!"

"I was just trying to be honest with you, Lee. I was trying to let you know what I was feeling." I hiccupped, tears streaming down my face.

"Feeling? Feeling?" He boomed, banging his hands on the steering wheel. "How do you *feel* about the fact that I'm supporting you through med school? How do *feel* that I bought a fancy house for you? How do you *feel* that I work my ass off for you?"

"I'm so sorry, Lee," I repeated, feeling lower than a lowly worm.

"Sorry doesn't cut it, Liz," he repeated.

"I'll do my best for you, Lee, I promise. I'll get over this. Give me time." I swiped at the tears and snot, my hands now soaked.

"Yeah, yeah. How I can trust you?"

"I promise," I repeated. I slouched down, devastated.

True to my self-loathing ways, I agreed with him. I had abandoned him at a time when he needed me. My husband's loose tongue and critical attitude had alienated his partners enough that his ER position in Salem was in jeopardy. He quickly responded by exploring alternate employment options in Seattle. Despite our relational crisis, Lee performed well in his Seattle interviews and he was offered a full time emergency department position. He could now be in the city he had longed to return to ever since his discharge from the navy.

§

When Lee moved to Seattle, I remained in our Portland area house. To help compensate for the extra costs of our now two living quarters, Lee had me rent an extra bedroom to a surgical intern, a Yale graduate.

"Come have a drink with me," Max would say with a swagger, his blue eyes gleaming. I was tempted, for he was a handsome, blond devil.

"I can't tonight. I have too much studying to do."

"What about tomorrow? Your husband's not around," he'd say, leaning against his doorframe, crossing his arms and ogling me from the bottom to the top.

"Sorry, unavailable," and I'd walk away with the slightest sashay to my hips, color rising to my cheeks. I felt flattered by his come-on, but remained loyal to my husband. Truth be told, I was still a prude, too hung up to explore any serious flirtation.

Our renter also completely charmed my mother, who stayed with me for a while, and who had a weakness for good-looking, blond men.

"Mrs. P, you look lovely today," he'd say as they met in the hall outside their rooms.

"Oh, you tease zees old lady." She'd flap her hand in dismissal but her face was shining with the compliment.

"No, I'm serious. You may have to lock your door tonight," he'd say with a grin and wink.

"You terreeble!" She'd grin back at him, and then pretend to stalk off.

I enjoyed watching their play, pleased to see how Anyu lapped up the compliments. With his lively bantering and frivolous flirting, our renter helped to brighten our days.

Anyu had come for an extended stay after her relationship with my brother had soured. She had been living in Paul's Seattle area home and had provoked him in a number of ways: she complained that he kept the house too cold; she threw out some of his cherished belongings; she hated his dog and repeatedly let him out of the yard, allowing him to roam around the neighborhood for hours. One time the dog didn't return and Paul couldn't find him anywhere. He was sickened by her repeated acting out, her meanness, and could no longer stand to be in the same house as her. He responded the only way he knew how: he accepted an engineering job on the East Coast, as far away from her as he could get. With no one left to pester, alone in the big house, my mother leapt at a more favorable option and accepted my invitation to visit. I felt sorry for her, and wanted to help her out.

For a few weeks, we got along and I wondered why Paul had had so much trouble with her. My mother began babysitting for the young family next door to me and they loved her "grandmotherly" ways. One weekend she stayed overnight at their place while the parents took a mini vacation. Just then, divorce papers from my father arrived in the mail.

My parents had struggled in their relationship for years, but their marriage really began to sour from the time we arrived in the United States and Apu left Anyu soon after. He then met another woman and settled into a new relationship that proved to be much more supportive for him. Apu asked for the divorce so he could remarry.

In the middle of the weekend, Anyu came by to get her mail, the two children in tow. She flew at me in the kitchen, leaving her charges hanging in the living room.

"You set this divorce up with your father!" She was seething. She waved the papers in front of my face, and then threw them on the floor.

"I did not." I squatted down to pick up the sheets, blanching when I saw the formal divorce document. "Please, Anyu, I had nothing to do with this."

"Of course you did." Anyu's voice was rising, and she began to spit out her words. "You are your daddy's girl. You and your father plot against me. Well, congratulations, this time you succeeded in ruining my life." She stalked out, motioned to the two terrified children. "Let's go."

"Anyu, calm down. You've scared the children."

"Don't talk to me. I'm done with you." She shooed them out of the house, slamming the front door.

My mother barricaded herself in the neighbor's house, as if it was a fort under attack. She refused to answer the phone and refused to open the door.

I was horrified that her outrageous behavior had extended beyond the two of us and I feared for the safety of the children she was caring for. At the very least, my mother's yelling and barricading had traumatized them. Fortunately, the weekend passed without further serious incident, but the children had already been exposed to the melodrama and they were shell-shocked. I felt horribly embarrassed when I had to relate to the parents what had happened. Their faces turned grim and they hardly said a word. In fact, they completely avoided me after that weekend – and I could hardly blame them.

My mother stayed angry, and I stayed aloof. We barely spoke. She soon moved out, responding to a newspaper ad for another babysitting job, this time as a live-in for a radiologist and his wife who wanted a nanny for their newborn. They adored my mother!

"They treat me like one of the family," she reported with pride. "They value my university education and my intelligence. They love me more and treat me much better than you, my own family," she pouted.

I recoiled with guilt. "Oh, Anyu, that's not true. We do love you."

"Oh no, you don't. You don't love me." She had dug her verbal dagger even deeper and I cringed even more.

My emotions flowed unchecked. I had such mixed feelings about my mother. I knew I loved her but I also didn't feel a lot of affection for her. She was hardly the approachable type, nor was she tenderhearted. Maybe my feelings toward her were more steeped in obligation than real love. Maybe Anyu was right. Maybe I didn't love her. My thinking fuzzed out as this realization dawned. My mother sensed my hesitation. She had gotten a rise out of me. "You don't love me," she said again. She smirked when she saw my cheeks flush, and my face droop. She knew her accusations had hit the mark – and I had allowed her to pull my strings. The rift between us widened with her every outburst. The only way I could cope was to stay away from her.

I wasn't the only one singled out with her criticism. She showered the same accusations onto my siblings, taking turns pitting one of us against the other. We talked amongst ourselves and agreed that Anyu behaved better with strangers than she did around us, that she remained on her best behavior in order to stay in their good graces. Her claws only came out with the family. We quipped that it was just another one of Anyu's crazy ways of acting out. Her meanness smarted and hurt terribly, though, for she was so adept at going for the jugular.

A few months later, Anyu moved to New York to work for Hungarian friends. He was a military academy colleague of my father's, and his wife a student of my mother's when she'd taught in Hungary. My mother stayed in their Westchester home and worked in their at-home rug and tapestry repair business. Three or four Hungarian ladies sewed and snipped on the rugs in the living room, gossiping and prattling about all things Hungarian, mostly reliving the past, the war, the step-down from the good old days. Here, too, my mother claimed she had found a "family" who took her in when her own children did not. She vowed she was being treated more kindly. My sibs and I couldn't win for losing. I felt relieved to have her farther away, yet guilty for feeling that way. I felt guilty that I wasn't doing more for her. I wasn't a good enough daughter.

§

Back in Seattle, Lee's parents were unhappy. Never one to talk about problems or feelings, Gus continued to lament his business failures and drowned his sorrows in booze. Arguments between he and Fern escalated. One day she left the apartment in a huff after yet another drunken uproar. She returned a couple of hours later, and found Gus splayed out on the bed, dead.

Lee called me in Portland. "Jesus H Christ, Liz, Dad blew his fucking brains out." With bitter staccato explosions, he continued his rant. "He was in a drunken stupor and he put the fucking gun to his mouth and pulled the fuckin' trigger." His voice was sharp but wet. I knew he'd been crying.

Blood rushed from my head. I felt faint and had to sit down. "Oh, no, Lee!"

"Mom found him in bed. She found him in bed, Liz, his fucking blood and brains sprayed all over the pillow and the wall. She's a mess, Liz. A complete fucking mess."

I reeled at his graphic description. "Lee, I'm so sorry."

"I'm glad he's gone. That fuckin' asshole. I hate him. Good riddance." He was sniffing now, his rage focused like a laser beam.

"Lee, you don't really mean that. Please, take it easy."

"I goddamn do mean it, Liz. He was a fuckin' asshole and I'm glad he's gone. He can't fuck with me anymore."

I couldn't get him to settle down.

A little later, as I was throwing a few things into a suitcase, my father called.

"Lee just called and I'm shocked. His language . . . his language was appalling. I've never heard swearing like that -- not even from the peasant enlisted boys in my battalion."

I was still shaking and emotionally numb from Lee's call, but with my father's disbelief and concern at Lee's harsh language, my husband's complete loss of control began to sink in. I got really scared.

"Apu, I think Lee's just reacting to the shock of what's happened." I tried to appease myself as well as my father.

My father's voice faltered. "How can a doctor behave like that? How can Lee be so disrespectful of his father?" I could tell Apu was beside himself.

"I don't know, Apu," was all I could say. I slumped down into a chair.

Lee's temper flares were not new to me, but this rampage had reached a new level. I feared he might lose it completely. He might not be able to function at work; he needed to stay composed and dispassionate in the ER, and I couldn't see him keeping his cool with how he was acting on the phone. I fretted the whole way up on my drive to Seattle.

Gus was the first close person in my life who had died, and I didn't know how to react or how to offer comfort. The next few days when family and friends gathered for the funeral, I mostly went around in a daze, on automatic. At the service, Gus's body was decked out for viewing, his face painted. That didn't seem right to me. Friends offered platitudes, euphemisms. To me it felt like a huge cover up, a blatant lie that hid the truth of a violent and gruesome act. Though I could understand the need to avoid re-traumatizing, I thought Gus's memorial a fake affair. It lacked authenticity. I felt conflicted and, as an in-law, didn't feel I could share my reservations or worries. Mine was a bit part, a supporting role in the whole affair. I stayed in the wings, my gut churning, but I held my discomfort and my opinions to myself.

Fern moved in with Lee. She remained distraught, unglued, and intermittently hysterical. Over the next several months, Lee supported her as she struggled with repeated nightmares and flashbacks. She never sought counseling. I returned to Portland to finish my sophomore year of med school, and began my clinical clerkships in my third year. Fortunately, I was able to spend some time in Seattle as Lee helped arrange for me to take some clerkships there. I completed an orthopedics rotation at the University of Washington Medical Center, clinical pediatrics at Group Health and urology at Virginia

Mason. We sold our lovely home in Lake Oswego.

I returned to Portland for a final clinical rotation in obstetrics and rented a room in the suburb of Beaverton. The dingy, cold basement had a concrete floor, smelled dank and had no kitchen access. I didn't even have a TV to keep me company and I felt like a prisoner in a desolate cage. It was the most god-awful living quarters of my life. Miserable and totally alone, I was distanced even from my classmates after my extended stay in Seattle. Many of them had also scattered far from the medical school, completing their specialty rotations throughout the state.

Not once did Lee visit me in Oregon. He had never liked it there, and was glad to leave it forever. I drove to Seattle the weekends I wasn't on call. I had reached a horrible low point: I was the one making every effort to see Lee; he was caught up in his new ER position; he was emotionally unavailable giving what little attention he could muster to his distraught mother.

§

I had a reprieve from the pall when Lee and I vacationed on the Hawaiian island of Kauai the spring of my senior year. Lee combined the vacation with the requisite tax break of attending a medical conference. We stayed in a condo right on the oceanfront in Poipu. As in my youth in Sydney, I again rejoiced in the sensuousness of the beach. I reveled in the sun, the trade winds rustling through the palm fronds, the rhythmic rumble of the surf, the smell of salt, and the sweet fragrance of the frangipanis. The sacred beach enveloped, nourished, and renewed my sore soul.

A longing for my youth returned in seeing the beaches and the flowers on Kauai. Beaches had been grounding resources, allies in an often lonely childhood, and I was lonely in my marriage too. My younger years seemed brighter in comparison as I recalled the happy summer days my father and I spent floating on our backs beyond the surf, savoring a rare moment of connection. I wasn't feeling connected to Lee. He spent a lot of time reading novels inside the condo – he inside – I outside in the sun. Separate. I invited him to join me. I wanted him to share the sensuousness of our surroundings. I teased him, I touched him. He gradually relaxed into island time and our relationship warmed.

Soon after, we conceived our son, Stephen.

CHAPTER 16 – WE'RE HAVING A BABY

Stephen, just one month old, and a somewhat weary mom.

My unplanned pregnancy was a couple of months along when I started my residency training. It wasn't the best timing at all, but I felt overjoyed to start a family and I was willing to do what it took to finish my internship year and also be a good mom.

Lee had often complained. "All my friends have kids that are already in school. I'm going to be a geriatric dad because of your career." At least now, he had less to gripe about.

I lucked out in landing a medicine internship at the Virginia Mason Hospital in Seattle. My physical separation from Lee was finally over. We were living in the same city again. I felt elated and excited to start a new life together. For the short term, Lee, I, and his mother moved into the University District rental house that he had recently purchased as an investment. The house was located next-door to the one my family had bought upon arriving to Seattle, the house that I had lived in when I met Lee – the boy next door – over a decade before.

"Look what I've done today!" Lee wielded a sledgehammer and smashed it into the dining room wall. A plume of dust puffed into the room adding to the already thick atmosphere. The acrid smoke filled my nostrils and stung my eyes. I sneezed and sniffed, wiping my itchy nose. I covered my nose and mouth with my lab coat.

"Looks good, Lee." I couldn't help smiling. My husband looked like a moving marble statue, enveloped in white powder from head to foot.

"I'm stripping all the lath and plaster off so we can rewire and re-plumb easily. I'm having a great time with the sledgehammer." He grinned, swinging the hammer with ease.

"Looks fun." I gingerly stepped over piles of plaster and thin slats of wood with nails spiking up that were littered across the floor. "And look! We have no need for doors," I said as I slid between two wall studs, barely making it through with my belly bulge.

"Yeah, this is fun," Lee added. "I love this stuff and you'll see, Liz, we'll have a great looking place and it'll be a great investment too. We can charge an arm and a leg once this place is fixed up." He always has to mention the money, I mused to myself, but I delighted in seeing him so thrilled. He was like a kid.

"Are the stairs safe?"

"Yeah, no problem. Mom's upstairs."

I plodded up and followed the welcoming aroma to the bathroom, my stomach growling with appreciation. "Hi, Mom, that smells really good." She was stirring Bolognese sauce in an electric fry pan perched on the sink and plugged into the bathroom wall socket. Water for spaghetti was boiling in a pan on top of the Coleman camp stove set on the chipped tile floor. The tiny window was open.

"Hi, Liz, dinner's almost ready. How are you feeling?"

"Pretty good," I said, feeling my growing belly. "The babe's moving around a little."

"I have the window open to let in some fresh air. I'm sure that plaster dust is not good to breathe. You must be careful with that baby and all."

"Thanks, Mom. That air was pretty thick downstairs for sure, but Lee is having a great time, isn't he?" I smiled.

"That Lee boy," Fern smiled back. "There no one like Lee. They threw away the mold when they made him," she said, repeating one of her favorite adages about him that she'd spout lovingly and with a little frustration.

"He's certainly plunged into this remodel with enthusiasm. It's all new to him and he's so fired up about it," I said. It didn't prove to be our last remodel and its novelty was soon to wear off.

§

We bought our second home soon after, a gracious home in the exclusive eastside neighborhood of Yarrow Point. We chose the Bellevue area because it had one of the best school districts in the region. Years before Lee had blossomed in the positive academic environment that the Bellevue schools had provided. We wanted that for our kids. The home had a mother-in-law apartment for Fern, who had lived with us since her husband's suicide. She needed us and – as it turned out – we also needed her to provide the childcare for our soon to be born son.

Fern's living quarters took up the whole daylight basement and that left us without a family room. We asked the home seller – who happened to also be a builder – to tack on a family room before we moved in. Lee insisted that the construction be done as quickly and as cheaply as possible. The builder resisted Lee's cost cutting ideas, but gave in to his persistent demands. The room didn't looked right; it never worked well for us, and the roof leaked from the get go. We learned the hard way that slipshod construction didn't pay.

We settled into our new home and I awaited motherhood with joy. I grew fatter by the week and hid my expanding belly by wearing looser and looser clothing to work. There, I used the excuse that my widening girth was because I couldn't resist the unlimited, free access to hospital food. By November, my front had ballooned out enough that I finally had to inform Maura, the residency program manager, that I was pregnant. The word spread quickly and stunned the residency administrators. I was the first ever intern or resident in the training program to become pregnant. Our group of interns distinguished themselves as the largest percentage of women ever accepted at Virginia Mason and with more women entering the medical field, it was inevitable that they would have to deal with a housestaff pregnancy at some point. To the medical center's credit, I was treated with respect and understanding. Their formal policy allowed for six weeks of pregnancy leave. I was lucky to stay active and healthy as my pregnancy progressed and I was able to continue my intern duties full time.

§

As the huge responsibility of bringing a child into the world dawned, I read baby books voraciously: Kaplan's *The First Twelve Months of Life*, Chilton Pearce's *Magical Child* among others. As I digested the child rearing practices they recommended, based on infant development research, I became more and more uneasy and uncomfortable. My body screamed with the truth of what I was reading. My nerves fired up and crackled, anxiety poured over me like a cold shower and one night I had to get up and pace around to diffuse the intensity. I headed to the new nursery, leaned over the crib and bawled.

I realized that what these books recommended was the exact opposite of how I was raised. For in my reading, I discovered for the first time that Anyu and Apu had fallen far short of healthy parenting practices. They held onto rigid ideas about what "good" childrearing was and touted them proudly and openly: "We had you kids on a schedule from the start . . . we fed you no more often than every four hours . . . we let you cry and didn't pick you up, so you were sleeping through the night in no time . . . we didn't spoil you by cuddling or coddling you . . . you were just fine all by yourselves . . . you were all such good babies." This attitude of "benign neglect" was by no means unique to my parents – and it was far from benign. Their generation accepted such austere childrearing practices as ideal, and growing up, so did I.

I had had no clue that my upbringing was unhealthy. I rarely got a spanking and there was no sexual abuse. Therefore, I had nothing obvious to point to, no red flag to alert me to the fact that the way my parents raised me may have affected my wellbeing. I believed that some highly personal flaw, a unique defect peculiar to only me, caused my lack of confidence and my unhappiness.

But now I realized that my father's belief – that military regimentation was the preferred way to raise children – contrasted starkly with published research. These studies, broad in scope, recommended spoiling babies with as much attention, cuddling, and play as parents could muster. They urged parents to respond to their baby's every whimper and demand. As I read these reports, I ached with the loss of not having experienced such cuddling and attention. I longed to fill the huge void, the deep need for affection that was never met as a child. The reports further stressed the near impossibility of spoiling a baby during the first year of life and how crucial the mother or primary caretaker's role was to be loving, affectionate and available to her baby. To provide this level of care, the mother needed to be aware and mature in her own right. And I wasn't there – not by a long shot.

It dawned on me that I needed to learn for myself what my parents had failed to teach me. If I wanted to bring up a halfway normal and happy child, I would first have to learn how to nurture myself, for then I would know how to nurture my babies. I needed to become a well-adjusted, happy person. My heart sank at the daunting undertaking ahead, but I vowed I would change and I would not do to my child what my parents had done to me.

I became even more motivated when I read about Patterns of Attachment research, which revealed how severe developmental problems resulted in babies who – like me – were left to cry, lacked physical contact, and who were so regimented. These included delays in milestones such as social engagement and learning and language development. Later in life difficulties such as poor self-esteem, anxiety, and depression were also common.

I became overwhelmed with a sense of dread and a sinking feeling in the pit of my stomach. I realized that my lack of confidence, anxiety, anger, and feelings of depression could have – at least partly – resulted from my upbringing. I became even more distraught when I learned that babies could pick up on and mirror the mother's sadness and anger. That meant that I could easily transfer my unhappiness to my soon-to-be-born baby. My heart sank. I had to do something. All this newfound knowledge made inherent sense to me. The truth of what I read, the validity of the attachment research resounded in my body and gave me no choice. In order to become a halfway decent mother, I had to work on myself.

I read and I planned. I tried to remain even-tempered and happy. I instructed my mother and mother-in-law on how I wanted my baby treated, for they were to be the caretakers after I returned to work to complete my internship. They were initially hesitant and doubted that I knew what I was doing – after all, they had raised many children and they had all turned out great, hadn't they? What was I doing coming up with new-fangled ideas that weren't "tried and true?"

Given how I was raised, I had real fears about my mother's ability to follow my instructions, but it helped some when she shared that it was my father who had laid down the law. It was he who had insisted that we babies be trained with military efficiency. She admitted that she had wanted to hug and hold us much more than him, but he wouldn't allow her to "spoil" us. If only she'd been strong enough to tell him to go to hell!

In the end, my medical training lent some gravitas to my recommendations and both my mother and mother-in-law agreed to carry out my wishes. I still worried about how they would actually handle my baby during my long work absences. I had no way to check up on them and had to trust that they would comply.

I might have considered the attachment studies to be new-fangled flash-in-the-pan fads, but the strong inner resonance convinced me of its core truth. My body wasn't lying. The truth sank in even more because, as a guinea-pig research participant of one and with lots of personal data to draw on, I had ample evidence of the damaging repercussions from a neglectful upbringing.

§

Not only did I want to be a good mother, I also wanted to be a model female intern. I wanted to do it all. As the first pregnant housestaff member, I endeavored to set an example: prove to everyone that I could not only cope with the strenuous every fourth night on call internship, I could do it all while pregnant – and with aplomb. I tried to become superwoman and super pregnant intern. I never asked for special treatment. I didn't take any time off for illness or discomfort. I remained reliable and robotic. As I did when growing up, I held my pain inside.

Late one night, I was called to the ER to admit a middle-aged woman with a history of advanced cancer. When I first went into the room, my heart revved and my face flushed: my patient was emaciated, ashen colored, and she was having great difficulty breathing. She looked to be on death's door! I stumbled about listening here, palpating there, gazing at the heart monitor, checking her labs, but nothing added up. I couldn't figure out what was causing her distress and I didn't know how to help her.

The nurse looked at me with concern, wanting direction. "Doctor, her breathing is getting more labored and her blood pressure is plummeting." The patient was indeed deteriorating before my eyes, becoming less responsive. Shaking and shivering, a wave of panic enveloped me. Confounded and overwhelmed, I paged the senior resident, asking for help. Even though I had woken her up, the resident's assessment was swift, her treatment immediate. The patient's heart couldn't pump effectively because of the pressure of the surrounding malignant fluid: cardiac tamponade. The resident jabbed a needle into the pericardium and withdrew some of the fluid. Almost immediately, the patient's heart and lung function improved. My heart sank and I broke out in a cold sweat. Nevertheless, I managed to help my resident stabilize the patient and get her up to the ICU. "Don't feel bad," she said as she headed down the hall. "This wasn't an easy diagnosis. We all miss stuff."

"Thanks," I muttered and headed for the elevator. Her kind words did nothing to appease my disgust. Once the doors closed, I choked back tears of shame and fear. I squeezed my eyes shut and balled my fists, sinking to the floor and I seethed. "You idiot! You damned idiot! You messed up. Boy, did you ever mess up. You're totally incompetent. You aren't the super-pregnant-intern you think you are. You're a miserable failure." I trudged to my call room, but lay awake, adrenalin razzed, for the rest of the night.

I didn't confide in Lee. I would have thought that I could have shared my feelings with my life partner. He was in the same profession after all. He knew exactly what I was going through because he had gone through it too. But Lee wasn't open to my sharing. He hadn't wanted to hear about my med school experiences and he continued to stay distant and detached when I became a resident. "I don't want to hear about your internship. You chose this ball busting profession so suck it up. You don't have to tell me about the demands. I know 'em all. I don't want to relive the training again so don't bug me. I'm working long hours, supporting you financially, putting up with your training and your hardly being around. Quit asking me for anything more."

And so I continued my internship alone, held my trials and pain inside, my nose to the grindstone.

§

In January, I rotated through the hospital cardiology service. On the 16th, I was to present a case on morning rounds. As I stepped into the shower in the early hours, my waters broke. I called my resident to report that I was in labor and that I wouldn't be coming in to work for a while. Later, he gave me grief for shirking my scheduled case presentation and leaving him to cover for me, but he meant it all in good jest.

Our son decided to arrive three and a half weeks before his due date. Lee and I had only attended the first childbirth preparation class and so we were ill prepared in the Lamaze breathing techniques. My contractions began soon after I arrived in labor and delivery and they were hard enough that I opted for an epidural. Stephen was born late that night.

I was over the moon, and basked on the hormonal high for days. My son was perfect and I fell instantly in love. Lee, a stunned and befuddled new dad, asked a friend what to get me on the occasion of our son's birth. Following her suggestion, he surprised me with a dozen gorgeous red roses. I was touched.

Our new little family trooped home to the delight of grandma and his Hungarian "Nagymama" (grandma in Hungarian). In preparation for their childcare duties, they observed how I cared for Stephen and I gave them last minute instructions. Once back at work, I made arrangements with the labor and delivery nurses to use the department's breast pump. I would sneak up during lunch breaks and nights on call to collect milk that the grandmothers later gave to Stephen. I often broke down and wept as I pumped. These were the only times – in private and alone – that I allowed myself to feel the anguish and pain of being separated from my baby. I otherwise held firm to my outer superwoman persona. I was the woman of iron who could do it all: have a baby, be an intern – and a darned good one at that.

§

Once I completed my internship, I took a year off to spend with Stephen. I was ecstatic to finally spend quality time with him and to be there for him once again 24/7. But a new conflict surfaced in our marriage.

One evening, after I had gotten Stephen settled, Lee announced, "It's time for you to start looking for a part time job – and you need to get your applications in for a residency next year." I slipped into bed next to him, taking a moment to smooth the soft, blue-striped covers.

"You know, Lee, I really want to take some time off to raise Stephen. It would be best for him." Lee shot out of bed and loomed over me.

"No way, Liz. I haven't paid for your education and put up with your lack of income for years, your not being around to have you quit on me now. What the hell are you thinking of?" he bellowed.

"Shh, you'll wake Stephen," I whispered. Lee began pacing the floor.

"You have to think of your career. It cost me too much for you to throw it all away now. Shit, don't you know that if you're away from medicine for even a year or two you're out of the loop? Advances move so quickly that there's no way for you to catch up."

"Well, I guess that's true."

"Damn right it's true. And if you're out for a time, no residency will even look at you. They want a hundred percent commitment. They'll see you as a half-assed professional – which you would be. You'll be completely unmarketable." I hung my head for I could see the truth of that as well. "No, no, not an option," he repeated as he took a firm stance in front of me. "You'll sign up for some shifts in a free standing clinic and that way, when you submit your application, they'll see that you are serious about your professional commitment . . . yes, that's what you'll do."

I sank down under the covers. I knew there was no chance for me to take as much time off as I wanted. I could see Lee's point, but I felt resentful and bitter. I felt completely trapped, like a hamster in a cage.

I found work at some freestanding clinics, euphemistically dubbed "doc-in-the-boxes." They were a new development in the world of instant-care, no-appointment-necessary corporate medicine. I worked shifts at various outlying clinics as the sole on-site physician. Having had only one year's clinical experience, I felt completely ill trained to handle the diverse and complex problems that patients filtered into the clinic with – everything from sprains to fractures, from colds to congestive heart failure. I did the best I could and spent a lot of time reading up on clinical issues, calling consultants and colleagues, and praying that I had provided appropriate care, which – by the grace of god – I had.

When Stephen was eighteen months old, I plunged into the last two years of a full time medicine residency program. Soon after my return to work, I experienced another personal crisis – a meltdown that led me to seek counseling with Father Jim.

CHAPTER 17 – LIVIN' ON A PRAYER

Coming home from the hospital with newborn Stephanie. Stephen, aged three, giving me a welcome hug.

"You might wonder what a priest is doing talking to you at a Marriage Encounter weekend – and rightly so!" Father Jim winked, his tall, thin body leaning towards us. We all smiled. I glanced at Lee. His lips were pursed. His arms and legs folded.

"Well, when I was asked to be a clerical advisor for Marriage Encounter, I was quite resistant. I considered myself to be an independent sort, a loner, a man who needed to focus only on God and not on human relationships. The image I flaunted inwardly was of myself as a cowboy, astride a horse, wearing a ten-gallon hat and chaps, cigarette in my hand. I saw myself as the 'Marlboro man.'" With that, he smoothed his wiry gray hair – what was left of it on the sides of his head – with a flourish. We all chuckled and I was relieved to see that Lee had at least broken into a smile. I relaxed a little.

Maybe this weekend was going to turn out after all. I was worried about our relationship and had asked Lee to join me for the Marriage Encounter workshop – not just to help us – but to benefit our young son. Lee had grudgingly agreed to tag along, but only as a concession to me.

"I needed no one," Father Jim continued. "I was happy riding through life alone. Then I met this crew." He smiled softly, turning to the couples that were leading the workshop. "And my barriers came tumbling down. The inherent nature of the program is to get closer to people. I struggled. I resisted. I feared sharing my innermost vulnerabilities." He grinned at his friends and they nodded. "But every bit of the pain was worth it. I am so grateful for my new found intimacy and connections with others – and with God."

I sat riveted. My eyes glazed over, my throat constricted, and my gut clenched. I realized how completely I identified with Father Jim's isolationism. I had work to do. I, too, wanted my barriers to tumble down.

As instructed by the program leaders, Lee and I wrote letters to each other. With newfound resolve that Father Jim had inspired, I poured my heart out. I wrote about my pain in my relationship with Lee, about feeling unheard, about wanting more connection, more intimacy, more respect for who I was.

Lee had no intention of revealing himself and hardly wrote a thing. His only reason for attending was to accommodate me, his needy, immature wife. It was I who needed the work. Yes, of course, I needed it – and this I readily acknowledged – but I also knew we needed to work on us as a couple. There was no give on Lee's part to consider this. I came away from the weekend with mixed feelings: I was heartened by what I had learned from Father Jim and the couples who led the program, but the chasm between Lee and I had hardly budged.

§

Soon after completing Marriage Encounter, I returned to Virginia Mason as a first year medicine resident. I again plunged into a crazy schedule of thirty-six hour stretches, every fourth night on call. The grandmas cared for Stephen in my absence.

Anyu didn't babysit for long. Fern intimated to me that she felt my mother's supervision lax and that she left Stephen alone too much. She may have had genuine concerns about my mother's care, however she was also guarding her territory. Fern lived with us, had her own quarters and she jealously and ferociously protected her position as chief babysitter. She effectively inched my mother out and I fully backed my mother-in-law's ousting. I feared that Anyu was using the same neglectful child rearing techniques that she used with me, despite my strict instructions to respond to Stephen's every need. I struggled with the decision to let her go. I thought myself an ungrateful daughter – though a good daughter-in-law for sure. My decision hurt my mother initially but she didn't seem to foster long-term regrets and for this, I was relieved. The struggles with my mother-in-law, however, and the boundaries around childcare and my relationship with her son had just begun to escalate.

§

Soon after I returned to work, I had a meltdown. I felt too much pressure at the hospital, too little support from Lee, too out of control with child rearing left in the hands of my mother-in-law, too little sleep staying up nights on call, and even less sleep staying up other nights with Stephen. I had absolutely no one to confide in, no confidants, no family, and no friends with whom to share my fears and pain.

When up one night with Stephen, completely exhausted and desperately wanting to get some sleep, I squeezed him tight to try to stop him from crying. I immediately recoiled; horrified that I'd lost control and that I had acted so forcefully. I began to weep, and soothed Stephen as best I could. I resolved then and there to get some help.

I remembered Father Jim's struggle to overcome solitariness and how he had offered the option of follow-up counseling after the Marriage Encounter weekend. For the first time in my life, I sought counseling. This was a huge step to take – a giant leap – but living a "Marlboro" solitary life, holding it all in was no longer a viable option.

At my first session, I tearfully unloaded my angst, unhappiness and overwhelm. And then Father Jim asked me to do something, the only activity in all our counseling time that he essentially ordered me to do.

"I want you to take a day off from work," he advised. I straightened up a little in the chair.

"I can't do that. I have responsibilities. I've never taken a day off unless I was really sick. That's unimaginable." I slumped back down and cried, pulling two more tissues from the readily available box and wiping my eyes. I thought to myself: *this is not a good sign that he has tissues right here. Is this what counseling's all about?*

Father Jim looked me straight in the eye. "This is really important, Elizabeth. I insist."

"Well, I'll consider it. I can spend a day with Stephen."

Father Jim raised his hand like a stop sign. "Oh no! I'm asking you to spend a day away from Stephen, away from all responsibility. Go for a walk in a park. Be outside for the day."

I shifted again in the chair. "I can't waste a day like that! I have so much to do. I can't do nothing!" I wailed, grabbing another tissue. I thought he was asking me to go to the moon. The concept of calling in sick unless I was deathly ill, the concept of not being with my son 24/7 when I wasn't working, the concept of taking time for myself – utterly selfish – seemed a foreign and terribly distasteful prospect. But Father Jim held firm with his request.

To my credit, I took his advice and called in sick. I walked around Greenlake in a daze. The gleaming water, the joggers flying by me, the moms chatting with their babes in prams, the piney fragrance of the evergreens, the roar of nearby Aurora highway traffic – all blurred around me. I ruminated about what I thought I needed to think about. I had no idea how to formulate thoughts, how to address what was happening to me. I shuffled about in a stupor, totally out of touch with my needs, with myself, with my place in the world. I began to face the depth of my unawareness. I was lost but at least I had reached out for help – and that was a huge first step.

In my counseling with Father Jim, I came to appreciate that my needs were real. More importantly, it was okay for me to have needs – and to work to have those needs fulfilled. It was okay for me to want love and attention from Lee. It was okay for me to have time for myself, to enjoy small pleasures such as movies and dinners out. I first had to fill those needs for myself. I had to create my own self-care program. What a novel idea! And yet, it felt oh so sweet to have someone validate my desires. Father Jim made it not just acceptable but essential to have desires, and to have them met in some way. And to know that I was *not* selfish in having such aspirations, and that I wasn't off the wall in the scope of what I wanted – this too was a revelation. And so began a long journey of listening to myself, of doing things for myself, and of backing off berating and criticizing myself. I had to counter what I so often heard from Lee and what kept repeating over and over in my head: "You want too much . . .

that costs too much . . . I don't have time to spend with you . . . I have all these projects I need to finish, projects that you don't help me with . . . Christ, I just worked three night shifts, how can you think of asking me to plan a dinner together, to go for a walk together, to watch a movie together . . . I am the main breadwinner, and I'm working my ass off for this family . . ." Lee's tapes had become my own: I wanted too much; I didn't contribute enough. And Lee's tapes had entrenched the ones I had played for myself since I was a little girl: I'm not good enough, I'm not lovable, I'm not worthy.

Father Jim helped place a chink in my armor of poor self-esteem, isolationism and self-loathing. I was so grateful to him for being that lifeline in my time of despair. Though he nodded off occasionally during sessions – no doubt from my endless whinging – he nevertheless provided me with the beginnings of a transformational foundation.

§

One crisis occurred during the time I counseled with Father Jim to which he was not privy. Later, he wished that he could have been there for me but in retrospect, I was glad to have gone through the tumultuous discernment process on my own.

The upheaval surfaced as another serious questioning of my relationship with Lee, similar to what I experienced as a medical student. I again thought about leaving him. During the earlier episode, I had acquiesced to Lee's needs: he was about to go on job interviews in Seattle and I didn't want to add more stressors, so I suppressed my relationship doubts. This time, I felt I needed to open myself completely to exploring whatever arose.

I immediately told Lee, cornering him in bed where he was reading the morning paper. I was trembling but stood firm as I began: "I'm not happy in my relationship with you and I don't know if I want to stay. I want to take some time to think things through. I'm sorry to put you through this, but I have to do it." I settled a little, pleased that I was being honest and forthright.

"Christ, Liz," Lee shouted, hurling the paper at me. "Not again. You're completely nuts." I flinched, a rush of heat flooding my body, but I held firm and I continued. "I need to isolate myself for as long as it takes to figure this out. I'm going to be in the storeroom." I walked away.

"Yeah, you do that, you bitch. You and your self-improvement selfishness." I cringed. This wasn't a new response from him, but it hurt nevertheless and I faltered as I walked downstairs. Was I nuts? I shook my head to clear my mind and trudged ahead with my resolve.

I holed up in the basement room of our house for a whole day and night, away from everybody, even Stephen. I cried. I fumed. I dozed. Disparate thoughts, memories, and images crashed through my mind: leave him . . . Marlboro man chasing me . . . I'm not worthy . . . Anyu smirking at me . . . flashes of indigo and red and coal black . . . I'm scared . . . I'm terrified . . . Stephen's pleading face . . . Don't give up, Elizabeth . . . Lee poking his finger in my face . . . Christ on the cross . . . I'm going crazy . . . hang on . . .

My head whirled. I heard Lee and his mother talking outside the room, moving about and that helped me come back into my body. I was drenched in sweat. *They think I'm nuts,* I thought ruefully. *I, too, think I may be nuts.* I got up from the floor and began to pace.

My mind hustled into action again. More fragments flooded in: phrases, images, colors and sounds. Through it all, I grappled with whether to leave or stay with Lee with the intensity of saints grappling with demons that I had learned about in Christian Doctrine classes so many years ago. I lost track of reality at times, where I was, who I was. *God help me, please help me, God help me. Don't abandon me again, not this time.* I wailed into a pillow. And then I remembered: God wasn't there for me when I wanted Mouseketeer clothes; he wasn't there for me when I asked for help deciding whether or not to marry Lee; why the hell would he come through for me this time? Anger overwhelmed me and I slammed my fists into the pillow.

My torment continued for hours interspersed with moments of fitful sleep. At last, as dawn was breaking – just like in the proverbial classic accounts – my suffering dissipated. My body settled into a peaceful, restful hum. My mind cleared with the grace of a single insight: "It is not time for you to leave Lee. It is time for you to continue to work on yourself. Right now, the issue is more with you, and less with your relationship."

I had entered the abyss, the death realms of questioning and I had resurfaced with fresh insights, renewed resolve, and new vigor. I had survived. I had received clear confirmation of a direction to take.

Lee was leery of my decision. He had ridden a second roller coaster because of my questioning, and this I understood. I had shaken the foundation of our marriage. With time, we settled back into our habitual ways, though I proceeded with a better understanding of my part in our dysfunctional relationship.

Instead of holding onto resentment and bursting through with bitchy anger and bouts of stony silence when at wit's end, I needed to learn to ask Lee for what I wanted. I attempted to make my requests openly and often – and I tried to accept when he didn't respond to them.

I continued to strive and work through my deficiencies. Most importantly, for the first time, I accepted the truth in some of Lee's complaints about me: my pride, my nagging, and judgmentalism. In acknowledging the less than flattering feedback, I had begun to learn humility.

§

I muddled through my residency, feeling inadequate and alone most of the time. Despite my new insights in therapy, I was still stuck in the role of superwoman and I tried to maintain a false façade at work – that of showing how together my life was. I wanted to project how strong I was, for that was part of the culture. I couldn't help but be submerged in the environment in which I spent so many long hours, day after day. I deemed a weekend off an exceptionally rare gift.

I was caught up in the indoctrination of medicine, the "good ole boys" mentality. The attending physicians were our mentors. They teased us about our "easy-breezy" call schedules and bragged how in their residency days, they had to take call every second night. They scoffed at how easy we had it with having call every fourth night. I gulped and swallowed the force-fed workaholic attitude. I had no idea there existed any other way to be in the medical world or any other way to become a competent physician.

Late at night, I had moments of near collapse where I heaved back tears, barely able to keep despair at bay as another patient assigned to my care took a turn for the worse. We residents had terms we used to cover up our feelings: "My patient just crumped" or "My patient is tubing it." With irreverence we could distance ourselves from the gravitas and the overwhelm of what we were doing. But my tears never flowed openly, and never – never did anyone know that I was in anyway affected by the intensity and severity of my work. I emulated the steely, unemotional persona, for that was what was expected of me. I kept up with the crazy game. Hell, not only could I do all the "male" things of residency, I could bear a child as well. I was beyond superman – I was superwoman and supermom!

It was all I knew how to do and how to be. I thought the chronic fatigue, the perennial fear of failure, the blocked off emotions, the judgments of not doing and knowing enough had to be. *I had no other world to compare and contrast my experience.* I had no other reference point. I raced about in this world for seventy to eighty hours a week, week after week. I deemed this to be normal and "as it should be." I imprinted and mirrored the pathologic energies that permeated the training program. I was in sync with its madness, fully absorbed in it and I obediently followed the drill without question. I didn't have a rebellious bone in my body.

While in the vortex of the residency training, my awareness of a healthy lifestyle was as foreign as the reaction of the native Indians when European ships first approached their shores. They had no concept of what ships were and so they didn't *see* them. I too had no concept of the possibility of a healthy lifestyle outside of the crazy medical profession. It wasn't until I moved away from the fracas of training and experienced repeated dosing of alternate ways of being, such as days off, and time for self-care and an attitude of personal reverence, that I realized how unhealthy my life had been. I began to comprehend that *it didn't have to be that way!* I had to pull myself away from the strong gravitational draw of that pathologic system to realize how unhealthy a lifestyle it fostered. That insight dawned slowly over several months and years after I completed my residency.

§

Twenty years after my medical training, when I had the great opportunity to mentor medical students and to coach physicians, I was saddened to see that these same attitudes still prevailed in the profession. Many physicians continued to work ridiculous hours, practiced with stiff upper lips, remained detached from their patients, and closeted their emotions. Those in medical school and residency programs competed as I did in the ever-present system of "one-upsmanship." They pored over the latest journal articles in the middle of the night, spouted forth the newest research minutia and statistics on rounds the following morning and at conferences, wowed attendings and fellow residents with their up-to-date knowledge. They sought to impress, worked to show strength, invincibility, resilience and brilliance. The medical training environment made little allowance for caring or mutual support. Those who survived and "succeeded" played the game, sucked it up, and they didn't challenge. They held in emotions, jauntily tolerated, and professed that they thrived on the atrocious long hours.

When I got involved mentoring med students, I had hoped that medical curriculums had made progress. It had been a quarter of a century since Meg, my medical school compatriot, had fought for and pioneered the brown bag humanistic medicine program at the University of Oregon Medical School. I was sorely disappointed. Yes, Dr. Rachel Naomi Remen's Institute for the Study of Health & Illness program was introduced at the University of Washington, but only as an elective and few students signed up for it. Even Rachel reported that gaining support for her programs proved an uphill and ongoing challenge at most medical centers.

The students told all too familiar stories. Half a dozen of them met with two of us facilitators in one of the University of Washington medical complex conference rooms. A fourth-year student, an attractive, no nonsense young woman with long blonde hair twisted into a clip related her story. "My attending surgeon dismissed my social work consult for a family that was clearly in crisis. I went ahead and got it anyway because I couldn't let the family down in their time of need. The surgeon retaliated by docking my grade." The other students around the conference table nodded their heads. I couldn't believe it.

"Is this common practice still?" I asked.

"Hell yes," another student answered. "That's exactly how things are around here: you toe the line or pay the price."

"How do you deal with it? Who do you have to confide in?" I persisted, hoping to hear they had resources which supported them.

"No one really. We pretty much keep to ourselves. We don't even share much with each other for fear of looking weak."

"Yeah, that's true," another young woman with soft Asian eyes, volunteered. "One time I was drawn to stay at the bedside of a patient who had just arrested and died. I felt strongly that I was to remain with him. My intuition was telling me to be a witness to the patient's passing. I felt uncomfortable being there and feared my attending or residents would come by and reprimand me. But I had to do it. Some inner calling spurred me on."

"You were using your intuition," my co-facilitator offered. "I use it in my practice all the time. Gut feelings are a valuable adjunct to my technical knowledge." Another student, this one an intense young man added, "Yeah, I sometimes have intuitive hits about a patient, but there's no way I'd say that to an attending. I'd be ridiculed or worse, accused of using hocus-pocus and so I don't go with it. I toe the scientific line."

"Do you guys really trust your intuition?" the Asian student asked, an amazed look on her face.

"Well, yes," I answered, "It's another tool I use all the time in assessing patients and it can be really helpful when factored in with the science and technology of medicine."

"Well, you're the first docs we've ever heard admit that," the male student replied. "That's amazing . . . really amazing. And helpful." He took a deep breath. "I'm relieved to have my hunches corroborated by someone who has lots of experience."

I was pleased to have helped these students share and validate their inner sensibilities. But what we offered was a drop in the bucket for we had reached only a few students – there was so much work left to do.

Medicine continues to predominate as a bastion of mechanistic science and technology, the domain of the masculine intellect. The profession has still to integrate the equally valuable feminine wisdom qualities of connection, caring, intuition and grounded-ness. The healthcare machine is moving towards wholeness much more slowly than I had hoped for as a medical student.

§

Toward the end of my training program I wanted to become pregnant again. Though I had not planned my first, Stephen was warmly welcomed and a huge blessing in my life, and I longed for another child. Lee showed less enthusiasm. Nevertheless, he agreed and was happy enough when he found out I was pregnant.

I completed my residency at the end of June, just as my legs began to swell. I now had time to lounge at home, to follow my obstetrician's orders and keep my legs elevated, but I delighted in chasing after my active three-year-old and, on the last weekend in July, I couldn't resist a stroll through The Bellevue Arts and Crafts fair. To my chagrin, I bumped into my obstetrician in the crowd. He gave me a bemused but caring look and I felt a hormonal rush of affection as I sheepishly grinned back at him.

Stephanie arrived close to her due date. I went into labor in the early evening and checked into the hospital. This time, Lee and I had actually completed the Lamaze classes and I felt eager to try natural childbirth. Lee got into the gusto of preparing my hospital bag, filling it with all the supplies that were recommended in the class: gum and mints, extra cushions, objects to gaze at while spotting during contractions. We would use none of them.

I went into heavy labor immediately after arriving at the hospital and soon felt an overwhelming urge to have a bowel movement. I sat and strained on the toilet without results. As I returned to bed, amniotic fluid gushed and sprayed all over the floor and walls. The fluid was olive-green – meconium stained – a cause for immediate alarm. The baby was in distress. The nurses flew into action, paged my obstetrician STAT and wheeled me into the delivery room. Stephanie was already crowning and I delivered within minutes. She had the cord wrapped around her neck and though her Apgar scores were normal, the pediatrician whisked her off to the nursery for labs and observation. (This was not good for mother-child bonding and attachment purposes, but I had no inkling of that at the time. Stephen, too, spent time in the nursery after he was born early and a critical attachment opportunity was lost with him too.)

Just like our Stephen, Stephanie was healthy and hearty and beautiful. I again rode a high of joy and elation. I had the summer off with my children and my only work task ahead was to study for my internal medicine board exams held in October.

The Virginia Mason residency program had prepared us well. Though the conferences and teaching rounds were geared towards quality, clinically relevant learning, our attending physicians also drilled us on historical board questions and drummed several esoteric test "pearls" into us. They trained us well in the peccadilloes of the board examiners. Though I worried dreadfully about how

I would perform, I passed the boards with above average scores. I rejoiced in my success, which I had achieved with the added challenges of mothering and pregnancy. I was now ready to embark on my own practice.

CHAPTER 18 – WORKING FOR THE MAN

Ready for the Context Training graduation gala in the dreamy dress that my sister had first worn to a ball in Sydney twenty years before.

I sat in the attending physician's waiting room, nervous, giving myself a pep talk. "You've done okay, Elizabeth. You're finished with your med school training, medical internship, and residency. You've successfully passed your specialty board examinations. It's taken seven long years but you can be proud to have survived. You're ready to begin working in a practice. Just let 'em know what you want." A slim, young office assistant approached me with a smile.

"Dr. M is ready to see you, Doctor."

"Thank you," I murmured, following her into a handsome, oak-paneled office.

"Hello, Elizabeth." Even though he reached across his huge desk and welcomed me with an outstretched hand, his face was pinched, his lips downturned. I felt the start of a shudder but collected myself enough to reach over to meet his hand.

He motioned to the seat. "Congratulations on passing your board exams." I thanked him and didn't waste time getting to the purpose of my appointment.

"I'm ready to begin a practice and would love to join Virginia Mason. Having completed my residency here, I know that quality medicine is the highest priority and I believe I can provide excellent service here."

"I agree with you. You were a fine resident."

"Thank you," I answered, peering in his general direction. The sun shone through the window behind him and made his face hard to see. I felt intimidated and took a deep breath before continuing. "I would like to work half time. I have two young children and want to be part of their lives growing up. Shared practices are developing in many medical centers and I would like to participate in such a program."

The physician looked down at his tented hands for a long moment before replying. "The partners here require nothing less than a full and complete commitment from all practitioners. Virginia Mason sees part-time practices as a slide in quality. If you are willing to apply for a full time position, we would be happy to consider you for you are a strong candidate, but a part time position is out of the question."

I thought this might be his response, but I felt sorely disappointed nonetheless. The male bastion of medicine was alive and well. "I appreciate your being so direct. I'm committed to being a good doc and a good mom and I just can't see doing both maxed out in a full time practice. I believe that shared practices will be more accepted in the future. I was hoping that would be the case here." I was pleased with standing up for myself, and for challenging him just a little.

"Our position is clear and uncompromising," he countered. "Full time or not at all."

I stood up. "I appreciate your position, but I, too, am firm in mine. Thank you for your time." I walked out disappointed, but with my resolve intact.

There was no way that I was going to work full time. I had already given in to Lee's demand to complete my residency, working over seventy hours a week, and I didn't wish to compromise my personal or family needs any further. Even limiting my scope to a half-time practice meant working about forty hours a week and that was more than enough. At least I had enough sense and fortitude to stand firm on this issue with Lee. I had to maintain my sanity – and I wanted to be a major influence in raising our children.

Group Health had already established shared practices and after a couple of months of locums work within the organization, I was offered a permanent position at a clinic close to home, partnering with another female physician. I worked in the office seeing patients two days a week alternating with three days. On the days that I worked, I came in early and stayed late to round on any hospitalized patients, and I took night call for patients on my own panel. In addition, a couple of times a month I covered evening shifts in the walk-in emergency department, and every twelve weeks I took hospital call 24/7 for a week at a time. I kept a plenty busy schedule but at least I had days off to just be a mom.

When I first began at the clinic, I was anxious with just about every patient who walked through the door. Did that teenager have more than a cold? Did I prescribe the right antibiotic for that lady with the bladder infection? Did I do enough of a work up on that smoker with chest pain? Did I miss something on that kid with the headache? I had plenty of resources at my disposal, though, and I didn't hesitate to use them: I kept a library of textbooks to refer to; I had cluster partners I could consult with, and I had access to specialists a phone call away. Even though it took a while, I was gradually able to settle into the flow of the practice.

§

When I began to work at Group Health there were no treatment record forms (TRFs) or billing forms to fill out. All I had to do was see patients and write good chart notes – good by peer review standards. My practice kept me jumping for sure, especially on days that I saw up to thirty patients in eight hours, but I spent most of my time coordinating patient care and leaving clear tracks in the charts. Back then there were no copays, no deductibles, no exclusions that patients were obligated to cover. All patients paid for were their monthly dues. That is *all* they paid for! And there was pretty much one single coverage plan

– no deluge of coverage options from which to choose, and through which to navigate. One basic healthcare plan served practically all. At the time, I didn't realize how lucky I was.

Twenty years later, myriad levels of administrative complexity had seeped into my practice. I had treatment record forms I had to fill out to document the level of care I provided, and to account for every procedure I performed, from paring corns to performing endometrial biopsies and suturing lacerations. A plethora of billing codes for every possible diagnosis and procedure inundated my work life. I could only charge higher diagnostic billing code levels if I followed the required documentation guidelines. I had to write my clinic notes in minute detail, using the exact mandated language. If I failed to follow the strict rules, I risked Medicare fraud charges: billing for work there was no evidence for in the chart.

The level of service billing codes determined my productivity, which the organization now carefully monitored and graded using system standards. Every statistic was captured: the number of patients I saw, the number of procedures I performed and the level of complexity of every visit. Our clinic chiefs paraded the statistics at our medical staff meetings and they admonished those providers whose numbers were below an arbitrary ideal. As a female provider my practice attracted more women, and as an internist I took care of more patients with complex medical problems than my family practice colleagues, and so my stats stayed high for the most part, but this didn't reassure me and didn't take the edge off my performance anxiety. Still later, the medical leadership introduced pay incentives, and these I abhorred. I wanted no part of being compensated for the number of widgets I billed for. Nevertheless, a portion of my salary now depended on these productivity measures.

Hundreds of administrative non-patient care positions and system "upgrades" surfaced to cope with the tsunami brought about by the new changes. I was astonished at the magnitude of the upheavals: clinics were remodeled to create registration areas where newly hired clerks collected copays and determined insurance coverage; business departments exploded with coding technicians, billing clerks, and computer programmers; huge infrastructures materialized to develop, monitor, update, and maximize data capture and optimize reimbursements. And to keep up with and compete with the nationwide healthcare chaos, Group Health expanded its insurance coverage options and now offered literally hundreds of plans – so confusing, that I no longer knew how or whether the tests, medications, referrals, and procedures I ordered would be paid for by my patient's coverage plan.

When patients asked me, "Is that lab test covered, doc?" I could only shake my head. "I don't know. You'll have to check at the business office. Do you know where that is? No? It's through the waiting room, down the hall and . . . yes, I can repeat that again . . . through the waiting room . . . " As they were leaving I'd say, "Call me when you find out and I'll order the test." A shadow would come over the patient.

"But, doc, you know I can't get through to you on the phone."

How true that was – the wait times for answering calls was shamefully long and even when patients did get through, they got put on hold, had to retell their story over and over to different people before they ever got a response from me hours later through my medical assistant.

"I'll make sure my assistant knows you'll be calling, I'll leave her a note."

"Well, all right, I hope that works," the patient would say with a dubious look on his face. I could hardly blame him.

"Thank you, Mr. Jones. Now do make sure you let me know what you decide, for if you can't afford that lab test, we'll need to find another less expensive option. It's very important for your health that we take care of this, okay?"

Patients would then have to decide what they could pay for and what they couldn't afford. I had to let them know the risks of not getting the tests done, or I had to scramble to find less expensive care options. All this required extra time, and inconvenienced both my patients and me. Care was occasionally compromised when patients didn't check back after heading to the business office, or if they waited until they could come up with funds to pay for the medications and tests that I ordered. Many times patients became disgruntled with the costs they had to bear and some became irate when the drugs or tests to treat their particular illness weren't covered. I resented having to spend more of my clinic time documenting widgets of care and acting as the gatekeeper and mediator with my patients.

I was sickened to see how, with all the new changes, the focus had shifted away from patient care. Our medical staff meetings that once provided educational case reviews and clinical lectures, were now replaced by coding and charting classes to train providers on how to comply with the Medicare standards and maximize reimbursements from the government and insurance companies. The coding specialist frequently showed up at our meetings, giving us the latest code changes. For diabetes alone, hundreds of coding options were created – and they were updated almost every week. The administrators had to make sure that we were entering the newest and most complete classifications. Learning these codes, taking the time to make sure all the parameters needed for the appropriate level of service were included in my charting, keeping up with the frequent updates and "corrections," consumed more and more of my time. It drove me nuts.

When the codes were first introduced, the office billing clerks corrected the ones that I had flubbed and added codes that I couldn't figure out. These employees were godsends! But when electronic charting was initiated, my backup system went poof! I had to enter every darn diagnostic code myself. To my chagrin, the computer wouldn't allow me to order any labs, prescriptions, X-rays, treatments, or referrals unless I entered the exact diagnostic code.

Many a time I would flounder when with a patient. "Just a moment, Mrs. Smith. I'll have to find the right code number so I can order your X-ray. Would you please excuse me for a moment?" I'd dash out the door and try to track down the coding expert. When I couldn't find one anywhere, I'd grab one of my colleagues. "Hey, John, do you know the code . . . ?" Racing back and forth, it took me forever to get the code I needed. I'd hustle back in with the patient. "I'm so sorry for the delay, Mrs. Smith. Let me quickly finish up here and get you on your way." But by now, I would be ten or fifteen minutes farther behind in my schedule. "Crap," I would think to myself. "I'm going to be here until all hours tonight!"

I didn't question that the electronic charting system improved access to medical records and therefore served patients and clinicians well. What I was at odds with was how most of us docs were staying at least an hour or two later to finish up with our charting and paper work. I had to ask myself if the high complexity level of billing, coding, coverage, and reimbursement systems also served to create better health, and I knew the answer to that – I didn't think it did! And that made my extra work harder to accept. My disillusionment with the medical system grew.

§

Despite the administrative challenges, I settled into a routine in my medical practice and got to know the patients on my panel. In addition to attending to their medical ills, I learned about their lives and began to realize that when I treated their symptoms, I was tackling the end-stage of a long-term, diffuse process. As I talked to my patients with flu symptoms, backaches or chronic illnesses such as diabetes or heart disease, I noticed that the onset of their symptoms or the control of their chronic diseases correlated with their life circumstances. Their angina, spikes in their blood sugars, or blood pressure came on or worsened when they increased their work hours, received a bad performance review, had an argument with their boss, or when they got laid off. Family problems such as marital discord or abuse, illness, in-law conflicts or child behavioral problems also had significant health effects. Underlying psychological issues such as anxiety, depression, poor self-esteem, trauma, and attachment disorders complicated these environmental stresses. Symptom control and compliance with treatment recommendations also depended on a patient's stress levels, their sense of worthiness, and their level of social support. Unfruitful health practices such as tobacco, alcohol and drug addiction, lack of exercise, and poor eating habits served only to cover up and compensate for these underlying stressors. They were the side effects and not the primary causes of ill health.

The connections between stress and disease that I noted in my patients I also found to be true with my own health, and the health of my family. I'd already correlated the onset of my thyroid disease with the stresses of medical school and a difficult time in my marriage. The times when I had grueling work stretches, or got caught up in family dramas were the times I came down with a cold or the flu. Tension headaches occurred when I invalidated myself, urging myself to toughen up: the critical self unfurled its rage by squeezing my neck and head muscles. I also noted direct correlations between acute stress and accidents. Stumbles, sprains and cuts occurred when I felt off center. One time I drove on the freeway, angry after an argument with Lee, and was rear-ended. Not my fault some would say. I knew better. I was upset and I sensed that in some way, I had drawn the energy and the stress from around me, and that helped to cause the crash.

With what I saw day after day in my medical practice and what I experienced in my own life, I knew there had to be ways to improve health at its very core and I wanted to find out how. I wanted to learn ways to avert symptoms by dealing with the precipitating stresses that caused them. I also wanted to continue my own growth process that I'd begun in my counseling with Father Jim.

I believed that the "Context Training" self-improvement classes, developed by a private company, would provide these opportunities for growth and learning, but the reason I actually signed up for the course was in self-defense. I was surprised that Lee had agreed to take the program, as he had been so unwilling to participate when we had taken Marriage Encounter. It was a friend's recommendation that led to Lee's decision, and I was worried because my husband had begun to spend a lot of time with this friend, Sarah. She was the wife of his high school buddy, a soft-spoken, mousy blond, with shapely long legs that I envied. I thought that by taking the Context workshop, I could discuss my learnings with Lee, just as he had spent hours with Sarah, debriefing and sharing their experiences. Lee had hardly shared anything about his Context weekend with me. I felt a widening rift between us and I wanted my husband back.

I loved what I learned in Context Training. One of the program's requests was to fully participate and after dipping a toe in and speaking in front of the whole group of two hundred in a huge hotel conference room, I leaned how to jump in with both feet and participate more fully in my life. Another learning point in the class was keeping commitments and I practiced making promises to myself and to others. The class hall had a big banner across the stage area with "Tell the Truth" and I began to notice when I was telling myself the truth and when I was kidding myself. In one of the teaching pieces I was pleased to discovered a new way of looking at responsibility: it was no longer a burden – as in "I'm responsible for that" – but rather a choice – "I can choose how I respond." I became empowered by choosing, and began to let go of being the victim or feeling guilty. I also learned how to visualize and be creative and I began to pay attention to – and to trust – my intuition.

A portion of the Context program, called The Commitment Clarification Process, was devoted to exploring and solving a troubling life issue. It was part of a three-day retreat held in an austere ski area hostel. I sat on the floor of the pine-paneled common room surrounded by twenty or so other participants, all of us with a pile of sheets in front of us that outlined the steps of the process. Of course, I had chosen my troubled relationship with Lee. I wasn't sure how to love him. I gazed at the sheet that listed my next prompt: *I am committed to creating* . . . Well, yes, I wanted to create a loving relationship, but what was that? I had no idea. I stared into space, my brain completely blank. Love. A word. A word for which I could find absolutely no association. I glanced around. Others were pouring over their sheets, writing, smiling. Some were staring into space like me but then a glimmer would appear in their eye; they would break out in a smile and pour over their notes again, writing furiously. Some were reaching for a box of tissues, wiping tears away. It seemed like I was the only one stuck on the assignment.

The handful of workshop assistants sat at the edges of the room, ready to help if needed. Not one to ask for help – "Marlboro woman" that I still was in so many ways – I finally got up the gumption to approach one of them.

"I'm stuck right here," I said, showing him my work. "I want to create a loving relationship with my husband, but I don't think I know how to love." I flushed with shame. I could hardly believe I'd admitted such a horrible deficiency out loud. The assistant didn't seem at all fazed – at least he didn't show it.

"Well, I suggest you make a list of what love is it you – fill a whole page."

"What . . . what does that mean?" I replied, even more flustered.

"Just think about the many, many ways love can be expressed." He smiled, bemused by my confusion.

"Oh . . . okay . . . thanks," I muttered, and shuffled back to my spot on the floor.

I wrote the title, "What is love to me?" and stared at the sheet of paper for a while before an idea floated up: it's letting go completely. "Damn," I groaned as I wrote that down. "Letting go is so bloody hard to do." I had to think of more ways to love – ones that I could follow through with more easily. Other ideas came to mind: it's opening yourself up; it's being vulnerable. I wasn't convinced that they were any easier to achieve. I began to lose confidence, but then the floodgates opened and a list poured out of me: it's sharing, it's laughter, it's playfulness, it's being there when the other is in trouble, it's accepting. A small smile spread over my face. I could do some of these things with Lee. In fact, I had been doing many of these things with him for a long time. Then it dawned on me: I already had a loving relationship with my husband. My body settled into a calming hum and I knew what my next steps were to be: I could work to expand and deepen that love.

The following day, we took turns sharing our experience with the group. After we had spoken, the assistants played a song that they felt resonated with our story. For me they chose "Let Your Love Flow" by the Bellamy Brothers. The lyrics showed the many ways love could manifest. The song fit, and while I had remained pretty stoic telling my story, my tears flowed unrestrained as I listened. I basked in my new insights. My neck and shoulders relaxed, and a warm glow settled in my chest.

As was the custom in the program, those who had sponsored us greeted us with flowers at the end of the three-day retreat. Lee showed up and handed me a bouquet of daisies.

I choked up. "Oh, thank you, Lee. How lovely. I can't wait to tell you all about my weekend." In the corner of my eye, I saw Sarah talking to another participant. Her gaze met Lee's and she walked towards us.

"Hi, Sarah," I said, determined to keep from getting in a huff. I was still on a high from my weekend. Moreover, I had, after all, learned that I had the ability to choose my response. I chose to remain open and cordial.

"Congratulations on completing the course, Liz," she said with a smile.

"Thank you, Sarah."

She glanced at Lee. There was an awkward pause.

"I'll check with you later, Sarah" Lee said, and we said our goodbyes.

As we drove home, I couldn't stop grinning. "I want to tell you all about what I learned and discovered, and I'd love to hear about your experience, now that I know what the course was all about."

Lee glanced at me. He wasn't smiling. "Tell me about it now. I've got things to do once I drop you off." He turned his attention to looking in the rear and side view mirrors, speeding in and out of traffic, as if he couldn't wait to be rid of me.

"Oh . . . I see." My smile faded, but I was determined to stay positive. I began my accounting, trying to draw him out.

"What did you think of the oatmeal-only breakfasts? I loved it but some in our group refused to eat 'the slop.'" I smiled, looking expectantly at Lee.

He looked straight ahead. "It was okay."

I forged on, shifting in my seat. "And what about the mile? I assumed it was a race and ran as fast as I could. Several of us did. I was surprised when the facilitator clarified that we were to "do" and not necessarily "run" the mile . . . what about you?"

"It wasn't a big deal," he said as he made a sharp left turn.

I lurched towards the door. My face fell but I plowed on, still trying to engage Lee. We arrived home before I could recount the heart of my discoveries. My sharing time had fallen far short of the hours he had spent with Sarah. I felt hurt but undaunted nonetheless. At the retreat I had learned about some of the ways that I loved Lee, and I was prepared to build on that foundation.

§

Lee and I attended the Context Training graduation ceremony together. During the previous months, I had lost all the pregnancy weight I had gained with Stephanie. I was jogging regularly and even ran a few 10Ks. I was proud of myself and relished how fit I felt. For the graduation event, I was able to squeeze into the gorgeous turquoise chiffon evening gown that I had coveted as a teenager, the one that had been fashioned for my sister for the Hungarian White Rose Ball. I had never before worn a gown so beautiful and I felt joy and pride as I slipped into the hand-me-down dress. It was a fitting culmination of a long ago dream: I had worked hard on myself; worked hard on my relationship with Lee. My svelte figure and gorgeous gown symbolized all of that and the progress I'd made in my life. Lee wore a tux – the only time besides our wedding when he did. Sarah also graduated at the same ceremony.

§

A few weeks later, Lee took off without telling me where he went. At first, I thought nothing of his absence: Lee leaving unannounced for several hours wasn't new. I spent the afternoon sitting in our backyard, weeding our dandelion and clover infested lawn – a losing battle.

I looked up and smiled. Eight-year-old Stephen and his best buddy, Sammy, were hammering in earnest. My dark haired son and his blond friend loved building forts next to my bedraggled vegetable garden. Lee allowed them to use bits of plywood and two-by-fours left over from his many shelf and fence-building projects.

Over several days, the boys had constructed a handful of platforms – "rooms" in their fort – to which they were adding.

"Look, Stephen. Let's build a bridge here," Sammy said as he dragged a plywood remnant over a dip in the ground.

My son looked up from hammering a wobbly rail into place. He walked over to Sammy, studied the proposed site, and suddenly broke out in a grin. "We hafta make it a drawbridge and make a moat under it."

"Oh yeah!" Sammy chuckled. "I'll get the shovels."

For the next two hours, the boys slogged away, digging a trench, giggling and strategizing as they decided where each bend in the course of their moat would be. With amazing ingenuity, they constructed a pulley system with ropes to raise the drawbridge up and down.

Stephen dragged the hose to their magnificent creation. "Turn the water on, Sam . . . no, no, slower. It's coming too fast." Sam did his bidding and scampered back.

"Look, look!" They squealed, jumping up and down.

"Look, Mom," Stephen cried. "Look what we made."

I got up off the ground, happy to get a respite from the dratted weeds, a hand clutching my aching back.

"Well, well, that's a great moat and you figured how to make the drawbridge go up and down. That's pretty cool." They straightened up and stood taller, huge grins on their mud-spattered faces. I hated to spoil their fun but had to add, "You'll have to turn the water off though, before it floods the yard."

"No, problem, Mom. We can dam up the moat."

Stephen and Sammy worked at their fort every spring and summer until they hit their teens, only to have Lee tear it down every winter. "It's a goddamn blight," he'd say. Stephen would come home from school, and his face would blanch upon seeing his creation destroyed. He'd hang his head and disappear to his room without a word. My heart ached for him. He wanted his dad's approval and didn't want to show his disappointment. Nevertheless, after the initial shock, the boys rebounded, and undeterred, began an even bigger and better – and more sophisticated – fort the following year.

Later that weeding and fort-building day, as I fixed homemade macaroni and cheese, I watched five-year-old Stephanie with her little friend Janna in the adjacent family room. They were picking through several of my old dresses and scarves that were strewn all over the hardwood floor.

"Help me, Mommy," Steph said, pulling my well-used, hand-me-down aqua ball gown over her head. Her voice was muffled as she fought to pry herself out from the folds of chiffon.

"Hold on." I laughed as I attempted to anchor the billowing dress over her tiny frame.

"Put the belt on too, Mommy." I did as she asked, my eyes moist as I remembered how gorgeous my sister looked when she first wore the dress over two decades ago, and how lovely I had felt wearing the dress to the Context Training graduation celebration just a few weeks before. Now stained and faded, I could no longer wear the dress. It had served its purpose, and now my beautiful daughter was wearing it.

"Look, Janna. I'm going to a ball." Awash in the folds, she yanked up an armful and strutted about the room, her soft brown eyes gleaming with joy.

Her friend was struggling with my wedding dress. "Here, let me help you, Janna." She grinned as I zipped up the lace-trimmed gown. "Can I wear the veil as well?" she asked shyly.

"Of course," I answered, "That's part of the outfit."

"I'll help you," Steph said, as she plopped the matching lace edged cap and veil on Janna's head.

"Can we wear your shoes, too, Mommy?" I hid my smile as I went to fetch some high heels.

The girls took turns with the dresses, becoming adept at helping each other, their brows furrowed and their tongues on their lips as they struggled with zipping and buttoning. They giggled and pranced and tripped and fell. I hardly cared when I heard a loud rip as Stephanie stepped on the aqua chiffon gown that her friend was now wearing. Janna froze and my daughter's face paled as she stared at the huge tear. She looked ready to cry.

"It's okay, Steph. That's an old gown and I'm not going to wear it again anyway. It's yours to play with." She quickly brushed a tear away and was back to playing.

After dinner, My Little Ponies replaced the dress-up game. Janna stayed over that night, perched below Stephanie on the pullout trundle bed. I read them *Goodnight Moon* and *Ferdinand*, Stephen listening as he stood in the shadow of the doorway. Big brother was too old to "hang out" with little girls. I tucked my little man in, too, giving him some extra time and attention, since he didn't have a friend stay over that night.

The children didn't notice their dad's absence as he was so often away either at work, or running errands, or fixing up the rental houses. I was grateful they didn't pick up on my growing unease. Late that night Lee still hadn't returned, neither had he by the following morning.

The more time passed without hearing from him, the more worried and angry I became. I had no idea where he'd gone. I wondered about his being with Sarah, as they had continued to spend time together, frequently meeting for coffee or for a jog. I finally swallowed my pride and called her house and spoke to her husband, Rick. My hands shook with nerves as I held the phone to my ear.

"Hey, Rick, I hate to do this to you, but Lee's been gone for two days and I don't know where he is. Have you heard from him?"

"No, I haven't, Liz," he said, sounding a little bewildered.

"Well, I know he and Sarah have been spending some time together. Do you think she might know where he is?" There was a pause at the other end of the line.

"Sarah is away at our cabin for a few days," he volunteered, a guarded and shaky edge to his voice.

"Oh," I said, my gut twisting. My fears about the two of them being together may have been founded after all.

"The cabin has a phone," he continued, "I'll call and ask her."

"Thanks, Rick. I'm sorry to have bothered you with this."

"Yeah, I know," he answered, his voice a resigned monotone. Neither of us was willing to state the obvious.

Lee turned up at the house a few hours later. I didn't even wait for him to get in the front door. Fury billowed up from my craw and flushed over my face.

"My god, you have a family to be responsible for. I couldn't have reached you if something had happened to the children."

"Oh, come on," he cajoled, stepping into the hallway, looking behind him to make sure no neighbors could hear us, and closing the door. "I wasn't gone for that long and nothing happened to the kids. No harm done." He brushed by me with his head lowered. I refused to let it go and grabbed his sleeve.

"No, Lee, you have done harm. What you do with your own time is your decision. I don't like that you were with Sarah, but that's not nearly as bad as the fact that you didn't let me know where I could reach you. As a partner, that's bush league. As a parent, that's inexcusable."

"Okay, okay, from here on out I'll let you know where I'm going. Get off my back," he said, spreading his hands in front of him as if to defend my onslaught.

Then I knew I could no longer put off the elephant-in-the-room question. I clenched my fists at my sides, looked him straight in the eye and asked: "Are you having an affair with Sarah?"

He immediately answered. "Hell, no! We just like each other's company. She's easy to talk to and she doesn't give me a hard time."

"Well, yeah, it's no wonder you get along. You don't have years of history living with her. You're not married to her," I said, unable to keep the bitterness out of my voice. He shuffled a foot.

"Well, I'm sorry I didn't tell you where I was, okay?"

"Okay," I said. "Let's just leave it at that," and I walked away, leaving him standing in the entryway.

I was still angry. I thought Lee had been chastened, but not so much because he didn't let me know where he was, but because he was caught with Sarah – and both Rick and I had found out. The contrast was telling: my main concern centered on his disappearing without letting me know; his main worry was getting caught. He cared little about taking off and being unaccountable. Though Lee vowed that his relationship with Sarah was platonic, I felt crushed. Not only did he thumb his nose at responsibility, he repeatedly turned to, and confided in Sarah. I was the woman scorned.

Undaunted, I licked my wounds and smoothed my bruised ego. I continued on my personal self-improvement journey. I was excited about practicing the tools I had learned in the Context Training program and believed that they might also benefit my patients. I began to explore how I might share them.

Around the same time, I became intrigued when a friend told me about a workshop coming to town, taught by Alexander Everett called "Inward Bound." I felt ready to further my spiritual growth – which had grown dormant for several years – and I again thought that my learnings could inform my work with patients. Indeed, the medical education department of my workplace was in agreement. They provided educational leave and reimbursed my tuition costs for both the Context and Inward Bound programs, much as they did for any formal continuing medical education conference.

§

Some called Alexander Everett "the father of the human potential movement." In the late sixties, he developed "Mind Dynamics," a self-improvement seminar whose students included Dr. O. Carl Simonton of the Simonton Cancer Center, and whose trainers included Randy Revel, who later developed Context Training, Werner Erhardt of EST and Landmark Forum fame, and several other human potential workshop founders. Alexander's work progressed from the more mental and psychological focus of Mind Dynamics to the deeper spiritual roots of human potential, and he began teaching Inward Bound in 1977. Alexander titled the course as a takeoff on Outward Bound, a wilderness course developed to build confidence, self-esteem, and competency in the great outdoors. Alexander used the Inward Bound title to represent the exploration of the inner wilderness, the realm of the spirit. His background was eclectic and included spiritualism, Christian, and Eastern traditions.

I found Alexander to be an imposing man: tall and confident with a thick shock of combed back silver hair and a sonorous voice. He emphasized a personal connection with the sacred through meditation and through nature, and this he contexted from both a historical and mystic perspective. He drew on all religious disciplines, found the commonalities and mystic threads that pervaded and connected them all. He posited that all religions shared a similar sacred core, and gave examples of mystics such as Thomas Merton and Paramahansa Yogananda, who both explored and collaborated with pundits of other faith traditions.

Alexander's perspective made a lot of sense to me. I like that he talked about a spirituality that was eclectic and not limited to a single doctrine or religious tradition. His views resonated with what I had felt in an amorphous way for most of my life. Even as a grade school student, I dismissed the doctrine that Catholics were the only ones allowed to enter heaven. Later, as I learned about the Mormon, fundamental Christian and Muslim religions, the dogmas of salvational exclusivity became even less plausible.

Alexander opened up a new world of esoteric interpretation of scripture, drawing from the bible, the Hindu *Bhagavad Gita* and the Muslim mystic texts of the Sufis. I could now move beyond the literal meaning of the words in the bible, which I had learned as a child, and which fundamentalist traditions touted. Alexander stressed the importance of individual exploration and insight, suggesting that we not rely on the interpretations or edicts of gurus, popes or "experts."

This too resonated for me. I had never ascribed to the absolute power of the Church or that of gurus. I wasn't one to follow anyone hook, line, and sinker. At one time, I believed I couldn't completely surrender to any spiritual tradition because I was weak and didn't have enough faith. Now I was able to shift my perspective. I saw myself as a discerner, one who learned and who could make my own decisions. I could forge a direct connection to the sacred and the divine, without the need of intermediaries. This stance required more responsibility, yet provided solace and comfort. I was the one to make decisions about my spiritual life, independent of the Vatican, priests, gurus, or dogmas. I shifted according to my conscience, integrity, and values. Far from being selfish or misguided, this new path brought out my inherent goodness and harmony, and tapped into an inner noble courage.

Alexander also asserted that meditation practice served not only as a spiritual but also a health practice and that, too, made inherent sense to me. He cited physiological research that demonstrated how transcendental meditation (TM) practitioners had lower blood pressures, higher levels of beneficial neurotransmitters and hormones, and maintained a higher overall sense of wellbeing. I was eager to share this research with my colleagues and with my patients. As I began to meditate, I experienced the beneficial effects myself. I was able to keep my emotions on a more even keel so that some of my ups and downs were leveled out. I discovered I could access a mature "witness" part of me that could detach from my emotions and more readily cope with stresses and charged situations.

During a break at one of the Inward Bound workshops, a group of us gathered in the breakout room and I happened to sit next to Alexander on the couch. Neither he nor I were participating in the conversation. All of a sudden, I felt a radiance of love pouring out of my heart. My body was vibrating with joy in every cell. Alexander turned to me and smiled, his eyes shining. We didn't say a word. We didn't need to. We both savored the heightened field of love that surrounded and enveloped us. The glow stayed with me for hours.

This sense of expansion and connection felt similar to what I'd experienced before: on the Sydney beach as a teenager, receiving communion, on the Champs Élysées in Paris, and on the first day of medical school. Now it had occurred as an intimate connection with another person. I felt blessed. With Alexander's work, I began to fully appreciate and integrate how the sacred infused everything: not only could I find it in the traditional church setting, I could find it in nature, in my profession and in human connections – and the presence of the sacred was just as awesome in secular settings. Moreover, I felt every one of these experiences fully in my body. The sacred was somatic. The sacred infused me. My body sensations were the final common pathway for how the sacred manifested. I didn't have to deny my body, or purge it of pleasure as I had learned in my Christian doctrine classes and from the Church pulpits. The sacred was here, right inside me, right here on earth. It wasn't limited to residing far away in heaven; it was both imminent and transcendent.

§

As I learned more, and as my self-confidence grew, I began to reach out to others. I no longer felt alone. For the first time in my life, I made friends with whom I could share with deeply. I enjoyed being with people who were interested in personal and spiritual growth and we shared our journeys and insights. I started my own meditation group. We met weekly, mostly at my house, and I reveled in the sacred field that our group meditations created, reflected in the words of Christ from Matthew's gospel: "For where two or three are gathered together in my name, there I am in the midst of them."

I found a special friend in Kathleen. We met through work – she an ER nurse – and we hit it off immediately. We shared a goofy side: Kathleen could pull off a wicked impression of Mae West; I loved to ham it up singing the Aussie Vegemite and Aeroplane Jelly ad-tunes. We both loved drama and music and we signed up for creative thinking and acting classes, and we joined a local choir. We spent hours laughing and crying together as we commiserated about the challenges and celebrated the joys in our lives.

For her fiftieth birthday shindig at a fancy rented venue, Kathleen asked me to join her in singing Karaoke duets of Connie Francis' "Lipstick on Your Collar," The Shirelles "Will You Still Love Me Tomorrow", and Nino Tempo and April Chuckn's "Deep Purple."

"We need choreography to go with the songs," I pronounced at one of our rehearsals.

"Ooh, yes." Kathleen grinned. "Let's make it corny."

"What about this?" I demonstrated tracing my lips with my finger and grasping a pretend collar as I sang "Lipstick on your collar . . ."

"Yes, yes." She giggled. "And what about this for 'Bet your bottom dollar, you and I are through,'" she added, turning her butt and striking it, then pointing a finger out and in and swinging her arms to the side.

"We're nuts, but this is soo much fun," I sputtered with glee. We hugged. "We're on a roll. Let's figure out some moves for the other songs."

We rollicked in our party performance with more enthusiasm than finesse. Nevertheless a friend came up to me afterwards and smiled. "You know, if you ever want to give up your medical practice, you have another career ready and waiting." I was touched – maybe our performance was better than I had figured.

§

The more I settled into life with my friends and the more I learned about myself, the more constricted I felt delivering such a limited scope of health to my patients. In an attempt to encourage healthy lifestyles, and armed with my own learning and experience with Context and Inward Bound, I organized a series of classes for my patients on health and happiness. The initial turnout was excellent– more than one hundred and twenty-five patients from my panel participated. As I stood on the podium of the conference room and began my talk, I felt my body resonate and thrum with joy. I sensed that my work was being validated at a deep level.

At the end of the talk, I received comments from the participants as they were leaving. "I really liked the visualization. It was so relaxing," one of them said. "I thought the piece about my ability to choose my response really helpful. I can choose how I deal with my diabetes," said another. His wife, standing by his side added, "Thank you for the list of ways to relieve stress. I'm going to try them."

My friend, Barbara, remained in the back of the room until everyone had gone. She had asked if she could observe my class and joined me as I was collecting my notes. "Your face was glowing – did you know that?"

"Oh, yes." I chuckled with joy and a little embarrassment. "Was it that obvious?"

"No, but I could just tell you were on fire with what you were teaching. You were absolutely radiating! You are meant to be doing this work, Elizabeth." I was humbled and grateful that my friend had noticed what I had felt.

Though my patients gave me positive feedback, I had little support from the medical leadership. The funding for mailing out workshop notifications dried up and I was told I couldn't schedule a conference room to hold any further workshops. I lost heart.

A year later, I tried a different tack. I figured that health begins with the healer and if I could present my health and happiness workshop to my coworkers, then maybe I could gain their support and do more with my patients. I was successful in persuading the clinic leadership to allow me to present an afternoon workshop for the clinic staff. Though well attended, the workshop had mixed reviews.

Two of the staff came up to me afterwards. "I loved it," one said.

"Yeah, and I want more," the other said.

"Thanks," I answered. "We'll have to see what more the administration is willing to go for."

Others were skeptical, and didn't care for my relaxation meditation. "Too woo-woo," I heard them whisper to each other as they left the conference room. One physician hung back after everyone had gone and pulled me aside as I left the room. Looking in my direction, but not meeting my gaze, he said, "I couldn't participate in the meditation because my church teaches me that letting go of thoughts opens the door for the devil to enter the mind." I was stunned!

"I'm sorry, Dane, it was not my intention to challenge your religious beliefs. I just wanted to do a closed-eye visualization. It's being done at some medical centers, you know, like at the Simonton Cancer Center in Texas, and it has been shown to really help patients."

Dane looked down and shuffled his toe. "I can see where you were going with it, but how could I go against my pastor? I couldn't."

"I see your point, Dane. I'm sorry to have made things difficult for you."

"I know. Well, thank you for hearing me out – and I did appreciate some of what you taught us."

But the air was still charged. Clearly some, like Dane, were threatened by my approach. I again lost heart. Mine was a solitary endeavor than never really blossomed within my practice setting.

§

One day, well into my practice years, I had a telling patient encounter. A woman in her late thirties came in complaining of head and chest congestion that had lasted over a month, and that was getting significantly worse. As I listened to her heart and chest, I asked about her life. She related that she worked long hours as a retail manager, cared for two active children as a single mom, and housed her down-and-out sister who had taken over her bedroom, leaving the patient to sleep on the living room couch. I gently offered that her living and work stresses may have been a factor in her drawn out illness, and she readily agreed. Along with an antibiotic prescription for her secondary bronchitis, an inhaler for her asthma, and recommending that she cut down on her smoking, I suggested she think about what self-care might look like for her. I also asked her to consider taking some personal time. I didn't think much of the interaction, as this was how I worked with most patients, many of whom acknowledged that life stresses factored into their illnesses – even chronic and serious ones.

Two months later, I was finishing up in my office after a long day. I plopped the last completed chart in the now crowded outbox – and groaned: there in my inbox was a pile of papers that my assistant must have slipped in just before she had left for home over three hours earlier. I looked longingly out the window at the now dark night. I so wanted to leave, to be outside, on my way home. I turned back to my desk and pulled out the pile with a sigh. One by one, I painstakingly did what was required. I signed prescriptions, initialed reports, filled out work releases, wrote follow up instructions to my assistant. At the bottom of the pile lay a powder blue notepaper envelope with a handwritten address. I tore open the seal. As I began to read, I recognized the author of the note.

"Thank you for your wise counsel," my patient wrote. "I asked my sister to leave and have reclaimed my bedroom. I have shifted my work position to one with less responsibility and fewer hours. I have also quit smoking." I leaned back in my chair and gazed at the ceiling, my eyes filling with tears. I brushed them aside and continued reading. "I have not felt so healthy in a long time. I feel like I am living for the first time in my life." I folded the letter slowly, placing it carefully in its envelope and touching it to my cheek.

"Well done you," I murmured to my patient as I set her letter in my drawer.

I felt proud of her for having taken such significant steps towards improving her health. Her letter affirmed that what I was learning and had begun to teach was important. That day she had come in to see me, I had given her more than antibiotics, an inhaler, and tobacco cessation counsel, and this broader scope of health creation is what I longed to provide for everyone in my practice. I beamed with joy, my heart full as I took off my white coat, reached for my purse and briefcase. "Yes!" I cried, pumping my fist. "Yes, yes" I chortled, my voice echoing in the empty clinic as I skipped out to my car. The long day had ended with a most beautiful flourish!

As I drove home, I mulled over the impact of my patient's feedback. I hardly took in the all too familiar route as I pondered the implications of my patient's letter. I didn't want to treat end-stage disease, I wanted to work with the core of health development to *prevent* end-stage disease, and this of necessity had to include all areas of life: physical, mental, emotional, work, home, community, spiritual, and environmental. Symptoms of disease were the end-stage of suboptimal health practices, and I as an allopathic physician, for the most part spent most of my time putting Band-Aids on the outcomes of weeks'-long—often years'-long—poor health practices. Unfortunately end-stage disease is where the overwhelming bulk of healthcare costs and time were funneled. The resource allocations were completely missing the mark of health creation.

I banged my hand on the steering wheel in frustration as I exited the freeway. I took in a deep breath and tried to relax – it was time to let go of work. I gazed at the oak trees leaning into the road and prepared for my homecoming. I turned into my street and sighed happily. My children would be waiting, excited to see me.

But I had stresses threatening my own health and wellbeing, for storm clouds were gathering again in my marriage.

CHAPTER 19 – IT'S TOO LATE

At our motel in Phoenix, Arizona. Lee in the foreground reading, Stephen standing, me in the sun. Stephanie took the shot. Not a happy family.

"Now comes the hard part." The backhoe operator grinned. "Good luck with that," he shouted, waving goodbye as he jumped into his machine and drove off. Lee and I stood in our back yard and stared into the huge hole that the workman had just scooped out and filled with gravel. The grunt work was left to us: we had to finish the French drain system by digging a down-sloping trench from the gravel-filled hole to the street drainage collecting system a hundred feet away. I had agreed to help Lee with this project, for our backyard was a mucky, messy swamp that swallowed our footsteps year round, making it tough for the kids to play.

"Come on, Liz," Lee urged, grabbing a shovel and handing it to me. "We've got to get this sucker done today." He pointed. "We start here and we head over to that corner of the lot." He grabbed a pickaxe and heaved it over his head. He grunted as he struck the axe into the solid clay clomp. Mud splattered everywhere. "Damn," he muttered as he wiped the spray of gunk off his face. I hid a smile and began to shovel.

Two hours later, we hadn't gotten very far and my back and arms were aching, my hands blistering.

"This might take more than a day, Lee," I suggested, arching my stiff back.

Without interrupting the flow of his pounding, he said, "No, way. We've got to finish today. Don't stop working." He looked up and saw me stretching. "Shit, Liz, you can't slack off now."

I picked up the shovel and drove it into the ground, again and again. Memories of Pensacola and hatch-covers, and the stench of fiberglass fumes flooded in. I wasn't going there, to that resentful place I had hung out in for so long. I now had new life skills. I had agreed to do this project and I wasn't going to act bitchy. I persevered for another hour or two.

"Okay, Liz." Lee was out of breath as he adjusted the perforated pipe while holding the leveler in the newly dug ditch. "The pipe has to have at least a one percent downgrade from the drain to the street collecting system. That over there looks okay but this needs to be deeper."

"Got it," I replied, wiping the grime out of my eye and grabbing my shovel. I was numb with fatigue. We had been slogging away for over seven hours.

"This is the last of it," Lee announced with a wry grin. "We did it! I need to make one more measurement just to make sure." He grabbed the leveler and crouched down in the dark. "Bring that flashlight here, Liz." He began to crawl along the trench sliding the measuring device as he went. "Fuckin-A, it's less than one percent here." He shot up, hurling the leveler to the ground, kicking dirt everywhere, the expletives pouring out of him. "It's not gonna work. We're still going to still have a fuckin' swamp in our back yard."

I took in our predicament as we stood, exhausted, aching, soaked and covered in grime, and found our whole situation ridiculously funny. I held my tongue though, and smiled inwardly since Lee clearly wasn't appreciating the humor.

"The drain still has a downward slope," I offered in an attempt to reassure him. "I think it'll work just fine, Lee. Let's just see if it does. We can't do any more tonight."

As it turned out, his outburst was for naught. Our once swampy yard remained dry from then on, no matter how hard the rains came.

§

When I was a child, I had a recurring nightmare in which an indistinguishable hoard, similar to a herd of buffalo, roared towards me and trampled me. The onslaught was inescapable. I'd always wake at the moment of contact, terrified. In some ways, the dream reflected Lee's verbal and behavioral onslaughts: they too felt inescapable and often came without warning. That was part of the crazy making with Lee. His actions were unpredictable.

§

Lee often worked on projects in fits and bursts. He spent hours rearranging and clearing out the basement. He stacked and restacked lumber and firewood in the backyard. He erected fences and a variety of storage nooks and shelters. He built shelves and then more shelves in the basement, and rearranged some more. He always had repair and remodeling projects in progress at his rental houses. His constant busyness drove me nuts. He always wanted to involve me, harping at and berating me when I resisted. I hated that kind of work and I hated the time he spent away from the children and me. When I did help, I mostly did so reluctantly, bitching and moaning. As I grew to understand and accept my needs, I tried to choose the projects I was willing to involve myself in and I slogged along with Lee attempting to maintain an attitude of support and good humor – like I did with the drain project. For Lee, though, my contributions were never enough and he sulked if I refused to join in, when I opted instead to be with the children: to play with them, and to take them on fun outings. Rarely, I refused because I just wanted to take some time for myself.

One Saturday, I signed up for a storytelling class. I arrived home to a disgusted Lee who had spent the day wiring the do-over family room remodel: the first addition that we had built when we bought the house was a disaster.

"Jesus, you've been frittering around all day while I've done all this wiring work – and I'm working full time too. You're selfish and a slacker. Liz." He yelled with his face up against mine, poking his finger in my chest. "You don't know how to work. You're not a partner. You don't support me, and you don't support the family." The kids ran to their rooms. I followed them, calmed them down, drying their tears as best I could. I set them up with some projects they could do by themselves. Instead of spending time with them as I had planned, I gulped back tears, took up the wire-cutters and power plugs, and worked until well past midnight installing switches and power outlets. My thoughts whirled. Was I selfish in taking a day for myself? Didn't I deserve having some personal time? I felt conflicted: I thought I had betrayed Lee – but I also felt enraged.

§

Lee had an ally in his rearranging projects. In fact, his mother was his role model. When Fern became anxious, she compensated by completely rearranging her furniture – almost a biweekly occurrence. Unfortunately, her rearranging – in cahoots with Lee – extended into our separate living quarters. I came home from work on more than one occasion shocked to find our home completely redone. Lee and his mother had moved furniture and pictures around without my input, knowledge or permission. I thought it a huge put down that Lee didn't respect me enough to work with me. Yes, I had issues with decorating – I didn't have a flare for it like Fern did, and therefore avoided it – but I still felt horribly violated. I was angry that Fern had breached my territorial boundaries. Her after-the-fact apologies did little to appease me.

My mother-in-law was already such a huge part of my life. She walked through my entryway to get to her living area downstairs. She watched our children for hours and days while I worked. The kids ran down to Grandma in the mornings when she awoke earlier than I did. The door to her apartment was always open. They'd whine when I'd ask them to come up for breakfast. If I was tied up with cooking or cleaning and I didn't play with them like they wanted me to, they'd go find Grandma.

I approached Lee one evening as we were getting ready for bed. "I want the kids to learn independent skills," I began, setting my clothes in the hamper. "I don't think it healthy for them to always have an adult at their beck and call." I folded the bedspread back and continued. "Your mother is always around and ready to play with them. I don't think the kids have enough time where they fend for themselves."

Lee threw his clothes towards the hamper and climbed into bed. "I think you're right, but I don't think it'll be easy. The kids love their Grandma and they want to spend time with her."

I climbed in beside him and nudged his shoulder, gratified to have his support. I was now feeling encouraged. "We'll have to somehow keep the kids from going down to her place."

"We can lock the door going down to her apartment."

I felt some apprehension at his suggestion. "We'll have to have a talk with the kids and with your mom," I worried about how they would respond.

The kids did pretty well with the new rule – they moaned for a time but adjusted to life upstairs. To our delight, they began to figure out what to do with alone times. Fern, however, didn't cope well at all. Initially she fussed and bristled that we were "locking her out." A week later, Lee's brother called. "You've gone too far with this. What you've done with Mom is cruel." Lee's other brother agreed. How had we gone too far? Why was it cruel of us to want our kids to have time with just their father and me? Wasn't it reasonable for us to want them to learn how to manage alone time? Didn't Fern have plenty of time with the kids when I worked and when we all spent family times together? Lee and I ended up unlocking the door, and we continued to encourage the kids to remain upstairs as best we could. My boundaries, both physical and emotional between my mother-in-law and Lee and I, were constantly being stretched and breached.

Lee infringed on my boundaries in other ways. Even though I did all of the cooking, he rearranged my kitchen domain, moving food from their original containers into unmarked ones, and completely revamping how I set up the refrigerator and cupboards. It drove me nuts to constantly unload cupboards and refrigerator, to peer inside containers in order to find the ingredients with which to prepare meals. When I told Lee how his rearranging made it harder for me to cook, he agreed. I asked him to stop and he promised to do so.

When I – yet again – opened the fridge after my latest reminder and request, rummaged around, and found that Lee had repackaged milk, mayo, sauces, meats, and vegetables in unlabeled containers, I lost it. I let out a piercing yell, grabbed a china plate, and hurled it down the stairs – the steps that led to my mother-in-law's apartment. I felt a perverse pleasure as it flew out of my hand, spun through the air, and shattered on the wall. I felt even better when Lee ran into the kitchen and realized just how fed up I was with his kitchen antics. Maybe this time I had gotten through to him, I thought with glee. But when my ten-year-old and seven-year-old ran in and I saw the startled fear on their faces, I felt awful. I had made a scene just like the ones my arguing parents had made when I was growing up. My kids were as afraid as I had been then. I felt guilty and ashamed. I thought that perhaps I hadn't succeeded in becoming a better parent after all.

§

In 1991, on the kids' spring break, we took a family vacation, and drove to Arizona, then on to San Diego to visit Lee's brother's family, returning to Seattle via the Bay Area.

In Phoenix, after a long day of driving, we cruised around looking for a place to eat and discovered the Olive Garden restaurant.

"Can we go there, Dad?" eleven-year-old Stephen asked.

"Yes, please?" Stephanie, almost eight, whined.

"That looks like a fun place," I said to Lee. "The kids are pretty tired and hungry. What do you think?"

"Okay. Let's try it, but if it's too expensive, we move on."

"I don't know how long these kids can hold out, Lee. They've been awfully good."

"Get off it, Liz." I buttoned my lip and hoped the restaurant would meet his budgeting criteria.

We tumbled out of the car into a fiery ninety-five-degree oven.

"Look, Mom, there's a line waiting to get in and I'm so hungry," Stephen said. His face puckered up like he was about to cry. Stephanie, too, looked droopy, ripe for a meltdown.

"The line's a good thing, Stephen."

"Why's that, Mom?" Stephanie asked, leaning into me and taking my hand.

"It means that if people are willing to wait, then the food's really good here."

"Maybe," Lee said, speeding ahead of us to check out the menu prices.

"But it's so hot out here," Stephanie said. "I don't like it."

"Look, Steph." Stephen was lifting his face up and holding his hands out. A huge grin broke out on his face. "It's wet!"

Stephanie moved in close and mimicked her brother. "What is this, Mom?"

"It's a cooling mist, kids. See the pipes above us? It's to help keep us comfortable while we wait."

Stephen stuck his tongue out to capture the fine spray. Stephanie again aped her big brother. They giggled.

I breathed a sigh of gratitude as the kids frolicked in the mist. The time flew by and we were soon seated.

The kids tore into the breadsticks. "These are great. Can we have some more, Mom?" Stephen was licking his fingers. The waiter passing by heard us and smiled. "You sure can, if it's okay with your mom and dad."

"Thank you," I said, and turned to the kids. "But save room for the rest of the meal."

To my delight, the kids munched on the salad, which they were often picky about at home.

"This spaghetti is great." Stephen grinned, his face covered in sauce.

"So's this ravioli." Stephanie's words were muffled, her mouth full.

I didn't have the heart to correct their table manners. They were in such high spirits, and they were eating so well.

"My eggplant parmesan is really delicious, too. How's your dish, Lee?"

"I like it. This is a pretty good place," he said, focused on his food.

"This is the best restaurant ever, don't you think, Dad?" Stephen glanced at Lee with a hopeful look on his face.

"It's pretty good, Stephen. Eat up now."

"Do you think they have an Olive Garden in Seattle?" Stephen asked after another bite.

"I don't know. The menu showed other locations so I think it's a franchise," I answered.

"Ooh, can we find one in Seattle?" Stephanie wiggled in her chair.

"Sure, we can look."

"I ate all my spaghetti," Stephen said, pushing his plate away. "Can I have dessert?"

"Me too. I want dessert too." Stephanie looked down at her unfinished ravioli, her face serious.

"You've eaten quite a bit, Steph, so yes, you can have some dessert too." I smiled.

Lee reached over and ate up the rest of her ravioli.

As we drove out of the parking lot, I clasped my hands. I was hopeful. I thought our trip was off to a good start.

In Phoenix, we stayed at the Days Inn, close to Camelback Mountain. The kids loved the pool. Stephen dove in and swam laps over and under the water. Stephanie was a little more tentative, afraid of the headfirst dives, and jumped in feet first instead, her strokes more of a dog paddle. I horsed around with the kids.

"Marco," Stephanie called out with her eyes shut, sweeping her hands to and fro in the water.

"Polo," I answered.

"Polo," Stephen whispered, swimming farther away. I stayed still.

"Marco." Her voice was now a little whiny.

"Polo." I moved closer to her.

"Polo." Stephen's voice came from the far end of the pool.

Stephanie flapped about and I let her touch me, but she wasn't happy. "Stephen's mean. He won't let me catch him. He never gets caught."

"Just wait, Steph, I'll get him this time and then you and I will make sure he doesn't find us." Stephanie wasn't so sure, but she nodded.

"No way. You won't get me . . . Dad, will you come and play?"

Lee lay on a lounger at the other end of the pool, engrossed in a dog-eared paperback. "Not right now," he said, without even glancing up.

Stephen dove underwater to hide his disappointment. My heart lurched. I hated that Lee distanced himself. I hated that he didn't see how much his son wanted his approval.

The following morning, Lee was up at dawn, dressed and ready to go. The kids were still asleep.

"Where are you going?" I whispered.

"I'm driving to Tucson to see Bonnie."

I jumped out of bed. "Wait and I'll get the kids ready." I wanted to spend time as a family, and I didn't mind going to see his childhood friend again.

Lee grabbled the keys. "I'm going alone." He darted out the door before I could reply. I fell back onto the bed and pounded my fists on the pillow. Lee had left me stranded.

The kids and I spent the day by the pool. I was heartened to see that they were happy enough. The three of us were used to not having Lee around. It was sad but true. At bedtime, as was our usual routine, I read books.

"One more page, please." Stephanie's eyes flew open when I closed the book. I thought she was asleep.

"Okay, one more page, but then that's it."

"Is Dad coming back?" Stephen asked, sitting up in the extra cot the hotel had provided. His face was so serious. His pain added to mine, and I was hard put to keep from crying. I tried to keep my voice level and gave him a shaky smile.

"Yes, of course he's coming back. He's just visiting an old friend." He nestled down in the covers, seeming satisfied. I breathed a sigh of relief.

"One more page, Mommy." Stephanie poked me in the side.

Lee didn't arrive back at the hotel until after midnight, and shared nothing about his day. I wondered if he had grumbled to Bonnie about what a horrible wife and mother I was. Is that why he didn't want me along? I felt abandoned and my unease grew.

§

We drove on to San Diego to visit Lee's brother, his wife, and their six active kids. Bart and Beth were devout Mormons, and we joined them for Easter services at their Stake House. I had bought Stephanie and their daughter Katie identical outfits – pastel yellow skirts with suspenders over white puffed sleeve blouses edged in matching yellow trim. Beth showed me how to fashion a halo braid in Katie's hair and I plaited Stephanie's the same way. I felt happy that the visit was going well. We were enjoying warm, close family time.

One night after all eight kids were bedded down, the four of us adults were visiting in the family room. The conversation shifted to finances, as it often did with Lee. He started in with "Yeah, we're doing all right financially, but not because of Liz. She's been a burden for years, a huge liability, what with her college and medical training."

"But she's earning a great income now," Bart interjected, smiling at me, "Surely that counts for something." I grabbed my lemonade, trying to hide behind the glass as I gulped.

"No way," Lee shot back. "She wasn't working for years and that was a huge opportunity cost for me. I'll never catch up with the level of assets my classmates have accumulated because of that. And she isn't even working full time. I'm screwed both ways." Lee was focused on Bart and spoke as if I wasn't even in the room.

Beth shot a glance at me, a little alarmed. "But she's a mom, and such a good one."

Lee turned his gaze to her. "She's not even a full time mom like you are, Beth. At least you came into the marriage fully educated and weren't a financial liability. Besides, at our house, Mom ends up watching the kids most of the time. Liz takes off whenever she wants." Bart and Beth sat stock still, staring at Lee. But he was on a roll. "Christ . . . "

"Lee, please don't swear." Bart said. His tone was firm, as if he were speaking to a child.

Lee shifted in his chair, and stared at the floor. "Well, okay, okay. Got to stay squeaky clean around you Mormons, I know." He looked up again, now over his momentary fluster, and began again. "Anyway, Liz couldn't care less about our financial assets. I try to get her involved, I try to teach her, but she refuses. And she won't help at all with the rental houses. I not only work full time, I have to take care of every break down, follow up on every call." Lee's motor mouth had at last run out of steam. An excruciating silence filled the room. I didn't dare budge. Bart and Beth were gazing at their hands – probably invoking a silent prayer for their infuriated brother and his humiliated wife.

Bart broke the silence and stood up. "It's getting late," he said, turning to Beth and taking her hand. "We're heading to bed."

"Do you need anything?" Beth asked, with a caring glance.

"No, thanks," I muttered and headed to the bedroom. I felt so stunned and embarrassed that the skin on my face felt hot enough to burn and slough off. I had not said a word during Lee's tirade.

As we prepared for bed, we didn't speak. I had absolutely no comeback. I scooted away from Lee, to the far the edge of the bed. I couldn't sleep. Dear god, Lee had pulverized me in front of his brother and sister-in-law. My stomach roiled with pain and rage. I stuffed dry tears and heaves. How could I hold my head up ever again? How could I face them in the morning? I was making good money as a physician. I was the primary parent raising our kids. Why wasn't that enough for Lee? When was I ever going to catch up to his expectations of me? His outbursts kept coming without warning and despite all I tried to do. I had jumped through hoop after hoop that he'd asked for, but they didn't count because I jumped too late, and I never jumped high enough. I felt sickened with the growing realization that I could never measure up in Lee's eyes. The horrible mess of my relationship was like the cartoon sketches of fights depicted as a whirl of clouds with arms and legs sticking out. I couldn't see through the murky jumble of fear, rage, blame, and shame.

Yet, during that long night, I was able to gradually move away from the cloudy fracas, and examine my relationship from a distance with the witness part of me – and then I remembered what I had learned about responsibility: I had the ability to respond to what had happened. I didn't have to be a victim. I could choose to continue to work on myself, I could claim my own self-worth, and I could appreciate all that I was already doing. I could acknowledge the truth: I couldn't change Lee's expectations of me no matter how hard I tried and – even knowing that – I could still keep my heart open to him. With the dawn, I still felt like a Mack truck had hit me, but despite the inner bruises I had suffered the night before, I remained committed to my marriage.

The next morning, I didn't say much. As I was helping Beth fix breakfast, her only reference to the previous night was to suggest, "You might try defending yourself better." I couldn't come up with any kind of response.

Lee and I slipped into an uneasy détente us as we drove towards Oakland. We spoke only to relay essentials. I didn't want to provoke him and he perhaps realized that he had outdone himself the night before. I didn't ask him, and he didn't volunteer. He certainly didn't apologize.

We focused on Stephen and Stephanie. We wished to show them where their dad had completed his medical internship, and where we had spent our first married days. As we drove along Shattuck Avenue in Berkeley, I ached knowing that some of my initial hopes as a newlywed had so not come to pass. In many ways, my relationship with Lee had soured. I set aside my disappointment and began telling the kids about some fun times their dad and I had had when we were first married. "Hey, Lee, remember all the hippies that used to hang out here? There were tie-dyed shirts and beads you could buy on the street corners. Remember how we found that little hole-in-the-wall place that had great burritos?"

Lee didn't respond to my questions. My anger spiraled and this time I couldn't hold in the pain. As we slowed to a red light, I screamed. The caged wild woman, feral and furious, couldn't take any more, and hollered to be free. Nearby, pedestrians startled and hopped away. Lee scrambled to push the window buttons closed. "Jesus, Liz, keep your voice down."

I immediately regretted my outburst, not towards Lee, but only that the children had to suffer. I turned to soothe and reassure the now terrified kids in the back seat. "It's okay, kids, I won't yell again. I'm sorry." I turned back to Lee, sobbing. "I can't stand how you treat me."

"Calm down. Quit being crazy," Lee snapped. I didn't want to say any more in front of the kids, and we continued on to San Francisco without speaking. We rode a cable car, walked around Nob Hill, and took in the gorgeous Bay view. I remained civil towards Lee only to protect the children. We went through the motions as a family, but even the children were caught up in our turmoil, and they remained restrained and quiet.

"Wild woman" – Clarissa Estes Pinkolt describes her in *Women Who Run With the Wolves*. I mostly suppressed my wild woman in my relationship with Lee. She peeked through mostly as bitchiness and silent resentment. Rarely did I blow up in raging anger as I did in Berkeley and when I threw the plate in the kitchen. Nevertheless, the accumulating hurts and putdowns began to fray the edges of my composure and I yearned to express myself more fully.

§

Three months later we took a summer family holiday. We planned another road trip, this time going east on I-90 to Lake Roosevelt. As our Honda chugged over the Cascade Mountains, the oil light began to flash, the engine sputtered, and acrid smoke began to billow out from under the hood. We scrambled out and stood alongside the car, horrified. Lee opened the hood, swept the black fumes away, and yelled for a rag. I hurriedly tore off some paper towels and handed them to him. He pulled out the dipstick and wiped it off. His face reddened and he shook the stick at me "Christ, there's no oil in the car! This is your fault. You're the one that uses this car. You're responsible for its maintenance and upkeep. Fuck, you're a screw-up. You've ruined the engine. It's going to cost a fortune. Damn it, you're going to have to pay for it. You've ruined our whole vacation!" He kept yelling, and I couldn't get a word in edgewise.

At first I was stunned. Numbness seeped through me. Then came disbelief. How was this my responsibility? This was the first I'd heard that it was my job to take care of the car maintenance. I couldn't breathe. I felt light headed. My head buzzed and my ears rang.

We limped into a garage in Moses Lake. We had indeed fried the car's engine and it needed rebuilding. We holed up in a dingy motel room. I tried to reassure the kids: "This has nothing to do with you. This is between your father and me. I just need to be alone for a while." A huge pall engulfed me, and all I could do was to withdraw. Even my soul felt wounded, oozing swamps of pain.

I refused to interact with Lee in any way. I couldn't even bring myself to interact with the kids. Lee took care of them, fed them, and took them swimming. Crushed, hurt and numb with disbelief at how vitriolic Lee's attack had been, I checked out emotionally, physically, and mentally. I was beyond arguing, stating my case, or processing the episode in any way. I felt like a mortally wounded animal. All I was capable of was to crouch in the corner of the motel room for several hours, licking my wounds.

The engine rebuild took longer than expected and after two days, we ended up riding a bus back to Seattle. By then I had begun to interact more, but my contact with Lee remained strained, and the air charged. I left a beloved Sydney sweatshirt behind on the bus. The loss of that sweater symbolized the loss of the joyous parts of my youth and deepened my despair over this latest living nightmare. I felt sickened by the growing rift between Lee and me, and yet I desperately wanted to hang on, to work our problems out. I was still committed to making the marriage succeed.

§

Though Lee and I had blowups, it was those things that Lee failed to provide that also eroded our relationship. The only consistent compliment he gave me was to recognize my intelligence. Lee harbored a fear of not being smart enough, kept referencing how much smarter such-and-such a high school or med school classmate was, how above his league they were. No matter how much I countered with the obvious – that he was a very bright and brilliant man – I could never persuade him.

Lee wasn't much for flowers or other small gestures. He forgot birthdays. His mother would have to remind him. One Mothers' Day, he took Fern and I on a ferryboat ride for a "picnic." He thought it was a fabulous idea, and chuckled as he unwrapped box after box of deli food. My mother-in-law and I felt uncomfortable with the public display of so many food packages splayed out on the ferry bench. Lee didn't provide plates or flatware. Bemused, I humored him, but felt saddened that he never asked how I wanted to be celebrated. He had his own sense of how to gift and he assumed his great ideas were exactly what I wanted.

Lee rarely explored my desires or needs. There wasn't much to build on to counteract the tearing down, the eroding away of trust, self-worth, and sovereignty. There were precious few pluses to neutralize the negatives. With Lee, I often felt like I did as a child: alone, unheard and uncared for. I kept repeating to myself, like a mantra: if only he would change, then I could be happy. I harbored resentments, inwardly seething, allowing all the perceived injustices to accumulate, all the while feeling the weight of my unworthiness. As I grew with my personal work, I was more and more able to take charge and be responsible for my attitudes and actions. I vacillated back and forth between being the victim and taking responsibility.

§

With my crazy medical practice schedule, I couldn't help but feel lucky to have my mother-in-law care for the children. The kids benefited from having a doting grandma in their lives – and yet Fern had strings attached to her love. She used childcare duties as a way to keep busy and to avoid facing her own demons: her chronic anxiety, the spousal abuse she had suffered, and her husband's violent suicide. She feared living alone. She was a worrywart. Early in our relationship, Lee shared with bitterness how his mother had used him as a confidante when he was a teenager. "I was the surrogate husband. She'd cry on my shoulder about his drinking and his putdowns."

Lee's response to his mom ran the gamut: he could be touchingly protective and playfully joke with her; he could also be overprotective and often directed her life and financial matters. At times, he and she engaged in horrendous yelling matches. Fern had little sense of timing: she didn't know when to back off and when it was safer to approach him. I avoided getting involved in the frays as much as I could and I resented their arguments when the kids were nearby. I did what I could to get them away from the fracas.

In the fall of 1991, Lee exploded like a powder keg.

"Christ, Mom, I just got off a night shift, I'm exhausted. I need to get some sleep," he yelled one morning.

"Oh, Lee, you never have time for me. I just had a question about your payment," Fern answered with a huff.

I heard them upstairs and lay my head against the wall hoping – please, not again. At least the kids had already left for school. Lee continued his rampage, slapping the dining room table for emphasis: "You keep bugging me. You're so needy. Why the hell can't you be more independent? I'm tired of having to support you and everyone else around here."

"Well forget I ever asked for anything," she wailed. "I can't live like this anymore." She ran outside, stumbling on the deck. Lee raced after her and picked her up.

"Jesus, Mom stop it, stop it," he urged, trying to calm her down. Even he knew he had gone too far, but by then Fern's blood pressure had skyrocketed. Her speech became slurred, and she couldn't move her arm. She had had a stroke. Lee drove her to the hospital to be admitted.

CHAPTER 20 – MOVIN' OUT

Fern with the kids. My live-in mother-in-law was both a help and a hindrance in our home.

Fern's stroke symptoms quickly resolved. We were all relieved. She came home from the hospital after a day or two, and within weeks felt strong enough to resume caring for the children. She was left with only a slight slowing of her speech, made worse when she became too tired. Lee's need to take care of his mother intensified after her stroke. He didn't think she could live alone and believed she needed close supervision.

For years, our friends and family had suggested to Lee and I that his mother move out. They picked up on the tensions, how Lee kept getting caught up with her needs, how I got caught in the triangle of mother, son and daughter-in-law. They believed it would be healthier for all of us if Fern had her own place. She could learn to be more independent, and Lee and I could better grow as a couple and as parents. For a long time I told them that we were okay and I minimized her impact on our lives. I felt beholden to her for all the childcare she provided. I went along with Lee's conviction that she needed our support. I wanted to be a good and loyal daughter-in-law.

A few weeks after Fern's stroke, Lee and I sat on our deck after we'd settled the kids for the night. The glow of a beautiful Indian summer sunset spread its warm caramel light over our yard. I smiled as I looked out over the lush green lawn, remembering how Lee and I had toiled to transform it from a swamp those years ago.

"Bart called again today to see how Mom was doing," Lee said, following my gaze out over the yard. Both of his brothers lived a ways away from Seattle and called often to get updates on their mom's condition. Lee then turned to look me directly in the eye as if to challenge me. "He thinks Mom would do better on her own, thinks we should find her an apartment." I dropped my gaze, not wanting to set him off by agreeing with his brother. I did venture to offer, "Well, we've heard that before, not just from your brothers but from some of our friends as well."

"They don't live here," Lee immediately shot back. "They don't know what goes on. Mom needs us. She's too fragile to live by herself. She's not strong enough and she'll fall apart if she has no one to live with her. You have no idea what she's gone through Liz. Hell, she hasn't recovered from Dad's blowing his brains out. You don't know what she was like those first months after he died. She was a fuckin' mess." Lee's face was aglow, his eyes piercing as he leaned in towards me. I began to chill despite the balmy evening breeze.

"You're right Lee, I don't know what it was like. I was still in Oregon. It must have been awful, but maybe now she's ready to be on her own. She could be independent and not get caught up so much in our lives. You know you get into arguments with her, and even you get uptight with her constant rearranging . . . "

"Don't even go there, Liz. You haven't been the best daughter-in-law and I could go on and on about that, you know." He glared at me, pursing his lips. "I can curb my tongue no problem. Her leaving – it ain't gonna happen."

I held his gaze, my mind swirling with a forbidden question that refused to let me go. I tightened my arms around my chest and with a sinking heart worked up the courage to softly ask:

"Who comes first for you Lee, me or your mom?"

With no hesitation whatsoever, he declared, "My mom."

My breath hitched and I hung my head.

His was a clear statement. I had no wiggle room as to how I might interpret his declaration. I had finally asked, and Lee had articulated what had hung in the air between us for years. I felt deflated, like a limp balloon, for I realized that Lee would always choose his mother over me. In many ways, he'd already chosen her at the expense of our relationship.

A week later, I had an intense emotional insight in a therapy session focusing on my relationship with my parents. Another piece of the puzzle of why my parents had distanced themselves from their children fell into place. Afterwards, I rested quietly in a nearby coffee shop. As I was absorbing and integrating what had happened, I heard a voice as clear as someone speaking next to me: "The time has come for you to leave Lee."

I quickly glanced around me, but no one was near. This admonition served as a confirmation for what deep inside, I already knew. I had done what I could to work on my relationship with my husband. Now it was time to separate myself and continue to grow on my own path. Despite the horrendous implications of this declaration, my body settled into a quiet calm. I was at peace.

§

Later that afternoon, I stood in the doorway of our bedroom. Lee was sprawled out on top of the bedspread reading the newspaper, his favorite white flannel sheet covering him. As was his nervous habit, he was threading the edge of the sheet back and forth in the web space between his first and second toes. I had always thought his mannerism cute, and dubbed him "twinkle toes," a nickname he rather liked. We were way past endearments, I thought ruefully. It was time to tell him. Fortunately, the kids had gone out for a Baskin Robbins treat with Grandma.

I took a deep breath as I edged into the room. I didn't want any physical contact to mar my resolve, and I needed to keep a safe distance between us to dampen the explosion of what I knew was to come. "Lee, I need to talk to you."

"What's up this time, Liz?" Lee looked up at me with suspicion and flapped the open newspaper with a sharp snap. He didn't close it. His toes flickered even faster.

I was glad my voice sounded firmer than I felt. My insides squirmed like a clump of worms. "I need some space, Lee. I want to move out."

Lee slapped the paper closed. His face was red, as he spit out, "Not again." His voice rose. "You know, you're a real cunt, Liz, a real cunt."

Even though it wasn't the first time he'd used this slur on me, my face flushed with pain, but I stood my ground. "I'm not saying I want us to split up, Lee, I just want some space for a month or two to think things through."

"Yeah, well, if you move out, we're done." He hurled the newspaper on the floor.

My whole body was shaking but I held his gaze.

He got up from the bed and thrust his face up against mine. "Christ, Liz, what the hell are you thinking? Where the fuck are you coming from? You're crazy."

I took a step back. My legs felt like rubber bands. Lee had accused me before of being "crazy," and at times I had believed him – but not any more. I straightened up and kept my gaze steady.

"I'm not crazy, Lee. You know I'm not, and you know things haven't been good between us."

"Yeah, that's because you're a royal bitch, Liz."

"Yeah, I am some of the time. All the more reason for me to get some distance so I can figure things out."

"Christ, Liz. Why are you doing this to me?" His voice faltered. My face flushed again. I felt his pain.

"I'm sorry, Lee. I've tried every other way I know. I must do this."

He turned away. I leaned against the doorjamb, slumping a little, feeling exhausted but relieved. I knew he had ceded the fight – for the moment.

The kids raced in the front door yelling, "Hi, Mom."

Lee punched the wall next to me. "God damn it, Liz. You're ruining our lives." He marched off past me, past the kids, past his mother, and slammed the basement door. Fern scurried after him.

The kids rushed to my side, their faces ashen. I hugged them both, tears streaming down my face. "I have something important to tell you."

"What, Mom? What is it?" Stephen sounded frantic, his face now splotched with red. Stephanie had begun to cry and ran to fetch her blankie. I took my son's hand, took my daughter's in my other hand, and led them to Stephen's room. I settled them on the bed, one on either side of me, our backs against the wall. I wiped away fresh tears: how we were sitting was exactly how we read books at night. I felt a stab in my chest knowing we wouldn't be doing that for much longer. I enveloped my children in both arms, breathing in their sweet chocolate and strawberry ice cream scents.

"I'm so sorry, but I have to do this . . . I'm leaving your dad. It hasn't been good between us for a long time and I need to be away from him for a while." Their stunned silence and the tears streaming down their faces twisted my guts for I had just caused their world to crash down. "This has nothing to do with either of you. You've done absolutely nothing to cause this. This is between your dad and me."

"Will we see you?" Stephanie hiccupped with panic as she squeezed her favorite blanket close to her heart. I held her tighter.

"Of course you will. You'll be with me and you'll have time with your dad and your grandma too. That won't change." I held them for a long time, heartbroken, my energy drained, spent.

§

The following days loomed hollow. A somber air surrounded the house that sucked out every last drop of joy and laughter. Lee's arguments and challenges peppered the gloom. I stood my ground. Underneath, he knew of my resolve and his challenges fizzled after a few fuming forays.

Two weeks later, I found a rental house for the kids and me. Lee and I agreed to joint custody. I moved out within a month of my decision. Ironically, my mother-in-law found an apartment and moved out a few weeks after I left. It seemed she could be independent, and her son could let go of her after all. I felt like I had been slapped in the face.

Initially, I wanted to leave Lee in order to get some physical distance and a measure of autonomy. I still had the desire to work on our marriage, but I needed the separation and psychic space to do so. I wanted us to enter couples counseling. While we had been living together, Lee weaseled out of joint therapy at every opportunity, but now that I had moved out, my determination was proof positive that I would no longer budge on this request. Lee had no wiggle room, no room to manipulate. My only request, besides the counseling, was an agreement that neither of us would enter into any new relationships.

And this is where Lee found his opening. His wiggle room appeared after all. Soon after beginning therapy, he admitted in a session that he was having an affair with one of the ER nurses in his department. The die was cast. I could no longer turn back. I had to break free completely.

After I moved out, I suffered wretched nights filled with violent tears as I stomped around my lonely rental. I had times when I ached to see the children, when they would call, sobbing that they missed me. Other times I shook with anger after Lee unloaded yet another diatribe about how I abandoned him, how I was taking him to the cleaners in the divorce settlement, how I threatened to take the kids away from him – which I never did. His rage flared like a spark to dry tinder and erupted in the all too familiar accusations: I cost him time and money that he would never recoup.

Some nights were filled with urgent prayers. I asked for divine guidance, for consolation. I knew my decision to leave had been a sound one; I knew that it was important for me to break my marriage vow. At the same time I struggled with guilt – I was the one who had uprooted the children from their combined parental home. I was the one that had, yet again, unleashed Lee's ire that spewed everywhere, like acid eating into my gut and heart, and into the lives of our children. What I hated most was how Lee used the kids as a sounding board, including them in his tirades about how I was taking all his money, and how I had run out on the family.

I felt disheartened. I had failed in my marriage and had broken my sacred vows. I was to become a divorcee. I had always recoiled from that status, vowing that it would never happen to me. Now I had to swallow my righteousness.

One evening, Lee somehow made it into my rental house in the middle of the night while I was sleeping.

"I want you to come back," he begged, kneeling by my bed and grabbing my hand. "I don't want this other relationship. I want you." I sat up, horrified at his intrusion.

"How on earth did you get in?" I asked.

"Come home, Liz," he cried, "Please come home."

"I'm sorry, Lee. You and I both know that it's over." I got out of bed, and gently led him to the door.

"Please don't come into my home like this again," I said, closing the door as he stood there bedraggled. There was no returning for me no matter how hard he begged. From that moment on, he knew it too and no longer crossed that boundary.

Some days later, I found myself out in the back yard of my rental house gazing at the moon, grieving, wailing like a wolf – softly, so the neighbors wouldn't hear – and I began to sing. I sang songs about the moon, among them "Brother Sun, Sister Moon," written by Donovan for the movie of the same name. It was my prayer to the moon goddess, asking for consolation, begging for respite from my grief and my rage.

After some time, I felt some comfort seep into me. As if affirming what I was sensing, the moon winked at me from behind a cloud. I broke out sobbing, but these tears were of understanding and filled with gratitude and love. My racing heart soon settled into a smooth rhythm and my body thrummed with a calm knowing. I had come to a place of reassurance and a serene confidence came over me, abiding in my heart. I knew then that all would pass. I knew that something, something greater and more compassionate, had me in hand and would see me through. I found consolation, and all my agitated and disorganized cells that had been reacting to my turbulent anger and anxiety settled into a synchronized peaceful hum. A stillness and a slow rhythm spread throughout my body and being. My mind, emotions and soul settled.

These times of consolation helped to keep me centered, and helped me deal with the stress and strain of Lee's accusations. I was able to ride the turbulent waves of the divorce and child custody settlement discussions. I was able to differentiate Lee's criticisms from my experience. I was able tease out Lee's attacks yet own my own part in the pathology of our relationship. I came to understand how unhealthy my outlook had been. I hadn't realized how little nurturing I had received from Lee. I reproduced in my marriage what I experienced as a child. I chose Lee, albeit unconsciously, to continue the unhealthy patterns begun by my parents. I now took full responsibility for my part. I had mostly held back and had not expressed clearly what I wanted because I feared retribution and punishment. I owned my coping mechanisms of strident criticism and bitchiness. There was no question that I had partnered in the pathology of my marriage.

What I did strive for, and what remained largely unappreciated by Lee, was my willingness to work on our relationship, my desire to change. I did not feel I had a partner in that. Yes, he did accompany me to Marriage Encounter but he placed the onus of our marital problems on my shoulders. I was the one who needed the help, the therapy. I was the weak link. And for a time, for a long time, I believed it. Yes, Lee did the Context Training human potential program, but he shared his learnings with another woman, and not with me.

In moving out, I continued to make sense of our convoluted and enmeshed relationship. I had survived the deluge. After twenty-two years of marriage, I had finally gained the courage to draw a clear line in the sand. I had set my boundary, and claimed my individual and soulic rights. Now that I had broken free, I could try to live and to flourish more fully than I ever did before.

CHAPTER 21 – MEMORIES ARE MADE OF THIS

My father and I in Budapest in front of the Sandor Petöfi memorial, Hungary's beloved national poet.

My father pointed to a bare hillside. We were touring the tiny village of Nyitra, now in Slovakia, but part of Hungary when Apu was growing up. He spoke proudly. "My grandfather's great vineyard once flourished over there. I loved to walk with him as he inspected the vines stepped all across and up and down that hill." My children frolicked along the gravel country road as Apu told us of my paternal great-grandfather. He had been a country gentleman who had built up a sizeable fortune and who had developed a hardy grape strain immune to *phylloxera*, the root disease that had previously prevented the establishment of vineyards in the region.

Apu and I and my children took this trip to Hungary and the surrounding countries in 1993. The time seemed right for all of us. I was getting over my relationship with Lee. Stephen and Stephanie, then aged thirteen and ten, were both old enough to appreciate and remember the experience. I wanted them to spend time with my father and to learn about their Hungarian heritage. My seventy-eight-year-old father remained active and loved to travel. Indeed, he ventured abroad almost every year. The time had come to accompany him.

I wanted to learn about my parents, what their early lives were like, and what they lived through during World War II. Their history rippled through me, sometimes like a breeze, other times like a sudden gale and I longed to know more. Moreover I felt a most curious and inexplicable homesickness that drew me to "return" to a homeland on which I'd never before set foot. A gravitational pull urged me to make the journey and held fast like a dog wrestling with an intruder's pant cuff.

"That's the house where I spent my toddler years." Apu smiled as he led us by an old stone building in Nyitra. "I played catch with my nanny there." He grinned as we peeked through an old iron gate into a tiny courtyard. I was delighted to hear my father open up, as he had so rarely shared stories of his childhood. "This is all that is left of my grandfather's Greek-style villa," Apu continued, now more serious. "My father lost grandfather's fortune because of unscrupulous advice from family members and "friends." They were all jackals and hyenas," he fumed. We turned away from the house and strolled down a curved cobblestoned street. The kids skipped ahead. Apu's voice quieted. "Our financial misfortune spread like wildfire. When the debt collectors came, my mother turned her pockets inside out crying 'no money, no money.'" My kids giggled as Apu acted out the childhood scene, turning his pants pockets inside out and holding his head in his hands. They didn't understand. Apu dropped his head. "My schoolmates made sport of mimicking my mother in front of me." I was shocked to see how the shame burned my father's face – even seventy years later – as he recounted this story. I flushed in sympathy. I was touched to see his vulnerability, which I had so rarely experienced in my childhood. Then, he had mostly remained militarily detached and strong.

Apu shrugged and looked away. "But I had good times growing up. When I was nine years old, I was shipped to Ypres, Belgium, as part of an outreach program." Always one for teaching us about history, Apu began to recount the political circumstances surrounding his summer travels. "Hungary was economically devastated and struggling after World War I. The Flemish, despite sustaining devastating casualties and destruction in their own right during the war, took on a huge humanitarian undertaking. The country reached out to aid our defeated country – their previous enemy – by providing Hungarian families with an opportunity to have their children vacation with foster families. My parents by then had pretty much lost all their fortune and their economic hardship enabled me to participate in the program. I lived with the Serruys family and they treated me so well, providing food and clothing. I played with their kids and learned how to speak Flemish. They were good times," he mused with a faraway look on his face. The fact that my father recalled his Belgian summer with great affection spoke not only to his adventurousness, but also reflected on his contrasting miserable, poverty-stricken life at home. Amazingly, Apu became fluent in Flemish during the few short weeks he spent in Ypres and this fueled his lifelong love of learning languages.

I began to fit together the puzzle pieces of my parents' lives in Hungary. My father's memoir, which he was in the process of writing at the time, helped fill in some of the historic details.

For instance, I did not know until I read his book that Apu was just fifteen when he lost both his parents. Hounded by debt collectors and duped by opportunists, his father's health failed from the financial ruin. His mother died a few short months later from heart failure and thrombosis. Apu hardly knew his maternal aunt and her husband, who took on the responsibility for raising him. His guardians placed him in a boarding house adjacent to the high school he attended. He spent miserable years here with what he described as "cold faces and cold hearts."

I learned more about Apu's life as we toured. The locales stimulated his memories and his stories poured out. One of them surfaced in Vienna when we took the kids to see one of the main tourist sites: the Schönnbrun Palace. Apu had taken me there as a teenager in 1967, when I had spent a semester in Paris. I remembered how he had pointed to the mural ceiling in the main hall and scornfully announced, "See the cattle in the corner? That's how the Habsburg dynasty depicted the Hungarian people."

This time, twenty-five years later, Apu stood firm at the ornate wrought iron gates of the Schönnbrun Palace grounds and stubbornly refused to enter. "You all go ahead," he said and motioned with a dramatic wave. With the words exploding through pursed lips, he said, "I no longer wish to admire or to support the excesses of the indolent Habsburg rogues. They built their empire on the backs of the Hungarian peasants." He turned and marched away. My kids looked down at the ground and shuffled their feet.

"Nagypapa (grandpa in Hungarian) has always rooted for the little guy," I explained. "He hated how the royalty had all the money, all the opportunities, and all the power. Let's go inside the palace, and I'll show you what Nagypapa meant."

Apu's experience gave him a lifelong aversion to upper class privilege and he always championed those of low birth with intelligence and a strong work ethic. It was one of the reasons he was so attracted to my mother when they met at a dance in Galánta in 1939, where he was stationed and she taught high school. In his memoir, he describes Anyu as "typically self-made, ambitious, efficient, and pretty." He admired people like her who pulled themselves out of humble beginnings. He had seen "peasant" classmates and military recruits just as smart and ambitious as he, who never had the opportunities to rise above their lower class status. Apu was privileged to attend the Ludovika Military Academy and become an officer solely because he came from gentry.

I loved the grandeur and luxury of the Schönnbrun palace, and marveled at the exquisite craftsmanship and the astonishing beauty of its artwork. But I, too, felt for the less fortunate working class that paid for, and sacrificed their lives by the millions to support the arrogant aristocrats. In this, I supported my father.

In Hungary, we drove to the famed resort area of Lake Balaton. Here, my conversation with Apu turned to World War II. He and I sat on a bench by the lake as we watched my children wading in the brisk water. The sun was shrouded in a misty fog as Apu began. "In late 1942, I was promoted as a company commander and I received orders to mobilize to the Russian front along the Don River. The Hungarian Second Army troops were poorly trained and equipped with outdated firearms and artillery, much of which was resurrected from World War I stashes and drawn by horses." He grumbled. "Most of the soldiers wore threadbare clothing insufficient to counter the brutal Russian temperatures of 35-40 degrees below freezing. It was horrible." I shivered and drew my arms around me.

"We didn't have a chance. We Hungarians were used as the front line cannon fodder. The Germans followed right behind and they were well equipped with state of the art weapons," he added bitterly. "In less than three weeks in

January 1943, the Hungarian legions were decimated. No nation lost as much blood during World War II in such a short period of time." He paused. "Less than two dozen of the battalion I commanded survived the Russian front." He fell silent. I glanced and saw his watery gaze fixed on the expanse of the lake. Apu was back in his devastated, war-torn world, his face twisted in anguish, his usual military bearing now perceptibly sagging. I flushed despite the cool air. Finally he breathed a sigh and whispered, "I don't know why I was one of the few singled out to survive."

I feared looking at him again, wanting to honor the gravitas of the moment, afraid that if I looked I would break its spell. My mind whirled, searching for the heartfelt words that would convey my love. Finally, I responded. "You returned from the front because you were needed in the world. You had much to do for your family and for so many others. I, Geza and Tom wouldn't be here if you had not returned. I have been blessed to have you as my father."

Neither of us dared shift our gaze from the water. A charged silence filled the pocket of air around us, broken only when my daughter trotted up, shivering and asking for a towel. Somehow, my father and I knew no further words were necessary. We had affirmed our love, gratitude, and mutual understanding. We finally looked at each other and smiled.

My father felt guilty that he had survived when thousands had not, ashamed that, though ordered to retreat, he was unable to continue fighting to try to help save some of his men. One of the troops my father was ordered to leave behind was his batman (personal assistant) and good friend. When Apu broke the news of his death to the batman's wife, she attacked him with pounding fists and screamed obscenities. My father was crushed. Years later, when he first returned to Hungary, he sought out his fallen comrade's family and worked to make amends by providing financial support, but even this generous gesture never completely assuaged his guilt.

§

A highlight of our trip was the time we spent in Budapest, staying with my tall and serious Uncle Zoltán and his second wife. They lived in a tasteless, high-rise condo building on the outskirts of the city, constructed during the era of the communist occupation. Marika Néni, plump and talkative, made the most delicious chilled sour cherry soup (*meggy leves*) decadently thickened with sour cream. I couldn't get enough of it.

One of our must-see sites in Budapest was the famed Buda Hill overlooking the majestic Danube River. As we strolled through the Fisherman's Bastion atop the hill, my body softened and my eyes and nose prickled with tears to see the picturesque bridges suspended across the river, the gorgeous parliament house that edged the far bank and the flattened Pest district beyond. I felt overwhelmed to finally be in my homeland and to see in real life what years before I had seen only in seen pictures. The Hungarian names flowed on my tongue in sweet remembrance as I took in each beloved landmark: *Lánc híd, Margit híd, Országház, Halászbástya, Mátyás-templom*. I stood mesmerized, in complete awe. I pointed with excitement. "Look children! See, there are the Chain and Margaret bridges over the great Blue Danube River." I became even more caught up in the emotions as I chatted. "And look! We are standing in the Fisherman's Bastion that I learned about when I was your age at Hungarian summer camp. I'm amazed to be seeing it for real. Isn't it awesome?"

I struggled to convey to my children the magnitude of what I felt. The physical draw was magnetic, overwhelming and inexplicable. At age forty-three, I had come home to a land that I had never before set foot on, and yet I felt connected to it in my very soul. I felt crushed that I wasn't getting through to them. Stephen was caught up in getting the sites recorded on video. Stephanie smiled and nodded but then quickly walked on, wanting to see the next attraction. Their attention wavered and their looks remained blank, even a little put off as I attempted to explain with more and more animation. Even Apu failed to take in the depth of my emotional reaction, caught up in his role as tour guide. Mine was a solitary communion with my homeland.

We moved on and stood in the square of the old Buda Castle, which now housed the Budapest Historical Museum. Apu swept his arm around the area.

"This was all bombed and mostly rubble during the war," he said. "It's all been reconstructed."

"You're kidding," Stephen said, peering from behind the camera.

"Not at all," Apu replied, smiling at my son's disbelief. In a more sober and measured voice he turned to me. "Under here, in the cellars is where your mother and siblings spent weeks during the bombings."

Anyu's experience during the Budapest siege, one of the longest and bloodiest battles of the Second World War, proved nearly as horrific as my father's time on the Russian front. The Russians surrounded the city in late October, 1944. Nearly thirty-three thousand German and thirty-seven thousand Hungarian soldiers, as well as more than eight hundred thousand civilians were trapped within the city. Refusing to authorize a withdrawal, Hitler declared Budapest a fortress city, which he vowed had to be defended "to the last man."

My mother, two of my older siblings, and my Uncle Zoltán moved to the cellar shelters under the royal palace. Apu had asked his brother to do what he could to help the family in his absence. Caught up in the perils and anguish of the war, Zoltán rose to the occasion, put aside the personal disapproval of my mother that he had demonstrated by failing to show at their wedding, and had harbored for years. When the bombing began, he helped to ferry the family to the shelter of the cellars.

As I stood in the Buda Castle square, I recalled the tale Anyu told as I was growing up and shared it with my children. "Once Nagymama realized the bombings were coming, she baked dozens of hard cookies, the kind traditionally hung on Christmas trees. These she hid away and when they moved to the cellars, she gave them out at night – just to your Uncle Paul and Aunt Irene – while the other people slept. In his hunger, Paul would cry out for 'little stars and moons,' the shapes of the cookies. The other people were curious as to what he meant, and Nagymama told them, 'Oh, it's just the child's illness. He's hallucinating.'"

Though my kids smiled, they also began to get a gist of the hardships my family endured during the war. Now a mother myself, I appreciated what a fierce survivalist Anyu was and how ferally she protected her children. I admired her courage and tenacity. I drew Stephen and Stephanie about me and hugged them tight. Neither my children nor I had had to endure what Anyu and Paul and Irene had suffered. I felt humbled and grateful for the privilege of living in a country where wars didn't rage on our doorsteps.

Anyu had kept her family alive in those cellars when others died of hunger, disease, and wounds. Their bodies were carted up to the street surfaces every morning. Infant Irene, ill with tuberculosis, coughed into her damp pillow, covered with green mildew. Two-year-old Paul struggled with tonsillitis and bronchitis. My mother braved artillery fire and bombs daily as she traipsed upstairs to use the cooking facilities in order to provide meager meals for the family. Uncle Zoltán wrote of all this in a diary that he kept of those weeks in the cellars. He wrote tenderly of my mother, how she continued to care for him and the children despite being ill herself, how she starved herself and gave the little available food to her family. Uncle Zoltán's disapproving attitude towards my mother had indeed softened since his failure to show at my parents' wedding.

We next drove through the busy streets of Pest, and Apu's stories moved on to events after the war. He remained in the military and maneuvered about and around the communist Russians who had occupied and retained control in the country since the war. He was able to skate the convoluted politics for a while, and he avoided joining the communist party. Many of his associates were imprisoned or executed during those years – capriciously it seemed – as membership in the Communist party didn't confer any particular protection.

By 1947, though, Apu's luck had run out. He responded to a demand to report to the MP headquarters and there, authorities detained and questioned him. They falsely accused my father of ordering a subordinate to hide loaded weapons rather than distributing them as ordered. He spent three days in a cell, petrified, hearing the cries of men being beaten. Through the intervention of some friends who still had influence with the communist regime, he was at last released.

"Stop here for a moment." Apu motioned and I pulled over in the heavy traffic. He pointed to a narrow alley. "Here's where I took that interminably long walk out of the detention center after they released me." My children's chatter in the back seat quieted. "My legs were shaking. I thought for sure I'd be shot in the back, as some of my colleagues had been before me. The communist officials had justified these executions stating they were shooting escapees. All I could think of was to pray." Apu's voice caught as he continued. "See, you can still see the bullet pockmarks in the sides of the buildings." My eyes filled with tears. An impatient car honked behind me. I drove on in a blur.

A few weeks after his first detention, my father was served another order to report to the MP headquarters. This time, he did not respond to the summons. He gathered his family and arranged to be immediately smuggled across the border to Austria. The smuggler drove the family in a wine wagon, the three children hidden in barrels. My parents drugged baby Geza, my third sibling born just a few months earlier in March of 1947. They were hoping to keep him from crying and alerting the sentries, but he just ended up vomiting the medication and crying anyway. Nonetheless, the family safely made the hairy border crossing and settled temporarily in an Austrian refugee camp.

There my father's righteousness imperiled the family's safety. He reported personnel who were selling much needed drugs – drugs that should have been distributed free of charge. That, coupled with rumors accusing my father of being a communist, caused Apu to be blacklisted, in effect forcing the family to move out of the camp.

In Austria, we travelled to Salzburg. The kids and I danced through the Mirabell Gardens, one of the settings for our favorite movie, *The Sound of Music*. We were thrilled to stomp around the fountain edge and run through the trellis as we sang, "Do, Re, Mi," though we warbled with a lot less aplomb than Maria and the children had in the film. Less caught up in our light-heartedness, Apu humphed, "It's time to move on. I want to show you Attendorfberg." This was the tiny hamlet my family relocated to after they were ousted from the Austrian refugee camp.

"We lived here for a year," he told us as we drove up to an old stately house sitting alone atop a hill. "The widow of the local doctor lived here. The house was a mess and smelly – she was very dirty. The doctor's servant bought the place after she died." The house had been passed on in the family and it was now the granddaughter who welcomed us warmly. She showed us up to a tiny dingy attic room that had a single gabled window. The view of the yard below was half blocked by the roof overhang below. "This was where all five of us lived," Apu quipped. "We had no heat." I found it hard to imagine how the family could have squeezed into this cramped dark room. The granddaughter smiled. "You didn't have it easy here, I know."

Back downstairs, Stephen and Stephanie chased rabbits in the garden while Apu continued his story. "We were hungry most of the time. I worked odd jobs, from chopping wood to serving as an orderly for a pompous English officer. I had to ride the train to Graz every day." My heart sank at the shift in his life circumstances. The tables had turned. My father who had been a major and a staff officer, was no more. He had now become the batman, the assistant to a low ranking first lieutenant. I was moved, and gently touched Apu to express my empathy. My father shrugged, dismissing the obvious irony, and pulled away from my arm. He motioned to the surrounding woods and said, "We even sold mushrooms that we collected in those woods."

Apu realized he couldn't make a living in Austria and that he had to move the family. He had always hoped to settle in the United States, but American visas were in demand and hard to come by. He therefore applied for, and received an Australian visa. With travel funds forwarded by the Australian government, the family rode trains to Naples and from there sailed on a newly refitted ship, the *Anna Salen*, along with hundreds of other European immigrants, all part of the huge diaspora following World War II.

In his memoir, my father describes the family's journey into Sydney Harbor in June, 1949. "Sydney's environs are frighteningly steep stone cliffs, abundant tree and bush covered hills, and lavish villas and parks in a story-like harmony . . . In the middle of winter, the green colors shouted out from every shade. Fluffy, blindingly white clouds alternated with sunshine . . . there is no face in the world that would not have smiled . . . With one set of clothes and two suitcases filled with a change of underwear, a few memories, books, papers, an old fashioned camera, a few tools for repairing radios, children's clothing, and some three pounds sterling in my pocket, I stepped onto the shores of the promised land."

§

I pondered my parents' odyssey as I jetted back to Seattle with my kids. Apu didn't return with us, having decided to stay in Europe a little longer to visit with friends. My time with him had been ever so precious. Apu was still my stolid, politic spouting, rigid father, but on this trip, I had begun to glimpse his emotional turmoil, his vulnerability and the pain of his childhood and war traumas. My father had become more real and more approachable.

I gazed at Stephen and Stephanie as they dozed in the seats on either side of me. I hoped that they had grown and learned from the experience. I longed to take them to Sydney, to show them my origins. How might their view of me shift upon seeing where I grew up, where I both faltered and thrived? That would have to be another odyssey. As I leaned my head into the tiny cushion and adjusted my cramped body, my thoughts flew ahead to Seattle and to a relationship that was beginning to heat up.

CHAPTER 22 – AT LAST

Joseph & I soon after we began dating.

"I want one more weekend to look around, Lee," I said as we were driving home. It was two weeks after I had announced that I wanted to move out and he and I had just looked at a house for me to rent.

"That one looks okay, Mom" Stephen reported from the back seat, "My friend, Kara lives across the street."

"I don't know what your problem is." Lee huffed. "It's practically brand new and the rent is fine."

"Yes, I know, but it's really close to the freeway and I'm not sure breathing smog is that good for the children."

"Ha!" Lee scoffed. "Good for the children. You've got to be kidding. You've chosen to leave me. How good is that for the children?"

"Lee, please," I begged.

I hadn't wanted him to come along on the rental house search but he had insisted and I didn't want to make any more waves. I just wanted to move out with as little hassle as possible. What I didn't tell Lee is that I had imagined the rental house I was to move into in a meditation and the house we had just looked at wasn't it. The following weekend, I found it.

The three bedroom modest bungalow with the L-shaped entry had just been listed in the classifieds and as I drove up to it, I was elated. It was exactly as I had envisioned! "I apologize for the mess," Joseph offered as he wiped his grout stained hands on a rag. The slim, handsome soft-spoken man in his early fifties, with a thick shock of more-pepper-than-salt hair immediately put me at ease. I felt relieved for I had met some surly and even shady landlords in my housing search the previous two weeks.

Joseph led the children and me through the home. "I'm completely redoing the bathroom and I'm painting the kitchen cupboards. It'll all be done in a couple of days." I glanced at the cabinet doors laid out on tarps, the odors of stain and lacquer prickling my nose.

"So will it be available to move in next weekend?" I asked with some hesitancy in my voice.

"Oh, yes, my son's a contractor and he'll lend a hand to finish it all up tomorrow." I smiled in relief as he led us through the three bedrooms.

"This is a pretty modest place, but it's a good family home. It's where we raised our three children," Joseph mused with a soft glow on his face. "The back yard is large and a great place for the kids to play." I immediately felt comfortable with this man and with the house.

Joseph remained an attentive, yet unobtrusive landlord. Initially, he only checked in to see if I had any concerns about the rental. As we became acquainted, we shared more of our lives. His wife had died rather suddenly of an acute illness a year and a half before. He, of course knew the reason for my renting. When he came over, he'd ask how I was doing. I could tell he didn't wish to pry, but rather felt genuine concern for my wellbeing. I began to open up as my hopes for a turnaround dimmed in my relationship with Lee.

I warmed to Joseph when he offered to loan me some tapes about loss that a friend had given him. "I didn't know if you'd be interested in these," he said with some hesitancy, "And you don't have to listen to them. They helped me to deal with my wife's death and I thought you might get something out of them with your loss as well." I thanked him and listened to the tapes. They were indeed helpful.

A few months after moving out, once my marriage had tolled its death knell, Joseph started to invite me on walks. I liked our easy conversation, his thoughtful, non-judgmental listening. At the end of a walk one evening, as we were nearing my front door, he stopped, turned to me and asked, "Would you let me take you out to dinner?" Before I had a chance to reply, he added, "I haven't done this dating thing in decades and I'm not sure I even know how – if I ever did – but if you'll bear with my bumbling, I'd love to give it a try with you." His face flushed and he broke out in a befuddled grin.

"I'm in the same boat, you know." I smiled. "I haven't dated in years and I feel just as awkward as you. I'd love to go out to dinner. We can muddle together."

"Wonderful." He sighed with relief, giving me a hug. We said our good byes and after I closed the front door, I clapped with glee and jumped up and down.

§

Joseph picked me up the following Saturday evening. He looked polished in a smart navy sports coat and tie.

"You look lovely," he said as he opened the car door for me.

"Thank you." I smiled at him as I swept my legs into the car. I thought to myself, "Brownie points for you for dressing and acting like a real gentleman."

"I wanted to take you somewhere special," he said as he backed his Buick out of the driveway. "I called Salty's at Alki but they were full. I hope you don't mind that we're driving all the way down to the other Salty's at Redondo Beach." He glanced at me and then averted his gaze, busying himself with adjusting the rear view mirror.

"Of course I don't mind. Salty's is a great place and I haven't been to the one in Redondo. My brother lives down there, you know." The twenty-mile drive sped by as we filled the time chatting lightly about Tom and our families.

All the seating in the tiered restaurant faced the expansive waters of Puget Sound, now dusky with a few twinkling lights in the distance on Maury and Vashon Islands.

"This place is great," I whispered to Joseph after the hostess seated us.

"Oh, I'm so glad you like it." He gave me a shy grin before burying his face in the menu. After we ordered, there was a pause in our conversation. I glanced around the bustling restaurant. It seemed like there were only couples there and they were all at ease, animated and smiling.

"Well, this is awkward," Joseph said, adjusting the napkin on his lap.

I shifted in my seat. "We did say we'd muddle along on our first date, didn't we?"

"I guess we did say that." He chuckled and met my gaze. I smiled at the warmth in his eyes and my shoulders relaxed.

"Tell me about Australia. I've always wanted to go there." I told him about my love of the beaches and the balmy weather.

"Did you see koalas and kangaroos?"

"Only at the zoo."

"You mean they didn't hop along streets in the city?"

I grinned. "No, but my brother used to go kangaroo hunting in the outback with his university mates. He saw lots of them."

He looked surprised. "You're allowed to kill kangaroos?" I nodded.

The server interrupted, bringing our salads.

"Okay, now it's your turn," I said, attempting to pierce a wiggly piece of lettuce. "Tell me about growing up."

Joseph set his fork down, taking a moment to collect his thoughts. "Well, I was raised in Decatur, Illinois. My favorite times were when Dad and I went fishing."

"You know, I've gone fishing a few times and I've never, ever caught anything."

"You've got to be kidding. Really?"

I laughed. "Really. Stephanie hooks a fish every time she throws her line in. She loves to kid me about my failures."

Joseph chuckled. He again thought a moment, studying his salad plate before saying, "I'd like to take you fishing sometime. Maybe I can change your luck."

"You're on!" I laughed, pleased that Joseph liked me enough to want another date.

Joseph smiled back but then he became quiet, his face serious and sober. He met my gaze.

"You mentioned Stephanie. You know, my parents divorced when I was nine. That was really hard. I can imagine a little how it is for your kids." He turned to the window. I followed his far away gaze and stared at the murky waters of the Sound. I felt a twinge of excitement course through me. This guy knew how to empathize. He understood what my kids were going through. I was touched.

"Thank you. That means a lot to me."

"They'll get through it. They've got a good mom." His brown eyes settled on me, soft and steady.

"You're kind." I chased the last of the now droopy lettuce onto my fork. I wasn't so sure I deserved the complement and wanted to change the subject. "Tell me what else you liked to do as a kid."

The waiter interrupted our conversation with our steaming pasta and grilled salmon dishes. The aromas made my mouth water.

Joseph gently teased a tender flake of salmon onto his fork. "This looks great . . . hmm, what else did I like as a kid . . . well, my dad would take me to St. Louis to baseball games. It was a long drive but I loved it and I loved talking baseball with him."

I could relate to baseball. Stephen was totally into it and the Seattle Mariners had had some recent memorable winning seasons. We chatted on with ease, and not just about baseball. Our awkwardness disappeared completely by the time we had finished dessert.

§

We went our second date a week later on Labor Day. Joseph took me on one of his favorite hikes to Ebey's Landing on Whidbey Island, a short ferryboat ride away from Seattle. It was my first of many times on that hike.

We walked along the beach and climbed up the bluff. I felt an immediate connection with the stunning landscape, patchwork farmlands, vast expanses of water, evergreen forests and rugged mountains in the distance. Awed by our surroundings, we walked mostly in silence. At the top of the bluff, Joseph pulled me into the copse of trees and tenderly kissed me. It was perfect. "Let's go find a place to eat." He grinned. We found a wonderful restaurant in Langley overlooking the water. We held hands in the car on our drive, on the ferry, the whole way home.

The next time we saw each other, Joseph came by the house to drop off something. As he kissed me, I felt a wallop in my pelvis of such a magnitude that I had to sit down. The erotic in our relationship was stoked and we soon became lovers. My body awoke with his tender touch, and my starving soul was nourished with his attention and respect.

§

My time with Joseph was a celebration. We ate out often, went to plays, the symphony, and the ballet. We went away for weekends and for one of our first getaways we headed to Vancouver in British Columbia.

"Where would you like to stay?" Joseph asked me as we approached the city.

"I don't know," I answered. "The last time I was here, we stayed at an outlying motel to save money. I don't mind doing that."

"How about the city center? That way we'll be close to the sites and we can walk everywhere." I nodded with an eager smile. Joseph added, "There's an old stately hotel that's part of a historic chain like the ones at Banff and Lake Louise that I'd like to check out. Are you up for it?"

"Well, sure," I grinned.

We soon drove up to the stately Hotel Vancouver, topped with a gorgeous green copper roof. I felt elated to be staying at such a luxurious hotel, the kind I'd coveted years before in Banff when traveling as a newlywed with Lee.

"We're in the process of redecorating all the rooms," the hotel clerk informed us as we checked in. "I don't think your room has been done yet." I followed Joseph to the elevator, thinking that the older rooms would still be stylish enough, but my heart sank as we entered the room. The furniture was bland and Fifties style – the kind my mother filled our home with and that I hated. Joseph immediately noticed my disappointment and put his arm around me. "How about if I call down to the front desk to see if we can stay in one of the redecorated rooms."

"Oh, would you?" I cried.

"Of course! I'd like to stay in the new room too."

When we entered the freshly decorated room a few minutes later, we both looked at each other with huge grins. The furniture was traditional with a velvety rich, dark oak finish. The luxuriously colored floral design on the plush bed shams and coverlets oozed elegance and out our window, we had a gorgeous view of the city. I flopped on the bed, giggling with glee.

"This is heaven." I sighed, "Thank you so much for doing this for me."

"It's my pleasure." He grinned as he joined me on the bed with a knowing look. "My pleasure," he repeated slowly as he began to unbutton my blouse.

In Vancouver, we took in a Canucks ice hockey game. We laughed at the player's antics, and cringed at their bloody fights. The hotel concierge got us tickets to see the *Romeo and Juliet* ballet. My heart swelled to see the young ballerina fly across the stage with the quickest *en pointe bourré* I'd ever seen. Her tiny, rapid steps as she raced to her Romeo were unbelievably sensuous.

I squeezed Joseph's hand and drew closer to him. I was on a perfect romantic getaway, and I was so grateful to be with Joseph. He delighted in every outing we went on and never, not once did he hold back or mention cost. We commemorated our trip by purchasing a beautiful poster of the Vancouver skyline featuring the copper roofed Hotel Vancouver.

§

I loved the attention I received from Joseph. He valued my opinions. He noticed things about me, complimented me, and loved to celebrate with me. He brought me flowers. He loved to have fun. And he was attentive not just to me, but to my children. He listened to them without judgment. He attended Stephen's baseball games and took videos of Stephanie's rides in every horse show in which she participated. Joseph was a calming and grounding influence for my kids, a positive older male figure who listened, cared about, and respected them. This was not the experience they had with their father.

I married Joseph at his parish Episcopal Church in February, 1994, two and a half years after we met and a month after my divorce was finalized. It was a small wedding with mostly family and a few close friends. I wore an ivory crepe midi dress gathered below my hips in almost flapper fashion yet quite modern when cinched at the waist with a belt of the same fabric. My head was bare and I carried a bouquet of pink roses. Joseph looked elegant in his dark suit. His admiring look when I approached made my heart sing. I felt beautiful.

We included a celebratory Eucharist in the marriage service. This time, in stark contrast to my first marriage, taking communion in the ceremony made complete sense. Holy Communion was a central element in Joseph's faith practice and complemented the deep connection I'd first had, receiving the sacred host as a teenager. As we carried the offertory bread and wine to the altar, I felt a rush of sacred love and turned to Joseph as he turned to me. We sensed the blessing of our union at the same moment and beamed at each other. Receiving communion became a loving, holy ritual we shared as a couple.

I thrived on Joseph's love and attention. I had some great years with him, years of being nurtured and celebrated for who I was. Our vacations both with and without the children were filled with fun. We explored and laughed and played together. Even though our combined incomes were less than when I was married to Lee, we spent within our means with a carefree sense of delight. We were able to enjoy great times with no worries about expenses or lost opportunity costs.

§

When Joseph's old car was close to its last gasp, we made the rounds to look for a new one. As we headed over the West Seattle bridge to the last car dealerships on our list for the day, I took in glorious Mount Rainier peeking out from the clouds to our left. My face softened to feel its majestic presence.

Joseph looked at me with a grin and announced, "We have to get a car with enough room for Stephen and Stephanie. They're close to grown up and getting tall. They'll need lots of leg room." I was touched. My children, now aged fourteen and eleven, were indeed growing up.

"They're not always with us, you know, so I don't know if their needs should be a high priority," I answered, not wanting to burden him too much.

"Nonsense!" He gave a wave of his hand. "They're family." Joseph always included the children in our planning and he never felt them to be a burden. "We'll also need a car with a little zip – Stephen will want to rev the engine when he gets his license," he added with a chuckle.

That evening, we found a handsome Buick that measured up to our criteria. As we were driving it off the lot, Joseph glanced at me with a knowing look. "The first person to put a ding in the car gets taken out to dinner," he declared. Puzzled and shaking my head I clarified, "You mean whoever dings the car gets to take the other out to dinner."

"No, no." He laughed. "The person who dinged the car feels bad enough already. They're the ones that need to be treated."

I was floored! All I had known was Lee's angry responses on the few occasions that I had banged up the car. I also recalled the awful blowup that he orchestrated accusing me of frying our Honda engine. I struggled to take in the huge contrast of Joseph's caring reaction. "You are an amazing man, Joseph, and I love you," I replied grabbing his hand and gently kissing it.

I gradually became less on edge with mishaps or dollars spent on "frivolous" entertainment. With each gift Joseph bestowed, I allowed myself, little by little, to fully enjoy and settle into receiving. And I no longer feared the blaming outbursts like the ones Lee peppered out with regularity. I no longer felt I had to be always on guard, ready to protect myself from insults.

My faith that a relationship could be loving and nurturing was restored and grew with each passing day that I spent with Joseph. I was so grateful! I was giddy with love and I began to write poetry.

Elizabeth C. Fowler

Your Touch

Your touch is exquisite
Soft, sensitive, slow
Ever reaching new and wondrous places
Places I never thought could awaken
Such patience, such tenderness
How do you know where to go?

At times I'm not with you
My mind flies away
And I am gently, sensuously
Brought back

Do you know when I'm not there?
If you do, I sense no judgment
Only acceptance
Of who I am

I thank you.

§

Three years into our marriage, dark clouds appeared. Joseph began to struggle with what we believed to be chronic prostate symptoms and after several months his discomfort was severe enough that he opted for surgery. He underwent a prostate resection in August 1997.

In an unusual, not strictly ethical twist, his surgeon gave me permission to access the path report: I was a colleague and he was about to leave on vacation immediately following the surgery. Two days later, I stopped off at my office to look up the results before visiting Joseph in the hospital. My fingers trembled over the computer keys as I punched in my provider access code and his medical history number. Yes, I had managed to pull up the right report: there was his name and the origin of the biopsy tissue: prostate. I scrolled down through the morass of medical jargon to the diagnosis printed at the bottom of the report: invasive transitional cell carcinoma.

Joseph had bladder cancer! My stunned brain flew to la-la-land, uncomprehending, but my body understood immediately and broke out in a cold sweat. My mind was swimming in a riptide but gradually kicked back into gear and began to make sense of the path report: bad, bad bladder cancer. I hadn't expected this at all. Where was the diagnosis of prostatic hyperplasia? I

260

must have the wrong report! I checked the name again. Yes, it was Joseph. Well then, they must have switched specimens – there must have been a mix-up in the path lab. Why would the surgeon have allowed me to access the report if he suspected cancer? My mind whirled. It was a complete shock. I became light headed, my ears began to ring, and my throat choked up.

I stumbled out of the office, barely able to remain upright. I must have looked like hell for my office assistant became alarmed and immediately rushed to my side to hold me up.

"What's wrong, what happened Elizabeth?"

Confused and barely contained, I muttered, "No . . . no . . . nothing . . . I'm . . . okay." I fled from her arms and raced off to see Joseph.

"Why even try?" were the first words Joseph uttered with disgust when I gave him the dour diagnosis. He fell into a stony silence. I sat beside him for the longest time. I couldn't think of any consoling words. Not yet. The stark reality was sinking in for both of us.

Despite his initial outburst of angry frustration and hopelessness, Joseph rallied and he fought hard. On CT scan, his tumor was shown to extend to the pelvic wall and therefore, surgery was no longer an option. The oncologists recommended alternating courses of radiation and chemo and Joseph willingly complied with all their suggestions. In addition, he embarked on a flurry of alternate therapies including vitamin and naturopathic supplements and exotic mushroom preparations shipped directly from Hong Kong. He went for acupuncture treatments and took yoga classes. The combination of all these modalities served for a time and kept our hopes alive.

§

Life changed after Joseph's diagnoses. One afternoon, I was playing catch with Stephen in the back yard. He hurled a fastball directly into my glove.

"Ouch, Stephen, that really hurt," I said, removing my glove and rubbing my palm. "I can't catch any more of those."

Stephen sped to my side to check on my beet-red hand. "Sorry, Mom. I'll ease up."

"I'll do a few more catches, but then I have to start dinner." I felt uneasy. If he had the chance, Stephen would play until it was dark and the stars were shining. Why wouldn't his dad ever take the time to play with him?

"Good throw, Mom." I was pleased at his compliment and smiled.

"You're just buttering me up so I'll play longer. Three more catches."

"Aw, Mom, come on. Please can't we play longer?" I felt heat rising up. I hated it when Stephen pushed.

"Five more catches. That's it," I said, my tone stern. Stephen knew he couldn't push any more. I could see his shoulders sagging and I felt like a heel.

"We can play again on Friday, if you like."

"I have baseball practice after school . . . but maybe over the weekend?"

"You bet!" I smiled and was heartened to see his grin.

"You know, you really are getting good at throwing, Mom. I mean it."

I tousled his hair. My earnest, seventeen-year-old was turning into a fine young man.

Joseph appeared at the door with a scowl. "Are you going to fix dinner? You know I need to eat by six." He turned with a huff and I followed him into the kitchen.

"I'm getting to it right now. It'll be ready," I said to his back.

Stephen gave me a look, and then headed to his room.

Joseph took a seat at the kitchen table, wincing slightly as his rear end made contact with the chair. The tumor in his prostate area was bothering him again. I wished I could ease his pain. I felt helpless. "That chicken dish you made last night was too spicy. I can't eat that stuff any more. It bothers my stomach."

I washed my hands in the sink. "I'll keep your food bland, Joseph. The kids like my Hungarian dishes, though, at least every once in a while."

"That's fine, you fix it for them but fix me a bland dish: grilled chicken and fish and lots of broccoli."

"Okay, I got it." I felt put out, like a short order cook and pulled hard on the refrigerator door. I began to plop packets of chicken breasts, bags of carrots and green beans onto the counter.

Joseph lined up his stash of herbs and supplements on the table and began to methodically swallow them one by one. "Your kids don't do much around here. I pick up their messes all the time. The least they can do is pile them up in their own rooms so I don't have to see it."

I wiped my brow and let my breath out, trying to calm down. "I'll talk to them," I finally said, chopping the carrots harder and faster, but managing to keep my voice even.

The kids were already getting earfuls of putdowns from their dad. Joseph's piling on the criticisms did not help. I felt torn, caught in the middle. I wanted to be there for Joseph and yet I desperately wanted to counteract Lee's lambastes. I needed to be the supportive parent for my kids.

Dinner was a solemn affair. The kids picked up on Joseph's mood. I got down to business, orchestrating schedules.

"Stephen, what time are you done with baseball practice? Can you pick Stephanie up from the barn at 6:30?"

"Yeah, I can."

"And don't be late like you were last time." Stephanie glared at him.

"Too bad, Sis."

"Zip it, both of you," I said, weary of the tension at the table. Joseph was staring at me. I felt I like a pincushion. "I'm meeting Kathleen after work, so I'll be late getting home."

"What about my dinner?" Joseph asked with a frown on his face.

"I've made extra tonight, so you'll all have plenty of leftovers."

"Well, okay, but you're sure gone a lot." The kids both looked down at their plates.

"I do what I can, Joseph," I said, picking up the plates and carrying them to the sink. Joseph got up from his chair and grabbed the newspaper.

What had happened to my loving, attentive husband who supported my kids and me at every opportunity? Since his cancer diagnosis, it was as if Joseph had turned into a chameleon, shifting his emotional colors from warm pastels to dour charcoals and burned out maroons. He had become more withdrawn and self-centered. His illness became his first priority and my needs were lower on the list. "He wants me at his bloody beck and call," I muttered to myself. Disheartened and near tears, I loaded the dishwasher.

Later that evening, thirteen-year-old Stephanie made a face as I entered her room to say good night. "Joseph hates me," she said, "and you spend all your time with him. I'm not important to you anymore." My heart ached to see her near tears, clutching her worn blanket to her chest as she climbed into bed.

"I understand how hard it is for you to see Joseph sick and needing me more, but I'm here for you too, Stephanie, and I love you, you know that." I hugged her and held her tight. She softened a little in my arms.

"Read to me." She pouted. "Read to me a long time."

I understood her viewpoint, for I was often torn between her and Joseph – even that night I knew he was waiting for me, wanting to discuss some new treatment modality that he had researched. It was getting late and he'd be irritated because he'd want to get to bed. I was irritated because I was tired and had to get up early for work. I was also irritated that Stephanie was testing my love by asking me to read for a long time.

After three pages of *The Golden Compass*, I gently closed the book but her eyes immediately flew open. "More," she insisted. "One more page," I countered. My irritation smoldered, my faced flashed with anger. I felt I was being stretched in too many directions and I was losing it. "No, read until I'm asleep," she whined. "I can't do that Stephanie, I'm getting tired too." She turned away from me with a frown. I felt wretched. I wasn't meeting her needs, Joseph's needs, or Stephen's. Nobody was happy, least of all me.

§

At times, I had to get away from the pall of emotions in the house. I'd take off to meditate at a nearby park, across the street from the Episcopal Church where Joseph and I had wed. One time I sat in the car, staring at the ducks in the pond, jealous of the couple strolling by smiling, arm in arm. What had happened to our relationship? I had just begun to accept Joseph's love, become at ease with his consistent attention. I had finally begun to let my guard down. My metaphorical arm wasn't shooting to my face moment to moment to ward off verbal blows like I'd received on a regular basis from Lee. Now, I had to become defensive again. I had to ward off Joseph's criticisms of my children and me. I pounded the steering wheel with my fist. What the hell had happened to him?

I reasoned with myself that he faced a horrible diagnosis: non-curable cancer. He was ill and in pain. His whole world had turned upside down. I had to be more understanding. I had to give him some slack. But the ache in my heart grew and angry tears streamed down my cheeks. I mourned the loss of what we had and I wearied of being the mediator, the peacemaker between my kids and Joseph. I tried to focus on meditating and instead dozed off, exhausted.

I awoke startled, hearing a tap on the car window. A young mother with a child in tow was breathless and anxiously blurted out, "Are you okay? Oh, Oh, I'm so sorry to disturb you. I thought you might need to be resuscitated!" I muttered that I was all right and thanked her for checking, but maybe she was right. As I drove home, I mused that maybe I was heartsick enough that I did need to be resuscitated. I didn't feel much better.

§

At age forty-six, in the midst of my shifting relationship with Joseph, I hit menopause. My thyrotoxicosis recurred, not an unusual occurrence in the setting of hormonal changes. As with my earlier bout, I was placed on anti-thyroid medication.

Over the years, since my initial thyroid event in medical school, I had gained some perspective on my thyroid problems. I found it intriguing that I developed a thyroid disorder, the gland that sets the metabolic rate for the whole body. There were times that my body believed that I needed to rev myself up to rise to some unfathomable challenge. In med school, it was the challenge of my troubled relationship with Lee as much as the intensity of medical training itself. With the menopausal recurrence it was my extreme stress and frustration at the loss of my healthy second husband who, once diagnosed with cancer, shifted from being an attentive, loving partner to a more needy, self-absorbed one. I was back in a relationship that was not feeding me. My body's way of coping was to ramp up the pace in an effort to overcome the pain of the losses.

As an autoimmune illness, Graves disease was part of a spectrum of illnesses that recognized the body's own tissues as foreign and set up a rejection process. My immune system saw my thyroid as the enemy and was attacking it with a fervor that caused the poor gland to jump with overactive zeal. The autoimmune process was a way that I physiologically whipped myself into a hyperactive furor. I was literally "beating myself up." My thyroid dysfunction and self-destruction served as an embodiment of the harsh critic within that mercilessly punished me at every turn: not good enough, not strong enough, not smart enough and, above all, not deserving enough.

Finally, my thyroid gland resided in my neck, the anatomic byway between heart and head. My disease symbolized a roadblock, a lack of communication, a lack of resonance between my heart and my cognitive brain. For years, I had fostered my intellect: it was how I sought attention and approval from my parents; it was one of my qualities that had attracted Lee; and intellect was what medicine worshipped and rewarded above all else. It has been my life path, my soul's journey to reconnect my disparate head and heart, to learn how to open my heart and have it work in conjunction with and enhance my intellect, rather than allowing the mind to run amok without the benefit of love and compassion to guide it. Above all, I lacked love and compassion for myself. As much as I was able, I metered these qualities out to those around me.

This bout of high thyroid levels again responded quickly responded to anti-thyroid medications. I was grateful, extremely grateful that I didn't have to undergo total thyroid ablation necessitating lifelong thyroid replacement pill taking.

§

In the midst of Joseph's illness, we continued to have moments of intense connection. At his first treatment, after the nurse had hung the IV bag and the chemo agent began its journey into Joseph's body, he and I gazed at each other filled with love. We reached out to hold hands, partners fully aware that this moment marked the beginning of a new and perilous journey. We felt the sacred infuse and bless us. We smiled softly, our faces glowing. We needed no words. We held onto and cherished the reverent connection.

A year into his treatment, when he had had a partial response and some of his strength had returned, Joseph joined me on a jog. We chuckled and reveled in his resilience. Around and around the track we sped, filled with the hopes and joys of his remission.

Later that year we celebrated Christmas, welcoming our families into our home. Anyu and Apu sitting far apart from each other; Paul with his wife and two children; Irene and her husband; Geza and his wife and two children and some of Joseph's family -- all settled themselves in our living room.

I had taken up playing the violin again and had practiced carol duets with Stephanie. "I don't know if I can do this, Mom," Steph whispered to me as we tuned our violins by the baby grand piano. Everyone awaited us.

"No sweat, you'll sound great." I whispered back, "I'm the one who should be worrying. I've hardly played in thirty years!" That brought a smile to her face.

"Quiet, everyone," Joseph announced, his face wan yet beaming, his head now completely bald, his gorgeous hair completely ravaged by chemo. "The ladies are ready to perform."

He moved away and stood by the glowing fireplace, his gaunt body leaning into its warmth. Steph and I looked at each other, smiled and then with a nod focused on our music and began to play *Oh Holy Night.* The arrangement and harmonies were simple yet touching. Steph sounded great, her tone clear, her intonation spot on. I was pleased that I managed to stay mostly in tune.

"Well done," I said to Steph as we took our bow. She gave the audience and me a shy grin. I then announced, "Stephen has prepared a special treat for the Palotás crew." I smiled looking at Joseph, and continued. "As long as I can remember, *Mennyből Az Angyal* has been a family tradition. We sang this carol every Christmas Eve before opening presents," My voice cracked with emotion. "The translation goes . . . " Apu, Paul and Irene helped me out when I faltered and bumbled with translating the lyrics.

The angels came down from heaven to you, shepherds
So that you may hasten to Bethlehem and see
The son of God, who has been born [and is lying] in a manger.
May he be your savior.
May his mother Mary be beside him;
The holy boy lies among cattle, he sleeps in the manger.
Let them go at once to greet him,
Taking beautiful gifts with them in their hearts.
May they worship little Jesus alike,
May they all bless God Almighty for such a great boon.

We were all grinning by the time we had reached the end. Stephen settled at the piano and began to plunk out the tune along with some matching chords. All my family joined in and began to sing: my father, his face beaming with pride; my mother and sister – both still off key but endearingly so – my brothers Paul,

Geza and Tom. I was so touched I could hardly bear it. I had never felt such loving harmony in all the years I'd sung that Christmas carol with my family. The Fowlers gave us a round of applause.

Caught up in the warm festivities, my father then motioned to Geza and whispered in his ear, handing him some keys. My brother returned, lugging an old cello. Apu beamed.

"I picked it up at a garage sale. Listen, it has a really good tone," he said strumming a few notes, searching and sliding for the right intervals, trying to stay in tune. "Ah, my hearing has gone," he huffed in frustration. "Here, Geza, you were the one who took cello lessons. Play us a tune."

Geza sheepishly took the instrument between his legs and bowed over the open strings before hesitantly trying a few notes. He even managed a little vibrato.

"It's been eons," he lamented. "I don't remember hardly anything at all."

"Well let's sing some Christmas carols," I suggested. "And you can strum along."

Steph and I began "Jingle Bells" on our violins, Stephen on the piano, Geza hitting every fourth or fifth note – not always quite in tune. Nevertheless, we were all singing along, all beaming and having a marvelous time. As I looked about the room and took in our melded families, my heart warmed and my eyes glowed. My gaze met Joseph's and his face shone with love.

The evening was getting on but I wanted to celebrate one more tradition. I walked up to my brother and touched his shoulder.

"Pali, you have to play us some honkytonk. Please?"

Paul grinned, happy to be asked. Like Joseph, he appeared gaunt, his belly swollen from the bile duct cancer that was ravaging his body. Both he and Joseph were undergoing chemo. My brother limped to the piano, favoring his arthritic hip, but once he began to play, his energy rebounded: he blasted out "In the Mood" without any hesitation, his fingers flying over the piano keys. I chuckled with glee, swaying to the beat. We all clapped and cheered after he finished.

"No biggie," he muttered, using a phrase that he so often threw out, but his radiant face told a very different story.

After we had said our goodbyes to our guests and were walking up to our bedroom, I took Joseph's hand. "Thank you for tonight. Your love for holiday traditions has spread to my family. This has been my sweetest Christmas ever." I leaned over and kissed him.

Connected times like this held us together and helped to stem the resentment as he became weaker and needier, and as he withdrew more and more. By the time Joseph grew too weak to be up and about, I was able to let go of my needs not being met, and I was able to be there for him.

When Joseph slipped into a coma, our Episcopal priest came to the house to administer last rites. As I accompanied him to the front door afterwards, he remarked with a soft smile, "Love is in this house. I have no worries about Joseph's transition. I have no further work here." I appreciated his observation, for it affirmed what I felt.

That evening, my dear friends Kathleen and Judy visited. We gathered around Joseph, now unresponsive, and sang, "This Little Light of Mine," and "Amazing Grace." Even the much-maligned "Kumbayah," the often parodied "hippie" refrain, felt sacred and totally appropriate, and our soft voices mixed with our smiles and tears as we opened our hearts to Joseph's transition. My friends had both experienced the passing of loved ones. Their support helped me cope and their presence filled the room with sacred wonder. Their love and hugs gave me the strength to carry on with Joseph to the end.

Joseph's son and daughter-in-law sat with him through his last day. Exhausted, they left in the evening. Alone, I lay next to him listening to his cheyne-stokes respirations: increasing gasps followed by long pauses. In the early morning hours, he breathed two agonal breaths that brought no air into his lungs – and he was gone. His three and a half year struggle with pain and disappointment was over. That was a consolation, but my heart ached to see my love pass away, for Joseph had bestowed an invaluable gift. He had given me the experience of being fully loved, respected and celebrated.

§

One of the many gifts Joseph showered on me was to help me reconnect with sacred music. For Joseph's funeral service, I asked the choir to sing the version of the 23rd Psalm I had learned and had found so thrilling in grade school. The words to this psalm were powerful, and made so much more sense than it did in my youth, for I now had experienced the death of a loved one very close to me. The words consoled. The melody and the sweet descant tugged at my heart, and my tears flowed.

Classical church music had always moved me. I found Gregorian chants hauntingly beautiful. Christmas carols such as "O Holy Night" consistently brought on a heart surge and a full throat. The Episcopal parish church that Joseph and I attended had a topnotch music department. After his death, I became more active in the church choir. Under the masterful direction of its music chorister, David White, I became captivated by the ancient hymns and services of Compline and Evensong. David's genius and passion for music infected all of us in the choir. He inspired not just amateurs like me. Four choir directors and several professional singers joined the choir just to experience his brilliant direction and teaching. Hidden and safe among the many choir members, I sang my heart out without feeling self-conscious like I did as a youngster singing solos.

Our choir toured England in 2002 and performed for a week as the choir in residence at St Alban's Cathedral just north of London. I reveled in adding my voice to the other altos, sopranos, tenors and basses. Our harmonized sounds soared and reverberated through the hallowed heights of the ancient edifice as we sang the haunting words of the "Magnificat." The words are from St Luke's gospel where Mary, newly pregnant with Jesus, greets her also pregnant cousin, Elizabeth:

My soul doth magnify the Lord,
And my spirit hath rejoiced in God my Saviour . . .

The Evensong service continued with the "Nunc Dimittis," The Canticle of Simeon, also from Luke's gospel. Simeon, an elderly Jew praying in the temple, recognizes the baby Jesus as the Messiah and exclaims:

Lord, now lettest thou thy servant depart in peace,
According to thy word,
Because my eyes have seen thy salvation . . .

Singing these sacred motets in an ancient cathedral that echoed centuries of hallowed Evensong services was a huge thrill.

Soon after returning from England, David moved back to his hometown of Chicago. The choir had lost its inspiration and I along with several other members left. I also stopped attending services. Joseph's devotion to the Episcopal Church had rekindled my love of the Christian liturgy. I loved the service of the Mass, the sacrament of Communion, the sacred music, the rituals and the incense. Attending church with Joseph had helped to enhance our relationship and created a sacred foothold. I marveled at how similar the Episcopal Eucharist was to the Catholic Mass and warmed to the saner church laws: contraception was acceptable, as was divorce, and priests were allowed to marry. Episcopalians did in fact enjoy "Catholicism without the guilt." But even with its less stringent rules, the Episcopal Church, like the Catholic Church, fell far short of encompassing the whole of my spiritual life. For me, Christ wasn't the only answer. Neither was repetitive ritual. The Christian world was too small. What about nature? What about the sacred potential of my mind and body? What about the vast realms of the non-physical worlds? I longed to find a seamless, inclusive way to incorporate all aspects of creation.

I found that broad approach when I met David Spangler. I had heard about David's work from Brugh Joy, another spiritual teacher that I had met a few years before, so when I learned that David was doing a signing for his new book *The Call* and that the event was at my favorite hangout – the nearby University Bookstore – I decided to go meet him.

I arrived late at the bookstore. David had just finished his talk and was engaging his audience. A plump, jovial man with thinning hair, he must have known some of the attendees as he gave them big hugs and grinned as he talked. With the copy of his book clasped in my hand, I approached him shyly and introduced myself.

"I have worked with Brugh, and he often mentioned your work," I said.

"Oh, that's great that you got to work with him," David smiled. "Yes, Brugh and I led the yearly Asilomar conferences for quite some time. It was a wonderful collaboration." I passed him my book and he inscribed it, "To Elizabeth – with blessings – may the call of your heart always resonate with the contours of your life!" With a twinkle in his eye, he handed me the book and gave me a bear hug. I was touched by his openness and the caring love that he radiated.

Soon afterwards, I signed up for one of his workshops. David described himself as an "everyday mystic" and that title fascinated me. He was sensing spirit in the ordinary and I longed for that as well. Moreover, his work confirmed what I knew deep inside: every aspect of our being and our environment is sacred and has consciousness. We humans are part of the universe, and all of it is a seamless continuation of the sacred, which infuses plants and animals, manmade edifices, earth, universe, as well as nonphysical realms. This wholeness is what I perceived as I communed with the ocean, basked in the glow of the sun, cherished the blush of a rose, when I listened to Mozart or a robin's call, when I sensed the presence of Christ in the communion host, when I gazed with love at my children or my lover. Everything was sacred. At last, I could seamlessly meld all my disparate experiences into the all-encompassing scope of the all-pervasive sacred. At last, I also received confirmation of what I sensed about myself: the holy infused all aspects of my being – body, mind, emotions and personality.

I resonated with David's Incarnational Spirituality work and was honored to join the faculty of the Lorian Association. This organization was begun by a group of expatriates from Findhorn, an eco-spiritual community in Northern Scotland where David had served as director for a time. We launched Deepening into Spirit, a two-year, masters level spiritual formation program. In helping to teach this program, I had the privilege of learning and deepening my own sacred connections. I became more and more drawn to my spiritual work. At the same time, my medical practice obligations were becoming more and more stressful.

CHAPTER 23 – THE TIMES THEY ARE A CHANGIN'

A formal work photo taken around the time I was clinic Chief.

"Elizabeth," my clinic manager cornered me in the hallway, "Do you have a moment?" The handsome, self-assured young man, at least a decade younger than me, motioned me into his office. I had always appreciated his directness, his humor, and his no nonsense way of getting things done, but the serious edge to his voice alerted me. I had a few moments before my next patient was due and so I took a seat.

"As you know," he began, "We're in dire need of a new clinic chief and your name has come up." He began clearing a pile of papers off the desk so he could see me better. I slumped a little in my seat. Of course, I knew about the vacant chief position. Everybody at the clinic knew. I, along with all my partners, cringed at the thought of taking on the administrative and bureaucratic hassles that the position entailed. The leadership vacuum, however, was becoming more and more of an issue and the management were pressuring us all. I sat in stony silence, not wanting to look at him. "We'd like for you to apply for the position, Elizabeth – *I'd* like for you to apply. I think you'd be a great chief and I'd love to work with you."

"Thank you," I mumbled, "I'm flattered."

"Flattery has nothing to do with it. You have a good sense about the clinic goings on and I need you advocacy and support. Things are heating up around here and you being chief would help me immeasurably. Please consider the position." I could see he had begun to buckle under the pressures of the organizational politics and I knew I had the ability to provide some support.

"Let me think about it for a day or two and I'll get back to you," I finally answered.

"Thank you." He leaped up and took my hand in both of his, shaking it enthusiastically.

"Sure." I smiled ruefully.

That night, I pondered the clinic manager's proposition. It had been a year since Joseph's passing and I was looking for some new direction in my life. I felt some draw to take on this additional responsibility. Leaning on the transformational work I'd explored for years, I took the question into meditation and opened to the possibility of taking on the chief position. When I felt my heart radiating warmth in my chest, I took it as a sign that I was to accept the chief challenge. Little did I realize what was to come.

§

As soon as I became chief, the organization introduced a new electronic chart system and embarked on new efficiency initiatives and austerity measures. Clinicians were instructed to increase the number of patients on their panel sizes and to see more patients each day. I recoiled from these edicts for I had hoped to develop and promote healthy and holistic practice environments. I wanted physicians to have more time to spend with patients, not less. I rolled out the stern requirements with less than rah-rah enthusiasm. I was an uninspired advocate for the new changes. The clinic manager quit soon after I began as chief, for he could no longer abide by the harsh organizational policies. I had lost one of my like-minded colleagues and became disheartened and disillusioned.

Along with my chief duties, I continued in my shared practice, but as time went on I realized just how burnt out I was on medicine. The grind of seeing ever more patients, the extra time learning and using the new electronic chart system wore me out. I had twelve hour and longer workdays, and that, along with my hard-hitting obligations as chief left me irritated and exhausted.

The *coup de grâce* occurred a few months into my chiefdom. The organization leaders piled on stringent cost cutting measures on top of the new efficiency initiatives. In a rare move for the organization, they began to lay off clinicians. I had the unsavory job of terminating two clinicians. I was able to prevent the layoff of a third physician by applying for a sabbatical myself. After a year and a half as chief, I had at last found a way to escape the leadership politics and the practice grind. For years, I had dreamed of taking a sabbatical and my opportunity had arrived at last. At the same time, I was doing a good deed by saving one of my partners from the layoff chopping block. I had no funding for my sabbatical – the austerity measures summarily dispensed with that benefit – but I could care less. Nothing could keep me from forging ahead with my decision. I craved a complete break from medicine, my first since beginning medical school twenty-seven years earlier.

In retrospect, I realized that the distasteful chief experience served to propel me towards a major shift in my life's work. Before taking on the leadership duties, my practice had maintained a steady state of stress. The chief position, coupled with the stresses of Joseph's death and my brother Paul's, five months later, brought about enough discomfort to enable me to really take stock, let loose, and plunge ahead into something completely new. The boondoggle of becoming chief helped to push me over the edge. The heart opening that had occurred in my meditation, which had encouraged me to accept the clinic chief position, hadn't been so incongruous after all. My intuition wasn't as capricious as I first suspected, for it served to give me the exact nudge to change that I needed.

§

On the last clinic day before my sabbatical, after closing out the final chart and packing the last of my belongings, I left the clinic late and alone. The rear receiving area door clanked as I pushed down the lever. The sound jarred and echoed disturbingly inside me. I suddenly felt confused. I realized that I was leaving not only my practice, but also my physician persona. I panicked as a sinking feeling of hollow emptiness overwhelmed me. I felt like a Jane Doe in a morgue, cold, lifeless and without identity. If I wasn't a physician, if I wasn't Dr. Fowler, who was I? That question was to haunt me during my off year.

§

The first week of my sabbatical, I spent alone on the big island of Hawaii. When I arrived I felt lethargic, out of shape, and I was horrified to see how frumpy I looked in a swimsuit. My thighs and stomach bulged like lumpy sausages and dull, dejected eyes stared back at me in the mirror. I walked around in a daze and had little clue of how to mobilize and put my year off to good use.

Then I felt the warm wind caress me and I began to pay attention. I soaked up the sun's love, marveled at the exotic flowers, and reunited with my beloved beaches. I found an isolated cove in which to snorkel, and delighted in watching the clown fish dart about the coral reefs. A pair of turtles swam up and serenaded me. They were giving me the nod and celebrating my new life.

One beautiful sunset, as I sat at the pool bar, a handsome man sat down next to me.

"What are you drinking? It looks lethal," he said, pointing to my huge goblet, garnished with an orchid.

Already quite mellow from the rarely imbibed surge of alcohol, I waved the bamboo backscratcher that was served with the cocktail. "It's a tropical itch, see? And it is quite lethal."

He smiled. "I'm Jim."

The alcohol loosened my usual shyness. This guy, with his deep-set, piercing eyes and perfect smile was a hunk and I was flattered by his attention. I thrust out my hand.

"Nice to meet 'ya. I'm Elizabeth. What brings you to Hawaii?"

"I'm celebrating my thirty-ninth birthday. I have to before I hit the big four-o."

This guy was a kid. What on earth was he doing, approaching a frumpy woman over ten years older? I took another swig.

"What are you doing here?"

I straightened up a little on my stool. If not with my looks, at least I could wow him with my accomplishments.

"I just attended a medical conference."

"Are you a nurse?"

"Nah, a physician."

"Sorry. My bad."

"No worries. I've heard it before." I smiled. "What about you? What do you do?"

"I'm an engineer from L.A. Where are you from?"

"Seattle. Hey, you have pretty great weather where you come from. What're you doing here?"

"I needed to get away and deal with my birthday alone. I'm really not looking forward to turning forty and I wanted to think some." He looked out onto the beach, lost in thought.

"Well, my birthday's later this month and I have a few years on you. Here's to birthdays!" I raised my glass and clinked with his. He smiled. He really, really was handsome.

"This should be a great sunset for seeing the green flash," he said.

"What's that?"

"It happens right as the sun disappears. The atmosphere causes the light from the sun to separate out into different colors. Keep looking at the horizon." Spoken like a true engineer, I thought to myself. I followed his gaze and watched. Sure enough, there was a momentary brilliant green flash with the last vestiges of the sun's curve disappearing. "Wow, that was amazing!"

Jim laughed at my delight. "Say, I'm getting pretty hungry. Would you like to join me for dinner?"

I was more than mellow by this point and plopped down from my barstool. "I'd love to. Lead the way." As he stepped down, John towered over me.

"Just how tall are you?" I asked, peering up at him.

"Six foot four – is that a problem?" He chuckled.

"Not at all." I nodded, soaking up his athletic physique that hung so perfectly in tropical shirt and shorts. *Oh my!*

We chatted amiably through our Hawaiian steak and chocolate lava cake dinner. We shared a bottle of merlot.

Jim put his arm around my back as we left the restaurant. A warm flush rose in my cheeks. *Good lord,* I thought, *this guy is a turn on.* He leaned in close and asked, "Would you like to come up to my room?" I was tipsy and tantalized. "Why not?"

We spent the next two days together. My first and only one-night stand proved to be restorative. Jim obviously saw more in my appearance than I did. He found me attractive and I turned him on. He was attentive and gentle. In his company I felt desirable and my emotions swelled like a blossom unfurling its petals. I became hopeful that I could be in relationship again.

I returned to Seattle, fired up to become even more attractive – inside and out. I resolved to get in shape and to lose weight. I jogged, sweated in aerobics and yoga classes, and shed several pounds. I boosted my meditation practice. By the time I joined my family on an Alaskan cruise a few months later, I had a new-found self confidence in what I had accomplished. I felt fit and svelte in my evening gowns.

In addition to my resolve to get in shape, I spent my sabbatical time musing, journaling, and soul searching. The kids were mostly gone, working and in college. I lounged on my living room couch, my back warmed by the sun streaming through the window. I read, gazed about, and noticed how my propped up legs twitched on occasion. Mildly alarmed, my medical persona imagined that I had contracted some dreadful degenerative neurologic disorder. My soul persona discerned the more likely cause of the restless legs: they were goading me to move ahead in my life – but to where? I knew I wanted to phase out of clinical medicine, but that scared the heck out of me. What kind of vocation could replace my medical practice? I loved my Lorian work, but I realized that spiritual teaching wasn't what I wanted to do long-term. How could I broaden my approach to helping people? And how on earth could I make a living?

Four months into my sabbatical, at the height of my dilemma, Suzanne – my dear friend and fellow Lorian faculty member – offered to coach me to help answer these questions. With her guidance, I came to realize fully a desire to listen to and to witness people – but I no longer wanted to do it in a medical practice setting. I already knew that the clinical time-constrained twenty-minute appointment environment didn't allow for deep exploration of the whole scope of a person's health. My common sense dictated that all aspects of being, from in utero to end of life, from body and mind to soul and spirit, from individual to community, from human to earth and beyond, all influenced wellness – and that totality is where I wanted to focus my work with people. Allopathic medicine was stuck at the far end, in a tiny corner of the life spectrum: the end pathway of symptomatology and disease. I felt this to be an incredibly shortsighted focus. I'd already attempted to bring a broader sense of health into my practice by providing self-improvement programs for patients and staff, but I had received little support from the organizational leadership. My attempts to work within the system had been unsuccessful. I was ready to move on.

I resolved to quit my practice. The decision to leave medicine wasn't an explosion of awareness. Rather, it simmered and simpered, a low grade, underlying knowing that I was to leave the fast paced medical world behind and shift to something new. Racing on the treadmill as I had for over twenty-seven years was no longer an option. The decision to leave settled quietly and surely in my soul.

As soon as I returned from my sabbatical, I submitted my resignation. I left at the end of December 2005. I was fifty-five-years-old, the earliest retirement age at Group Health and I was ready to embark on a new career as a life and leadership coach, and spiritual director.

CHAPTER 24 – I BELIEVE THE CHILDREN ARE OUR FUTURE

I and my granddaughter looking out onto blue skies. Photo taken by my photographer daughter: stephanieelizabethimages.com.

The Present.

It's my time at the ocean. Many years ago, I promised the sea I would meet up for an annual visit. I honor that promise. This time I am overjoyed for I am in Hawaii, my favorite tropical nature place. In the soft light of dawn, I sit overlooking the breaking waves. I clasp a frangipani in my hand and inhale its delectable sweet fragrance. I settle down, shivering a little in the trade winds that are somewhat cooler in the early hours. I am now quiet and I hear the pounding waves call to me: *let me love you.* Their counsel settles in my mind and I know the ocean is guiding me yet again. As usual, the words of the sea ring true, for that has been my lifelong challenge: learning to love and allowing love in. I send my gratitude out across the waves.

Some months later, I am at Mount Rainier, another sacred space where I often go to reflect. I have hiked about a mile up from Paradise Lodge with my friend Adrienne, delighting in the riot of summer color in the alpine meadows: carpets of magenta paintbrushes, blue lupines, and lilac asters. My friend and I settle side by side on a large boulder to meditate. I still. The bubbling voices and crunching feet passing by gradually fade away and I hear the mountain's call in my head: *I'm glad you are here.* My body begins to glow and settles into a hum. *Let me love you,* the mountain admonishes. My eyes glisten with tears and I clasp my hands in a grateful prayer, gazing at the venerable and powerful glaciered peak. A while later, Adrienne stirs. We hike back to the lodge for dinner, silent. The moment is too sacred to interrupt with words.

Later that fall, I am on Whidbey Island at Ebey's Landing – another sacred spot. I am about to spend the weekend with my dear friend, Suzanne. I hike along the beach, trudging over the water worn rocks and weaving around the scattered driftwood. The terrain is rough and I'm glad my ankles are well supported in my hiking boots. I sidle up to the water's edge and dip my fingers in, licking them to get the taste. I am receiving my salty communion. I bow to the lapping waves in gratitude. I continue on, past the lagoon and begin to climb up the narrow switchback trail that has been cut into the sandy cliff. This is a good workout, I think to myself as I begin to puff and perspire. Once I reach the top of the bluff, I take in the glorious view: Puget Sound, Olympic snowcapped mountains, Mount Baker, the farmlands below. Beyond lies the haunting grove of pines that had murmured to me some years before, letting me know how this too, in addition to Sydney, was my home. I smile in remembrance and nod my thanks to the evergreens. There aren't any people around on this gray fall rainy day. Luckily, I have managed to sandwich my hike between rain showers - and I am glad to be alone. I smile: the dreary weather no longer bothers me as it did when I first landed in Seattle almost fifty years ago. I am now completely at home in the drizzly Northwest. I settle on an almost dry log and close my eyes.

I am in the presence of my holy nature church. Despite the brisk breeze, I feel a stillness envelope me and in my mind, I hear: *let me love you.* I burst into tears! This is the third time, in a third sacred setting in less than six months that I have heard these same words. I gulp in the wind. *Get a clue*, I think to myself, smiling through my tears. *I'm getting there,* I whisper to my beloved landscape. *I know,* it replies, *I'm just reminding you.* As if in affirmation, it begins to drizzle. The drops dusting my face feel like a blessing. I scamper back down to the beach and to my car, chuckling and chortling with glee. The sacred communicates with me. My prayers no longer fall on deaf ears.

§

I have asked my sister to help me frame a wall hanging out of a needlepoint that I have just finished stitching. We are in her retirement home unit that overlooks a gorgeous downtown Seattle skyline and which is packed with shelves and shelves of quilting fabrics and accouterments. Irene has been figuring out loud, measuring, and cutting. I admire her ability to envision and calculate. She is masterful, has a keen engineering mind, and is an avid and skillful quilter. I hate sewing of any description, hence my request for her help, but have inherited the joy of needlepointing from my mother – *hüje le föl le föl munka* (idiot down up down up work) as Anyu used to quip. Nevertheless, I find the "no-brainer" pastime soothing and peaceful and I delight in the thread textures and colors.

We move to the sewing machine. I recite a much beloved Hungarian adage often muttered when embarking on a dubious mission: *"Most ugrik a béka a vizbe,"* (now the frog jumps into the water.) We both giggle. Irene stitches with precision and then I iron flat the edges.

We scrutinize our work. There is a moment of silence and then we burst out laughing, gasping, holding our bellies, tears streaming down our faces. Our measuring has been off by a quarter of an inch!

"Oh, oh, I have to go pee," I say as I waddle cross-legged to the bathroom.

I'm still chuckling when I return. "No worries." I smile, but my sister is bent over the project, already problem solving and measuring. "Hmm, look here. We can make an extra border, see?"

"Brilliant!" I say. "It'll look even better!"

Irene turns to me. "You know, this is fun spending time with you like this." I hug her and whisper in her ear, "I agree." I'm so grateful to have a warm relationship with my sister. It hasn't always been that way.

§

I sit with my friend, Suzanne, in her cozy Whidbey living room. We are signed up for a meditation workshop on the island and I am staying overnight with her. Her Caribbean roots and time spent in Africa are reflected in her brightly decorated home: vibrant trims in cool blues and aquas, warm reds and a scrumptious mango hue that I love. We enjoy a cup. Suzanne's a connoisseur of the finest tea blends, a taste that she developed during the years she spent in England. We relax and put up our feet. Her shock of silvery-gray shoulder length hair bounces about as she laughs. Her thick bangs frame intelligent eyes that don't miss a thing. She is open and honest and helps me to be the same. I am at ease with her and we gab about everything from work to family issues, from sacred experiences to world events, from TV shows and movies to lovers and laughs. We share our latest reads, our newest recipes, and our most embarrassing foibles

Suzanne and I have spent many joy-filled and challenging years collaborating as faculty in the spiritual formation and spiritual direction programs at Lorian. My dear friend was instrumental in helping me figure out and plan my transition from clinical medicine into coaching and spiritual direction.

We are both volunteering for One to One Women Coaching Women, a nonprofit organization that provides coaching for high potential, low income women. My work coaching women has been fulfilling. I have shepherded several clients toward finding their own brilliance and have been delighted to see them make fruitful choices furthering their education, moving towards more satisfying employment, and deepening their family relations. I have also been privileged to work with the coaches in the organization, developing training modules and a mentoring program.

This weekend, Suzanne and I spend some time finalizing a peer supervision program for the One to One coaches, a process that provides a supportive forum for coaches to explore personal challenges arising in their work with clients.

Our project planning is almost done. I type up the last minute changes on my laptop. We are ready to pilot our program at the next coaches training conference call. In the evening, we settle in for some raucous laughs. We watch *The Life of Brian,* the Monty Python classic.

Our sacred journeys, our work and our values have brought us together. Our firm friendship lovingly binds us. Not only have I found soulful work in my life, I have also been privileged to have developed deep, abiding friendships. I no longer hold hurts and fears inside. I have learned to trust and have found comfort in sharing deeply.

§

It's seven thirty in the evening and the phone rings. As expected, it's a call from my daughter. Stephanie, now thirty-years-old, has graduated with double majors in Psychology and Nursing and works in a pediatric ICU at a Seattle hospital. She is on her drive home from a twelve-hour shift. It's her time to talk. From the moment I hear her utter hello, the tone of her voice tells me exactly how her day has been. She may be upset about a child in her care who has died. She may sigh about her latest online date that didn't work out or rage about her father dissing her yet again. Sometimes she glows about her love of Crossfit and how her growing strength encourages her. Other times she's happy about receiving yet another photography gig, this time to do a family shoot in Discovery Park. I listen, I commiserate, I encourage and praise her. Sometimes, when she really gets down on herself, I tell my sometimes emotional daughter to shape up and get over it.

I am there for her as my parents were never there for me. This I have learned to do.

§

I hear a knock on the door just after seven in the morning. As expected, it's my son. Stephen is now in his mid thirties. He is married and a father. He, too, is a college graduate, in business, and works as the manager of an online computer component company. My son hugs me as I open the door. He is tall and lean with caramel eyes and dark curls like his sister. He drops off my nine-month-old granddaughter Adelaide. I will spend the day with her while her parents work. I glow when I see her. Stephen and I chat about her latest feats, how she has a new tooth, how she crawls everywhere, how she loves homemade carrots spiced with cinnamon. He asks if I want gates for my steps to keep her from tumbling. I tell him for right now, I'm free to watch her every move. He lingers for extra Ada kisses, hesitant to leave her, but his work beckons.

My son and his wife have been studying, sharing, and learning from the time they became pregnant. They shower Ada with attention, touch and love. The contrast to my upbringing is stark, and for this, I feel immense gratitude. I have learned how to listen and to nurture, crucial skills my parents hardly knew how to pattern for me, and I have imparted some measure of what I have learned to my children.

My day with Ada flows in the present. I talk, she babbles. We understand each other. We go for a walk, she in her stroller gazing about, kicking her legs with glee at seeing a crow or a plane fly by. She chortles as I push her in the nearby park swing. She wails when she's mad at having her pants changed, cries when she's tired. We read *The Little Red Hen, The Hungry Caterpillar*. She chews the edges of the pages and then turns them over. I sing and sing to her. She recognizes "Edelweiss" and quiets. She listens to "Ten Green Bottles" and "Kookaburra Sits in the Old Gum Tree" – tunes that I recall from my early school days. My favorite song to sing for her is "Getting to Know You" from *The King And I*. We are indeed getting to know each other. I cradle her as she guzzles her bottle. I gaze into her eyes, and she stares into mine. She shoves the bottle aside with her tiny hand and curves her lip with a knowing smile. It makes no difference if she's fussy or fine. I'm over the top enthralled with her.

§

The journey of learning to love and letting love in continues. Every step I take, one foot in front of the other, has been well worth it. I am no longer alone.

About the Publisher:

Starseed Books is an imprint of Lorian Press LLC. Starseed Books specializes in fiction but also publishes biographies, books for the Ancient Order of Druids in America and other material.

Starseed Books
Attn: Jeremy Berg
6592 Peninsula Dr
Traverse City, MI 49686

www.lorianpress.com

CPSIA information can be obtained
at www.ICGtesting.com
Printed in the USA
LVOW13s1047020517

532928LV00035B/1987/P